ALSO BY JACOB OLUWATAYO ADEUYAN

Let Us Walk Our Ways Back Into The Garden of Eden
Road Map to Business Success
Lord Show Me the Exit to the New Jerusalem
The Journey of the First Black Bishop – Bishop
Samuel Ajayi Crowther – 1806 – 1891
The Return of the Tidal Flow of the Middle Passage
Who are the Victims of Bad Governance in Nigeria?

Contributions of Yoruba People in the Economic & Political Developments of Nigeria

Jacob Oluwatayo Adeuyan

authorHOUSE®

AuthorHouse™
1663 Liberty Drive
Bloomington, IN 47403
www.authorhouse.com
Phone: 1-800-839-8640

First published by AuthorHouse 9/21/2011

ISBN: 978-1-4670-2483-9 (sc)
ISBN: 978-1-4670-2481-5 (hc)
ISBN: 978-1-4670-2480-8 (e)

Library of Congress Control Number: 2011916047

Printed in the United States of America

DEDICATION

This Book is dedicated to all the Sons and Daughters of Oduduwa worldwide - the Progenitor of Yorubaland.

Acknowledgments

This book would not have been able to see the light of the day if not for the support and painstaking contributions of the following people that surrounded me from the research table from all over the world to computer interpretations of some valuable data used in some of the contents of the book. The insights and attention of many talented and Godly collaborators made the writing of this book an experience of its message.

First are the inestimable contributions of my grand-children who immensely contributed their tender-age experience in computer manipulations of their generation and support to my ambition of getting this work across to my people: Ms. Oluwadamilola, Olayimika Oluwaseyi, Olamidipupo Jr. Olabode Jr. Omogbolahan, Olakitan, Oluwatayo Jr. Olatubosun Omolodun, Tayo Jr., Ishmail, Oluwaseun, Kemisola, David Oladeinde all of Adeuyan dynasty.

This book is a political and reference book to this generation and the Yoruba generations yet unborn in our corporate Nigeria and one of the series in the historical books already written by Nigeria writers for the maintenance of the status quo of our nation. My thanks, too, go to my beloved pastors and friends in my church – the Vine – Yard of Comfort, Lanham Maryland: Reverend David Olusegun Adenodi – the Senior Pastor of the American Parish, Pastor Dr Alex Oni, Pastor Dr Jide Aniyikaiye, Mr & Mrs Dotun Falade, Mr.& Prof. Apanishile, Mr & Mrs Muyiwa Oshinkomiya, Mrs Olu. Ajayi of Morgan State University and especially my son in the Lord Pastor & Deaconess Philip Ekoma who chaired the review & typesetting board of the book – your unwavering enthusiasm, your countless astute suggestions, your cheerful willingness to lend creativity and technical savvy – whatever it took – at any moment.

To my beloved children and their families for their love & financial support to me during my research trips to Africa, England and other nations of the world – I love you all. Same goes to my beloved friend Ms. Susan Aina Adefarakan who is always there for me in terms of free lodging and maintenance in England anytime I visit London for valuable information on this work – I thank you for your love and affection. My political brothers, friends & associates: Pa Reuben Fashoranti – Leader of Afenifere, Chief Olu. Falae – Former Secretary to the Federal Government of Nigeria & Presidential Candidate and also my childhood friend, Chief Bisi Akande, National Chairman of Action Congress of Nigeria & a loveable friend, Chief Henry Oladele Ajomale - Chairman Lagos State Action Congress of Nigeria – Old time associate & friend, Governor Babatunde Raji Fashola of Lagos State, Barister Dele Alade, Architect Oloye Awojodu, Mr. Kayode Ikuforiji, Olasende Akerele, Professor & Mrs Tenabe, Ike Isama Chairman Action Congress of Nigeria - USA, Mr & Mrs Jackson Falade, Colonel Olakunle Falayi, Dr. Wunmi Akintide, Samuel Owolanke Ogundare and very many others that space can not allow me to mention. This is not an intentional oversight as all of you make this journey a splendid fun. I thank you all.

Table of Contents

Some Nigerian Leaders of the Past and Present

(1) Herbert Macaulay – Father of Nigeria Politics.

(2) Dr. Nnamdi Azikwe – Ist Governor General of Nigeria and Ist President of Nigeria.

(3) Chief Obafemi Awolowo – Ist Premier of Western Region of Nigeria and Leader of Opposition at the Federal House of Representatives Lagos.

(4) Sir. Abubakar Tafawa Balewa – Ist Prime Minister of Nigeria.

(5) Mallam Aminu Kano – Leader of NEPU

(6) J. S. Tarka - Leader of UMBC

(7) Sir. Ahmadu Bello – The Sadauna of Sokoto and Leader of NPC

(8) Chief Samuel Ladoke Akintola – 2nd Premier of Western Region

(9) Oba Adesoji Aderemi – Ooni of Ife and 1st indigenous Governor of Western Region.

(10) General Yakubu Gowon – Nigeria Military Head of State

(11) Col. Adekunle Fajuyi – Ist military governor of the former Western Region.

(12) General Olusegun Obasanjo – Military Head of State and a Civilian President of Nigeria.

(13) Chief Fani-Kayode (Popularly known as "Fani-Power") Deputy Premier of Western Region.

(14) Chief Michael Okpara – 2nd Premier of Eastern Nigeria

Who are the Yoruba People?

Yoruba people have been the dominant group that resides for centuries on the west bank of River Niger, of mixed origin and the product of the assimilation of periodic movements of migrants who evolved a common language and culture to administer and control their day-to-day life style. Much had been written about their source of origin by the great historians of our time but as at yet we are made to be living in a confused state of many theories regarding this topic. The one to hold on to among these theories is the fact that the Yoruba people are the siblings of the great *Oduduwa* who was their primogenitor. Every other facts and theories that had been postulated regarding the origin of Yoruba people are welcomed for the moment and as well preserved for future scientific and technological development, which may par-adventure, shed more lights on the true position of the topic.

Like all other communities of the world that were in existence during the dark ages before the art of writing and development of knowledge were being brought to them by those already having them, Yoruba community cannot be exempted from having its own portion of this natural blackout. It will therefore be a nice suggestion that all we can do for now is to continue embracing all the previous scripts of our great historians on this topic and whenever there will be need to refer to or write about this topic, we can pick the one that is more comfortable to us and that will be more acceptable to our readers and make sense to the future generations of this great people.

Our undisputable home base of Ile-Ife, the cradle of Yoruba people was said to have been in existence for many centuries back before the Portuguese trading adventurers came to Africa in the fifteenth century on a trade mission to the city of Ile - Ife and Benin City. Some research papers revealed to us that by 900 AD, the Yoruba city-state of Ile-Ife had established itself as the dominating power in the land of the

Yoruba, which had complex states throughout the region that included the central and southwest of the present Nigeria, Benin and Togo Republics. The City-state of Ile-Ife, which according to the historians inhabited by Yoruba in the 4th century BCE, became the cultural center of the people and was acknowledged by all other Yoruba city-states as the primary source city of their existence.

The Benin Empire that was situated at the southeastern part of the home base of Ile-Ife, ruled by a dynasty that also traced its ancestry to this great city and its founder, the great *Oduduwa*. Apart from the fact that Benin City was largely populated by the Edo clan and other surrounding ethnicities, yet it held considerable sway in the election of its nobles and Kings similar to the practice in Yoruba land. Ile-Ife during the initial development of modern trade in Africa and unlike Benin and Oyo, it never developed onto a true kingdom but remained and maintained a city-state status that was paramount and important to the people of Yoruba land as their original sacred city and the dispenser of their basic religious thoughts. Other cities of Yoruba people established either by intent or by accident copied from the prototype structure of Ile-Ife to build their new locations in both spiritual and physical. We can confirm this through the control of the monarchs (*Oba*) and the councils made up of nobles, guild leaders and war lords that were in place throughout the land before the white-man arrived with their new form of government structures and system. Although some of the powers allocated to the monarchs of those days have now been severed and given to the people under democratic process and dispensation, but yet the traditional rights and powers associated with them still resides with the monarchs and their palace noble men till today.

Yoruba people of the past and present were organized in partrilineal descent groups that occupied various village and city communities. In the past, they lived mainly in the village communities and subsisted mainly on agriculture, but history told us that as from the eleventh century A.D., the adjacent village compounds with their detached or semi-detached houses began to coalesce into a number of territorial city-states in which loyalties to the clan chief-head became paramount and gradually transformed itself into dynastic chieftain level. Subsequently this system produced an urbanized political and social environment that was accompanied by a high level of intellectual ability to produce artistic achievements particularly in terracotta and ivory sculpture. The sophisticated metal casting produced by the early Yoruba craftsmen at Ile-Ife became the business source for international trade between the Yoruba people and their neighbors to the north and some far-away regions of Africa. The brass and bronze produced by the artisans at Ile-Ife from copper, tin and zinc became a significant item of trade to further develop their environment and its inhabitants. The raw materials of copper, tin, and zinc used to produce these ornaments were either brought into Yoruba country from the north of Africa through the trading caravan routes of this time or from the mines in the Sahara and northern Nigeria.

Formal traditions of the historical process by which Ile-Ife's ruling dynasty extended its authority over Yoruba land were significant and interesting. History affirmed that *oduduwa* had only a male child named Okanbi and that it was this male child that bore seven sons that later established independent city-states and dynasties throughout the Yoruba land where they reigned as priest-kings and presided over the cult rituals. Ile-Ife, being the center of as many as over 400 religious cults supported all the newly established cities that the young Oduduwa grand children came to established both with spiritual powers and structural assistance. They were as well protected as a parent would always protect its children. On their way out of Ile-Ife these princes took with them the most liked and most important ones among the numerous deities being worshiped at their city of origin to their new locations to establish their presence with them. This is why up till today in Yoruba land and elsewhere in the universe where Yoruba people may have migrated to there is always uniformity in their culture and the mode of their traditional religion.

The rise of Oyo Empire did not come as a surprise but as a result of its geographical location and its proximity to the people across the borders of Yoruba land especially those to the north of the territory. The slave trade business prop-up the importance of Oyo city-state at the end of the 15th century with the aid of the Portuguese guns behind it as its security pillars. In addition the expansion of the Empire at this time was equally associated with the acquisition of horses from across the Niger. This prestigious commodity actually enhanced and promoted their trade and also served as a source of mobility to them to travel faster and more comfortable than the traditional trekking on foot. This advantage, which other locations in the region had no access to, has increased the wealth and popularity of the monarch, nobles, merchants and the people of Oyo of this time.

Another spectacular point to note is the wellbeing and survival of those animals. Oyo city-state being a city located in the Savanna area of Yoruba land gives such opportunity to raise horses better than in the forest areas because of the deadly health effect on them through the bite of tsetse fly that is abundant in the forest areas. Unfortunately when the war broke out at Oyo at the end of the 18th century, the northern business friends and partners (the Fulanis), which Oyo people rested upon for help and assistance broke their backs completely as they ended up conquering all of old Oyo territory by 1830s. The Fulani invasion of the old Oyo territory pushed many Yoruba to the south where the towns of Ibadan and Abeokuta were founded. The city of Ilorin, which was one of the principal towns of the old Oyo Empire and some others within the territory remained Fulani dominated and ruled territory till today. The Afonja dynasty at Ilorin was completely replaced with an Emir – a Sokoto carlifate title.

The major trade of the old Yoruba people was agriculture because of the rich land advantage endowed them by their *Olodumare.* This trade enabled them to feed their families well and also exposed them to trading partnerships among themselves even before the arrival of the Whiteman's business opportunities and techniques. When they came and introduced new products from other areas of the world to them such as cotton and cocoa, it was easier for them to pick on the technology of growing these products fastly. The end result was that its agricultural input to the world economy when the British people were with us and after they had left was enormous. So also our cocoa beans, palm kernel produce, cotton, peanuts and beans undoubtedly contributed greatly to the economy of the colonial power that annexed us forcefully for sixty years. It may not be far from the truth that at a point in time in the life-circle of Yoruba people, over 70% of them were serious farmers while the remainder resided back in the cities to work as crafts people and traders. But as time went by, the centralization of wealth within the cities allowed for the development of a complex market economy, which encouraged extensive patronage of the arts.

It is no gain saying that the culture of Yoruba people spread across the Atlantic to the Americas and have some soft spots within the continent of mother Africa. During the slave trade era, many of Yoruba people were violently captured by Europeans and marched in millions to their plantations located in the Americas. During their hazardous journey on the sea and on the ocean, they were crowded together without any respect for human lives because of their interest in only numbers for profit gains. Many of them died on the voyage because of the condition of how they were stacked like bags of produce. Those that were fortunate to make it to the designated locations found themselves in various British, French, Spanish and Portuguese colonies in the New World. Interestingly in a number of the places where they were distributed to, the people made sure that their traditions and culture were maintained and preserved for their unborn generations. This impressive notion or ideology survived the slavery era and continued into the civilized era we see today.

In Brazil, Cuba, Haiti, and Trinidad, Yoruba religious rites, beliefs, music and myths are as new as they were in the slavery days when our people were in chains working in the plantations without any hope of freedom in sight for them. In Haiti for example, the Yoruba people are called "Anagos" and their religious activities concede to Yoruba religious rites and beliefs a honored place with the recognition of the numerous deities of Yoruba origin that their forefathers brought with them into the New World. In Brazil, Yoruba religious activities are called Anago or Shango, and in Cuba they are designated "Lucumi" meaning "Olukumi" in Yoruba expression and "my friend" in English language.

Practically before the advent of Christianity and Islam, Yoruba people believed in their own deities and the Supreme Being called "Olorun" or "Olodumare". These deities which changed with each geographical locations in the land are considered lesser gods who are capable of presenting the people's cases and problems judiciously in the courts of the Supreme Being in heaving and who will surely bring back to them undiluted answers clean and clear from Olodumare – the Almighty God. Some of these deities are Sango (god of thunder), Ogun (god of iron), soponna (god of smallpox), Aja (the spirit of whirlwind), Osun (goddess of fertility), Olokun (goddess of the sea) and other gods. They are all considered to be intermediaries between man and God – Olodumare. Yoruba proverbs and adages that came from rich philosophical background form an important part of their everyday language, and are extensively used in all forms of communication. The talking drum, which is the pride of the Yoruba folklore, still stands as a mystery to musical performers all over the world. The way its rhythm and sound is manipulated, controlled, and changed direction at will by the person drumming it could not be copied because of the dialectical messages of different versions its tone sends to the listeners through the beating.

The pre-colonial government administration of Yoruba people especially in the cities are something of interest to note. In the cities where monarchs had been established, the overall powers were vested in the courts of such monarch. He can absolutely use all the powers by himself or sometime he can seek for the advice of his noblemen called the chiefs or the palace officials if he wished to. But as time progressed especially when new cities such as Ibadan and Abeokuta were found after the defeat of Usman Dan Fodio, the militant Muslim leader who threatened to annex the whole of Yoruba land up to the sea shore at Lagos by the Ibadan military command at Oshogbo war front, new approach to government and social development were beginning to unfold itself.

The numerous Egba communities that later came together to form one political entity were notable example to site. In their system, the independent polities often elect an *Oba* while the real political, legislative, and judicial powers resided with the *Ogbonis,* a council of notable elders in the community. When Commander Fredrick Forbes, a representative of the British Crown in Nigeria visited Abeokuta in somewhere around 1853, he wrote in an edition of the Church Military Intelligencer of that year, describing Abeokuta as a city having "four presidents", and the system of government as having "840 principal rulers or "House of Lords", 2800 secondary chiefs or "House of Commons", 140 principal military ones and 280 secondary ones". He described Abeokuta and its system of government as "the most extra-ordinary republic in the world". This was the remark and observation of a strange person who only came but met the institution already in place at Abeokuta in 1853. The observation made about the high level of government and the rate of development by the Portuguese explorers in the 15th century when they first got to Benin City is similar to the one now made by Commander Forbes in the 19th century about Abeokuta's system of government and people.

The people saw the inherent danger lying behind the monopoly of power by the monarchs and this was why they put together such council members that comprised of notable men and women within the community and that were of the same influential status with the monarch to check on his abuses of the powers given to him by the people's collective constitution. This system about how to run the people's government as well developed among the other communities that fell under the Yoruba ethnic umbrella. In Oyo, which was then the most centralized of the pre-colonial Empires, the *Alafin* usually consult on all political decisions with his Prime Minister – the Bashorun and the council of leading nobles called the **Oyo Mesi.**

In the case of Ibadan a city founded in the 19th century by a polyglot group of refugees, soldiers and itinerant traders from Oyo and other Yoruba sub-groups, the people initially dispensed with the concept of monarchism but later embraced it in the 20th century. Before they finally embraced this system, the people preferred to elect their leader called **Baale** from the ranks of military and civil councils from the pool of their eminent citizens. By gradual development of such system, the city was growing in size and in democratic principle of governance. In not too long a time, Ibadan was astronomically swelling beyond everybody's expectation until it surpassed all other cities in Yoruba land both in population and size. Initially the city was regarded as Yoruba military republic and with the superior military experience and influence at its disposal, other people from other neighboring state-cities now preferred to move to Ibadan for the protection of themselves and their properties. This was the time that the inter-tribal wars among the Yoruba people were going on at different fronts; wiping out some communities completely in some instances and leaving some in serious devastation.

Arguably the white man did not bring anything new to the governing area of the people apart from their own commercial and business techniques that were established to serve their own purpose. Before they came with their brand of administrative system, we already had in place functional social organizations and by the time they came, they only took time to study the functionality of those organizations with the assistance of our people and then started to document them and where necessary expand or reconstitute some to fall in line with their own prototype. For example, occupational guilds, social clubs, secret societies, league of traders, religious units, and other progressive city organizations were on the ground functioning and moving the society forward before the white man's arrival. Unfortunately when they came to introduce their system to us, our people of the time thought that it was good and for that reason, they abandoned our established system to start learning the new system. We all can imagine the difficulty it will involve to learn a new system from its foundation. This diversionary method derailed our course, ran us into pitfall and completely changed our mindset to such an extent that we had to look forward unto England for every need we desired including the changing of our shoes and dresses when they are warn out.

Credit must be given to our past leaders, the nationalists and those of them that suffered in silence during the period of incarceration and degradation of our people in the hands of colonial lords. We must equally doff our caps for them for the wisdom, intelligence, patience, spirit of understanding, perseverance and all other qualities and virtues that they applied in dealing with the low ebb situation of the time. At last we gained independence through the hard works of these past leaders. Their names shall forever be remembered from generation to generation and also be written with golden ink on the plates of our walls, even at the gates of our cities and in the minds of our children. To them I say Bravo.

PART 1
YORUBA NATION

Chapter –1–
Yoruba Nation of the Dark Ages

Yoruba Nation of the dark ages may not necessarily refer to a very long or distant era of the past but which could have its beginning from somewhere around 800 AD, from whence the historians speculated as the birth century of Ile-Ife the home-city of Yoruba people. Though oral history through mythical belief predated the birth of this city to the time when God – *Oldumare* created the whole universe and made the city the center or core-city of the universe. Those who belonged to the school of thought that the father of Yoruba people – *Oduduwa* was sent down by *Olodumare* God the creator, to fashion the first human beings out of Ile-Ife clay soil and ruled over them could not be totally condemned for their belief. Those who hold-on to the other versions of the myth which posited that *Oduduwa* came from the Middle - East, somewhere around the city of Mecca as a mysterious sorjourner to rescue the people of Ile-Ife from the incessant raid of the rafian people with his magical powers too have their own reasons to believe this version.

The bottom line is that the early anthropologists confirmed that the city of Ile-Ife had been in existence before 900AD. By this time, according to their findings they remarked that the Yoruba city-state of Ile-Ife had established itself as the dominating power in Yoruba land which included all of the central and southwest of the present Nigeria and as far as to the territory of Togo. The mere fact that there was no way to properly record events of this time does not negate the oral history that was passed from one generation to the other until it came to our age when the history can now be documented and scanned. I am equally sure that future archeological discoveries would unravel more facts as to the true origin of our people.

In the dark ages and like in all other places of the world, people lived either in caves or on the land in small groups and fend for themselves by whatever means and ways available to them. Yoruba people too are no exception in this regard. History told us that in the forestlands of Western Africa south of the Sahelian states (the Sahel is the area immediately south of the Sahara), Africans lived in small villages that were tribal and ruled by chiefs. And sometime between 1000 and 1500 AD, many of these villages began to consolidate into larger units thereby transforming into powerful and centralized states; Benin City was recognized as the largest and longest lasting of these centralized states followed by Oyo.

Because of lack of adequate documentation, the city-states and kingdoms development around this time lost their histories in the jungle forests of the time. People of the time quickly migrated from one place to another for many reasons. One of such was the influx of grassland-dwelling people from the Sudan that were been driven south by the increasingly harsh climatic conditions in the desert areas. People from African desert region were known to be mainly cattle rearers in the past and because of their trade, they would need grazing land to keep their cattle and other domestic animals when the climate is too hot. This reason may have been their principal motive of drifting south in search of *Amazon* ground that would accommodate them and their flock of animals.

On their way to their new permanent places, they brought with them to establish their culture and the form of government that was being practiced at their original places including their hereditary monarchy which helped them to fuse together the villages in a particular district that later became state-cities. In this developmental lineage, Yoruba people were the first to expand the power of city-states over other territories. Ife people began a series of military incursions into parts of the Niger area in an attempt to set up monarchies for the people and to extend the powers of Ife dynasty to those places. Through this system, they were able to discover such place like Benin and established the city of Oyo both that later became powerful economic Empires of Yoruba territory.

Benin, which is located at the east of Ile-Ife was said to become a dependency of Ife at the beginning of the 14th century and by the 15th century, it took an independent course probably because of the visit of the Portuguese merchants to Benin city at the tail end of the 15th

2

century that transformed them to become a major trading power in their own rites, blocking Ife's access to the coastal parts of the territory. Benin was an area being occupied by speaking Edo people and according to them they claimed that the Edos have occupied this area for several thousands of years. Historically, record revealed that the Edo society is found on the village grouping like all other places in the region and was kinship organized whose authority is based on groups of males according to their age. With the abundancy of power and authority in the hands of Ile-Ife as at this time, it sent one of the members of its dynasty around 1300 AD to rule the Benin territory but fine enough the basic social and political structures that were being practiced in Benin before this time did not change profoundly. Because of this, the ruling period of the Oba sent to Benin was so short and strictly controlled by the Edo chiefs, called the Uzama.

Like all other Obas of Yoruba land of the time, political power and religious authority in Benin were vested in the Oba (king) who according to tradition descended from Ife dynasty. The Oba had as his advisers, six hereditary chiefs whom he consulted with from time to time on matters affecting his Empire and people. The perimeter size of Benin City around this time was estimated to cover around 25 kilometers with approximately a little over 100,000 houses at its height and with beautifully paved roads connecting each other. The city of Benin was then enclosed with three concentric rings of beautiful earthworks. The administration of the urban complex lay with sixty trade guilds, each with its own quarters, whose membership cut across clan affiliations. All of them owe their loyalty directly to the Oba.

At the Oba's court, the Oba presided over a large council in a courtroom richly adorned with brass, bronze and Ivory objects, which were the replica of the traditions of all Obas in Yorubaland. Benin too like Ife and other Yoruba states is famous for its sculpture and ornament producing techniques. From what has been said, Yoruba and Benin were closely interconnected from the beginning of existence. Benin Empire was recorded as one of the most powerful and extensive among the kingdoms of its time. It was one of the longest and lasting civilizations in West Africa and was still a powerful and imposing Empire when the Europeans came with their colonization program in the 19th century. It took the British a great deal of time and diplomacy to subdue the Empire in 1897 when the territory was invaded and the Empire finally dismantled.

In the case of Oyo Empire, which was extended to the present Ilorin and Yagba territories in the Savanna region between the forest and the Niger River with its capital city of Oyo-Ile was conquered by the Fulani Jihad conflict led by one of its militant Muslim leader and a Quranic scholar Uthman dan Fodio. The conflict drafted many Yoruba people from their original city base of Oyo-Ile further down south. Because the city was completely destroyed by the Sokoto Caliphate who in the course of the conflict also seized and occupied the city of Ilorin that was Yoruba border town to the north. The origin of Oyo may not be far-fetched because the city of Oyo was founded by the great warrior-son of *Oduduwa* named *Oranmiyan,* who reigned as an Oba in three distinctive kingdoms in Yorubaland – Ile-Ife, Benin City and Oyo Empire. Infact he was the first *Alafin* of Oyo and by the time he was leaving Oyo to return to his traditional base at Ile-Ife, left part of his kingship authority for his children he left behind as a symbol of Royal powers for those who are to reign after him. Ever since then his offshoots have always been installed as *Alafin* of Oyo, which included the legendary *Alafin Shango* the fourth Alafin of Oyo. The city was founded by Oranmiyan around 1350 AD and situated to the northwest of Ile-Ife.

History revealed that when Alafin Oranmiyan was on the throne of Oyo, his administration was the best in the continent of Africa, which could be likened to the British system of Administration during the colonial days. Oyo Empire of this time expanded up to the present territory of the Benin Republic. Oba *Oranmiyan* concentrated on establishing his authority at the southern territory and never bordered having anything to do with the eastern part of his kingdom because he left the administration of that part to his son Eweka of Benin to administer and control. Based on the good administration *Oranmiyan* left behind at Oyo, those that reigned after him and the leaders of the city built strong administrative pillars on his foundation to erect the tower building that the whole world witnessed centuries later.

Oyo now began to expand in size, power and trading activities that surpassed all other Empires on the west coast of Africa. Its economy became strong and rose to prominence through the wealth of gains from the slave trade and its possession of a powerful and important cavalry route to the sea. At a particular period in Yoruba history especially

The current Alaafin of Oyo Empire. HRH Oba Lamidi Adeyemi lll

4

from the mid 17th to 18th century, Oyo Empire was the most politically important Yoruba state, holding sway not only in the lesser Yoruba states, but also over the kingdom of Dahomey now located in the Republic of Benin. Its principal trading commodity, the slave trade was flourishing and the gains from it was to be used for territorial expansion of the Empire; but some people from the ranks of the nobles strongly objected to this idea and instead opted for personal wealth accumulation. The difference between the two groups was not resolved until *Alafin Abiodun Adegorolu* who reigned between 1770 and 1789 subjugated his opponents in a bitter war and then pursued a policy of economic development based purely on the coastal trade with the European merchants.

Early in the 16th century, Oyo was not just powerful because of the strength of power owned by its northern neighbors of Borgu and Nupe by whom it was conquered and weakened in 1550. But towards the end of the century, its military strength began to change through the efforts of the then reigning *Alafin Orompoto,* who used the wealth, derived from trade to establish a cavalry force and maintained a strong and trained army for the state. It was by the military strength of its army that made it possible for the Empire to subjugate the kingdom of Dahomey in two faces: the first between 1724 and 1730 while the second one was between 1738 and 1748. These victories gave Oyo the direct access to trade with the European merchants on the coast through the port of Ajase (Porto-Novo). No matter how powerful a nation is, yet its adversaries would always stay at its throat and this was the exact case of the old Oyo Empire.

Its decline was exacerbated by quarrels between *Alafin Awole Arogangan* who reigned between 1789 and 1796 and his advisers, which continued throughout the 18th century and extended to 19th century when Oyo Empire began to lose control of its trade routes to the coast. New power from Dahomey sprang up and invaded Oyo and soon after 1800, another heavy blow - deadly one this time around was punched at it by the militant Fulani Muslims from Hausaland when the militant group captured it. The end of the Empire that was once the largest state in the coastal West Africa came through the defeat by this militant group. The group permanently annexed all of the northern territory of the old Oyo Empire.

The people and its culture:

Yoruba being an indigenous people of West Africa belong to one of the African groups with the most diverse culture and thickly populated in that region of the continent. Their belief in the story of creation of the world which makes them the first creature to walk on the surface of this planet is yet to be disputed in strong terms or through any scientific discovery. As such we can still hold on to this belief until there will be other facts to disprove it with contrary views. The population of Yoruba speaking people in the Diaspora is close to between 50 and 60 million by now and the bulk from these numbers occupy a span of the coastal plain of the West Africa stretching to about 250 miles long from north to south and with approximately 400 miles wide from west to the east. The east to west territorial land mass cut across the political borders of Nigeria, the Republic of Benin, Togo, and some parts in the east of Ghana, which marks the eastern terminus of the old Oyo Empire in West Africa.

Their historically unavoidable and partial friendly neighbors fall into two major ethnic groups in the region and they are the Ewe and the Edos. The Ewe are presumed to be the largest and most diverse with their territory extending west and southwest from Yorubaland and cross to the political boundaries of the Republic of Benin, Togo, and Ghana. The Ewe people comprise of two major tribes – the Fon and Mahi and both of them are in close proximity to several Yoruba principalities. The Fon are the major tribe in Dahomey while Mahi peoples were in Dahomey sphere of influence. Both suffered defeat in the Yoruba Imperial expansion wars of the 18th century. Culturally these people share several deities with the Yoruba and at some times they mix together for religious festivals and lay claim to Ife dynasty.

The Edo people from historical perspective do not claim to have descended from Ile-Ife but accepted that one of the princes from Yorubaland and from Ife dynasty ruled over their territory at one time or the other in the past and left his footprint on the sands of Royal history in Benin. The Edo also had a mythic history similar to that of Yoruba regarding their state of origin. They too believed that they originated from God-sent ancestors who left "heaven" on the instructions of the Supreme God to come and populate the earth planet. Based on this belief and the respect they had for the spiritual powers, influence and the personality of *oduduwa,* the Edo people requested that one of the princes should be sent to rule over them. *Oranmiyan* a great warrior and the last born of *Oduduwa's* grand children left for Benin to fulfill their request. While in Benin as an Oba, he got married to one of the princesses who bore him a male child and whom he named as his successor to the throne before he left Benin to come back to his home base in Yorubaland. Ever since that time all reigning Obas in Benin City have their roots firmly planted in Oba Ornamiyan's royal field and with his blood to water their dynastic growth.

Two particular Benin Obas that reigned after *Oranmiyan* are worthy of referencing here because of their spectacular and intellectual administrative skills and the type of government they put in place during their reigns. Oba Esigie ascended the throne in 1504 and had a long and eventful reign of about forty-five years or more. During his reign was when the whitemen began to get in contact with the people of the region and much was written about his government. According to the world historical records, it was reported by a Dutch Chronicler a century after the reign of the Oba that he "undertakes nothing of importance without having sought his counsel". The message that this statement is sending to the whole world is that Oba Esigie was one of the founders of "Democracy" in the world if not the "founding father". Also during his time, the Oba commissioned many highly improved metal art works that reflected reality and have since then achieved worldwide distinction.

Of the best pieces of art works commissioned during his reign was the famous Queen Mother Idia bursts, which prompted Professor Felix Von Luschan, a former official of the Berlin Museum Fur Volkerkunde to state that: *"These works from Benin City are equal to the very finest examples of European casting technique. Benvenuto Cellini, the best Bronze metal technician of the time in Europe could not have cast them better, nor could anyone else before or after him.* These bronzes represent the very best possible achievement of the Oba's reign and the standard of development of our people of the time. The Portuguese king of this time was highly motivated and aroused Oba Esigie's interest in every possible ways including the procurement of firearms from Portugal for his future campaigns. In a letter that the king wrote to the Oba through his agent Affonso d'Averio, he thus explained to him that: "When we see that you have embraced the teachings of Christianity like a good and faithful Christian, there will be nothing within our realms which we shall not be glad to favour you, whether it be arms or cannon and all other weapons of war for use against your enemies; of such things we have a great store, as your ambassador Dom Jorge will inform you. In 1516 and without Portuguese arms, the army of Oba Esigie crushed the Igala army troops when they made an attempt to invade Benin and after the defeat they were compelled to pay reparations to Benin.

The second Oba to reference here regarding his achievements was HRH Ewuare of the great Benin who ruled from 1440 to 1473 AD. This great Oba is up till today remembered for his strong leadership and military prowess. He was noted to have marched against 201 towns and villages in the southern region of the present Nigeria, captured their leaders and made their inhabitants to pay tribute to him. Among the subdued regions included Eka, Ekiti, Ikare, Kukuruku, and Igbo territories in the west of River Niger. He was an able politician that used religious authority and intimidation as well as constitutional reforms to establish his powers over his territory. His reforms included a new tier of bureaucrats that created a strong centralized system, which he employed to administer his Empire. These bureaucrats were the Town Chiefs whom he appointed to undermine the control and authority of the hereditary Palace Chiefs and which is called the "Divide and Rule System" in modern day political premises. He picked his army commander from the Town Chiefs to lead his newly created standing army.

Controversies as to how this system worked perfectly at this age were raised among the intellectuals but Ifeka and Stride explained it thus: "Benin was apparently governed by the Oba, the Uzama and the Palace Chiefs. The Palace Chiefs were divided into three associations of title holders; the chamberlains, household officials and the harem-keepers and when Oba Ewuare found that the Palace Chiefs were becoming too powerful and for him to strengthen the authority of his Obaship, he introduced another association of chiefs that generally obtained their title on appointment by the Oba. He appointed four Town Chiefs of his choice and who were loyal to him to serve in his cabinet as his voting power in the council against the contrary decisions that the Palace Chiefs may have in mind on all matters affecting his administration or to act for him as a shield against coup de'tat.

The Town Chiefs who were the people's representatives in his government played an important role in the administration of the people while among them the Senior Town Chief, the Iyashere, was appointed the Commander-in-Chief of the army. The Town Chiefs now sat with the Palace Chiefs and the Uzama on the state council chambers to make laws and pass bills just as we have them in place today. If this was the system of government that was in place in Benin City over a thousand years back, what is then the significant difference between the government of Oba Ewuare and the system that Lord Lugard used when he claimed credit for the amalgamation of the various units of Nigeria into one federal unit? Who among the two will be more qualified to earn the prestigious title of "Divide and Rule" founding father? The judgment rests on the decisions of my readers.

Great achievements of the Yoruba people both of the past and the present including those of their brothers in the continent are beginning to unravel itself through the powers of modern information technology of the present age. Links are now better put in use than before among the people of the universe to get what is required of any question or questions and to ditch out clean information from its sources, which had hitherto been difficult to access in the past. Great thanks must be giving to the Internet inventors that made this possible for the whole world to be reached in one's living room to fish out whatever information required for the use of its users. It is through the power of this new technology that we got to know the following facts about Yoruba and other African's achievements of the past even at the time when our colonial lords were themselves still looking for a way out of the caves.

(1) In the pre-colonial era the cities in West Africa were walled to reflect their security intelligence. To support this fact, Winwood Reade, an English historian who visited West Africa in the 19th century commented that: "There are.....thousands of large walled cities resembling those of Europe in the Middle Ages, or of ancient Greece.

(2) Ibn Hankal, writing in 951 AD, informed us that the King of Ghana was "the richest king on the face of the earth" who's pre-eminence was due to the quantity of gold nuggets that had been amassed by the Royal King of Ghana.

(3) The Nigerian city of Ile-Ife was said to be paved in 1000AD on the orders of a female ruler with decorations that originated in ancient America. Naturally no one was able or wanted to explain how this took place approximately 500 years before the time of Christopher Columbus who discovered modern America.

(4) One of the greatest achievements of the Yoruba was their urban culture. By 1300 AD according to a modern scholar "the Yoruba people built numerous walled cities surrounded by farms". The cities were Owu, Oyo, Ijebu, Ijesa, Ketu, Popo, Egba, Sabe,

Dassa, Egbado, Igbomina, Owo, Akure, Ondo and the sixteen Ekiti principalities.

(5) Yoruba metal arts of the mediaeval period were of world standard. One scholar wrote about the Yoruba arts that "they would stand comparison with anything that Ancien Egypt, classical Greece and Rome, of Renaissance Europe had to offer.

(6) West African gold mining was estimated to be around 3,500 tons up to 1500 AD and worth more than $35 – 40 billion in today's market value.

(7) Michael Palin, in his TV Sahara series confirmed that the Imam of Timbuktu "has a collection of scientific texts that clearly show the planets circling the sun. They date back to hundred of years. There was very strong and convincing evidence that the scholars of Timbuktu of this time knew a lot more than their counterparts in Europe. In the 15th century in the same Timbuktu, the mathematicians already knew about the rotation of the planets, the eclipse, and they knew about the things we had to wait for almost 200 years to know in Europe through Galileo and Copernicus who came up with the same mathematical calculations as the scientists in Timbuktu had already calculated; but the two from Europe got the world fame for the same type of work while the bone fide researchers from Timbuktu and their research works were covered in the darkroom. There are many more achievements credited to people of Africa that were being kept under the table for many centuries that now needs to be brought out of their darkness and put on top of the table for the world to acknowledge and recognized.

Africa, in ages past, was acknowledged as the nursery of science and literature; from thence they are thought in Greece and Rome, and for this reason the Ancient Greeks represented their favourite goddess of wisdom – *Minerva* as an African princess. Pilgrimages were made to Africa in search of knowledge by such eminent men as Solon, Plato, Pythagoras and several of them who came to listen to the instruction of the African Eucvid, who was at the head of the most celebrated mathematical school in the world, and who flourished 300 years before the birth of Christ.

Chapter –2–

The Past Kingdoms and Empires of Yoruba Nation.

In 1960, Mali griot, Djeli Mamdoudou Kouyate, master in the art of eloquence delivered 13th century account of the people of Africa, which was orally handed down from generation to generation thus:

> *"Listen then sons of Mali, children of the black people, listen to my words for I am going to tell you of the Sundiata, the father of the Bright Country, of the Savanna land, the ancestor of those who draw the bow, the master of a hundred vanquished Kings".*

The past of the African people was full of interesting and fascinating events. For over three thousand years ago, the people of West Africa had been exposed to two important developments:
(1) Long distance trade and
(2) Their ability to manipulate stone, clay and metal to form sophisticated objects of ornament for decorations and historical events.

Through the developments of these skills from community like manner, they gradually transformed themselves into kingdoms, Empires and cities-states, which dated back to the 5th century as records could suggest through to the 16th century. The great Empires and Kingdoms had some things in common that binds them together as one people. These were the extensive trans-Saharan trade with the north of the continent, their large standing armies and an effective system of taxation.

11

The forerunners of West African Kingdoms and Empires of this time are as follows:

(1) The Empire of Ghana (which was some four hundred miles south east of the present Ghana site) was in the 8th century referred to by an Arab scholar as a strong, wealthy and highly organized Empire of its time.

(2) Two centuries later the Kingdom of Kanem came into being at the north of Lake Chad.

(3) In the 13th century, the Kingdom of Mali rose on its feet under the leadership of the Malinke Sundiata, a Kingdom which was recognized and respected for its wealth and learning. A century later the Kingdom of Mali fell into decline and became the target of Tuareg raids; but under the leadership of Askiya Mohammed the Songhay took over the territory. Trade was revived, as was the position of Timbuktu as a center of learning. The Songhay remained in control of the Kingdom until the Moroccan invaded and subdued it.

(4) In the 11th and 12th centuries, there arose two Kingdoms from Yorubaland. The two Kingdoms were Ile-Ife and Benin. These two Kingdoms remained two of the most powerful Kingdoms on the west coast of Africa. By the 17th century Ile-Ife was already eclipsed by Oyo that later became the most powerful and economically strong Kingdom on the west coast of the continent.

(5) During the 18th century, the northern part of West Africa was composed of city-states and Kingdoms with powerful economic status and further south arouse the Asante state (in the modern Ghana) into pre-eminence.

(6) In the 19th century, the Muslim reformers changed the political landscape of a very large part of West Africa including what is now known as the northern Nigeria of today under the leadership of Usman dan Fofio and built in this large area new Kingdoms and Empires of lesser status and international recognition to those already established and known during the past tens of centuries back.

These facts pointed to the premises of an understanding that Africa has not been isolated at any time from the rest of the world, as many books and papers would have erroneously led us to believe. For the Kingdoms and Empires in Africa to attain world recognition of any sort, it must have had strong economic ties or connections with other nations from other continents; be able to sustain itself with abundance of food to eat and essential goods for its citizens. Cowrie's shells from the Indian Ocean dating back to about 5000 BC have been found in Neolithic tombs in Egypt confirming that the Red Sea and Gulf of Aden coast as once one of the earliest sea trade routes for African merchants to the outside world. Arab traders have sailed the African coast since the 7th century AD, exchanging glass, spices, weapons and tools from China and India for gold, ivory, rhinoceros, slaves and animal hides.

Human beings do not evolve from nowhere and this is why Empires and Kingdoms of the world started their growth from collection of human point of view. Every human group in the world today therefore has its own mythical origins. In actual fact, if there is to be one universal culture, this will surely be it. All over the world, be it in Africa, Europe, China, Cuba, Japan, India or Singapore, we all have a variety of myths to offer. The most famous and easy to accept today is probably the Biblical creation myth, which many people in the world appear to prefer in translation. On the other side of it we have one very special and unusual story of origin, which is the scientific account of how we came to be what we are today, and it is also a story in which the continent of Africa plays a greater and central role.

Other mythical theories are timeless and unchanging probably in principle but the scientific story of myth is designed to be a transient one. Fortunately science is not set out to prove anything about the world and its origin; neither its statements are for the ages as most origin myths are intended to be. But what the science is all about is the continual refinement of the picture of the world, and of its components, and mostly how they all fit together into a functioning whole. In essence, science is surely about progress; and how then can we make scientific progress if what we believe today is not wrong tomorrow or at least incomplete? This is the course of serious headache to Anthropologists/ Archaeologists.

Similar problems face the geologists when they try to study the mysteries of the earth. These mysteries have fascinated the human race for thousands of years. The restlessness of the earth has transformed into landscapes, blackened skies and buried cities. But in the world of the past and present, our ways of life is dependent on the geologic resources that we take from mines, quarries and wells. Therefore our knowledge of our planet and learning the best ways to use its resources is critical to the welfare of our over-expanding population. The lecture delivered by Dr. Ian Tattasall at the Metropolitan Museum of Arts on the occasion of the symposium "Genesis: Exploration of origins" on March 7, 2003, which was made possible through the support of The Ford Foundation discussed on the origin of African continent and he said in one of the paragraphs of his paper that by 26,000 years and more ago, bone needles which announced the advent of tailoring, and early ceramic technology invented to bake in simple but remarkable kilns, hunting which became more complex, and fish and bird bones that showed up abundantly for the first time in food refuse was the product of Cro-Magnon achievements.

The Cro-Magnon he was talking about here was as the result of the evolutionary change of Homo sapiens, which occurred about 40,000 years ago. He said that around this time, the Homo Sapient in form of Cro-Magnon began trickling into Europe, probably from an initially African place of its origin. And by not less than 30,000 years ago according to him, the Neanderthals were gone from the entire huge swath of Europe and western Asia that they had previously inhabited, leaving the Cro-Magnons from the continent of Africa in sole possession. What is important here is the evidence that these people were "us" according to him, they possessed of a sensibility totally unprecedented in all the hominid history he had reviewed. This extraordinary record from Europe shows the human capacity that was already fully fledged. And quite evidently, this intellectual facility did not emerge in Europe. It was brought with them by the Cro-Magnons, whose new qualities had emerged elsewhere. Probably this was in Africa, for it is from this continent that we have not just the suggestions of the emergence of modern anatomical structure, but of modern behaviors as well.

Many objects and places of archeological interests dating back to between 70,000 and 100,000 years have been discovered in the continent, which actually depicted their civilization and the role they played in the development of the universe. Notable among these objects and places were the symbolic organization of space at the site of Klasies River mouth and also near the southern tip of Africa, dated at over 100,000 years ago. From the Porc-Epic cave in Ethiopia, pierced shells with strong implication of stringing of body ornamentation of about 70,000 years old were found. Bone tools of the kind introduced much later to Europe by the Cro-Magnons, are found at the site of Katanda in Congo dated to be around 80,000 years ago. In the economic and technological realm, such activities as flint-mining, pigment processing, gold and copper mining, and long-distance trade in useful materials were documented in Africa up to about 100,000 years ago. What then justifies this continent to be labeled as a backward place of the world? Your answer will be as good as mine too.

If it is possible to marry mythical ideas about the origin of people with the archeological discoveries in Africa, the product of such marriage would come near the belief of Yoruba people that Ile-Ife is the center-core of the universe and that the first creature also emerged thereof. During my research studies about world mythology, I found some similarities in Yoruba mythology and that of Greek mythology. The Greeks like their Yoruba family nation so to say were polytheistic in their religious beliefs. Polytheistic means that they believed in and worshiped many different gods. In Greek mythology, the gods often represented different forms of nature the way we have it in Yorubaland. Their religion or mythology had no formal structure with the exception of various festivals held in honor of the gods, as there was no sacred book or code of conduct to guide them.

The most powerful Greek gods were known as the Olympians and that these Olympians lived on the highest mountain called Olympus in Greece. These gods included the followings: *Zeus, Hera, Apollo, Aphrodite, Ares, Arthemis, Athena, Demeter, Hades, Hermes, Hephaestus, Poseidon, and Hestia.* Each and every one of the gods represented different forms of natural objects in the people's life-style. For example Zeus was regarded as the king of the gods just the way Yoruba people recognized Oduduwa as their most superior deity. Hera being the queen of the gods in Greek mythology has the same recognition as Osun in Yoruba mythology too. Ares and Ogun, Hephaestus and Sango, Poseidon and Olokun – all belonged to the same family member because of the similarities in their lines of duties to their communities. When one understands that the myths have been told for many centuries before they were written down, which first occurred in the case of Greek myths about 800 BC and in the 18th century or thereabout in the case of Ile-Ife, one can relish the differences in the telling and enjoy either the Yoruba's or Greek's brilliant and artful imagination throughout the ages. The retentive memories of the people must equally be respected in all of its ramifications.

The 17th and 18th centuries saw drastic changes in the Yoruba Kingdoms and Empires. These two centuries were the periods when

Yoruba sons and daughters were sold into slavery in millions by their own people just because of personal economic gains. This was the era when an un-necessary inter tribal wars were fought among the states in Yorubaland all in an attempt to catch their fellow brothers and sisters as commodities in Portuguese market squares. This was also the period when parts of their land mass and people therein were forcefully taken away from them and remained under the bondage and control of their conqueror at least up-till this age. The days of Ife hegemony were long past and if not because of Oyo's brave cavalry force that protected most of the areas to the north and west of Yoruba Kingdoms and Empires, only the gods of the land would have now be telling the story.

In 1441, it was reported that the beginning of slave trading in Africa started when ten Africans were kidnapped from the Guinea coast and taken to Portugal as gifts to Prince Henry the Navigator. In subsequent expeditions to the West African coast, its inhabitants were taken and shipped to Portugal to be sold as servants and objects of curiosity to households. In 1492, the Spaniard Christopher Columbus discovered the "New World", which marked the beginning of a triangular trade between Africa, Europe and the New World. European slave ships mainly those of British and French would take people from Africa to the New World particularly to the West Indies where they were to supplement the local Indians that were already decimated by the Spanish Conquistadors (one of the Spanish conquerors of Mexico and Peru) and this made the obnoxious business to grow from trickle to a flood, especially from the 17th century onwards.

As indicated above, the vast majority of slaves taken out of Africa to work in foreign plantations were sold by their own people particularly the rulers, traders and military aristocrats who all grew wealthy from the business not taking into account that the doors of future developments even in their own territories were being shut by their

degrading actions. The Portuguese Duatre Pacheco Pereire wrote in the early 16th century about how slaves were being acquired after his visit to Benin Kingdom that the Kingdom "is usually at war with its neighbors and takes many captives, whom we buy at twelve or fifteen brass bracelets each, or for copper bracelets, whichever they price more". An ex-slave "Olaudah Equiano" described in his memoirs published in 1789 about how African rulers carried out raids to capture slaves thus:

When a trader wants slaves, he applies to a chief for them, and tempts him with his wares. It is not extraordinary, if on this occasion he yields to the temptation with as little firmness, and accepts the price of his fellow creature's liberty with as little reluctance, as the enlightened merchant. Accordingly he falls upon his neighbors, and a desperate battle ensues. If he prevails and takes prisoners, he gratifies his avarice by selling them.

Equino was born in an area under the Kingdom of Benin in 1745. He was kidnapped at the age of ten by slave hunters who also took his sister. He was more fortunate than most other slaves in that after he served in America, the West Indies and England, he was able to save some money to buy off his freedom in 1756 at the age of 21 years.

Similar stories could be going on and on without an end to it. Even within the Yorubaland itself, captives were sold from one state-city to another within a distance of less than 20 kilometers to each other. A replica of such situation was the case of my great grandmother from my father's lineage. The story had it that she was a pretty little girl of less than 10 years old when the slave hunters captured her at the back yard of her father's palace. She was a princess and daughter of Oba Elekole of Ikole in Ekiti state and taken captive to be sold to would-be buyer outside her father's territorial command. She was brought to Akure with the hope of making much profit but nemesis caught up with them. By the time she was kidnapped, she was wearing her royal bracelet, which suggested that no merchants would be ready to put any price on her for being found on her a non-negotiable stigma. She was instead taken to the palace at Akure and handed her over to the palace officials for save keeping. There she grew up, married and never went back to her original place of birth which was less than 50 kilometers from where she grew up.

Mother Kingdom of Ile-Ife.

Ile-Ife being the sacred city and the dispenser of Yoruba basic thought has always been recognized as the founding city for all Yoruba sons and daughters throughout the world. It is said to have been standing on its present site for at least more than five hundred years with un-interrupted in its features before the appearance of Europeans on the west coast of

Africa. The founder of the great mother city – *Oduduwa* has always been accepted without any iota of doubt that he was the father of Yoruba people and that his spirit would always continue to guide them wherever they may find themselves on the surface of the earth. And it has always been so.

Much had been written about the origin and the first inhabitants of the city and the update of the information about this subject could be

accessed in some of the Yoruba history books or in the university libraries in the land. No matter how vary the stories of Yoruba origin may be, the fact still remains and always point to one direction that is closely related to their ancestor *"Oduduwa"* as the father to all Yoruba people, which cannot be disputed or distorted. How exactly he came to rule the people and where he came from should be left to the historians to sort out. A way forward

Ooni of Ife

that could lead us onto the highway (express way) was solidly constructed by our past leaders like Bishop Samuel Ajayi Crowther, Samuel Johnson, Omojola Agbebi and many others who took such an enormous pain to start the documentation of our history and people.

Ife Kingdom gave birth to other Kingdoms and Empires in Yorubaland and other coastal areas of West Africa. The Yoruba people that predominantly occupy the states of Ekiti, Ondo, Oyo, Osun, Ogun, Lagos and some parts of Kwara and Edo take their culture very seriously before and after the introduction of Christianity and Islam unto them. They are the type of people that are highly civilized and they always love to live peacefully among themselves and with their neighbors irrespective of ones religious belief. Yorubaland and its people from historical perspective has always been accommodating their fellow brothers and sisters from all ethnic groups in West Africa because they believe that what is good for the goose must as well be good for the gander. Hardly could there be any ethnic group in Nigeria that would surpass Yoruba hospitality in the realm of national understanding of sense of belonging. They have that strong believe that the people of Nigeria suffered together to win independence and they must live together to enjoy the fruits of their labor. When they sit back to review the noble contributions and sacrifices they have rendered to Nigeria as an entity, the people always feel proud of their successes and leadership positions that God has positioned them to fill.

Oyo Empire.

The geographical and cultural situations of West Africa divided the region into two major groups. There are the states belonging to the Western Sudan located in the area of Savanna vegetation and they are predominantly distinguished by their affiliation to Islamic religion after the Jihad revolution of the 19th century that swept across the West African territory. The second major group fell within the states that were situated in the tropical forest of West Africa with many Kingdoms and Empires and long existed before the advent of Christianity or Islam. These Kingdoms and Empires organized themselves into every sphere of civil order of the time. Freedom of trade in household commodities and other essentials were the form of trading pattern of the people before the Portuguese merchants turned this legal trade into an illegal slave trading in the 18th century. The people of this region around this time were farmers, fishermen, craftsmen, animal rearers, traders and they were peaceful in nature. The only friction that could possibly occurred between two clans or states of the time would probably be that of boundary rift and once such issue had been brought to the city or the regional council for adjudication, the verdict of the leader-in-council (the Oba and his advisers) remains binding on the litigants.

The Yoruba Kingdoms and Empires certainly belonged to the second group of our analysis and were profoundly influenced by the Islamic revolution of the Hausa states, which was inspired by their leader Usman dan Fodio subjecting many Yoruba people to the political and spiritual sphere of the Sokoto Caliphate. Equally too the Yoruba people were greatly influenced by European activities on the Guinea coast, especially through the changes from the slave to palm-oil trade, the availability of guns and powder, the trade in alcohol and the missionary and cultural influences coming from the recaptives from Sierra Leone, Liberia, Europe, and America. For very many centuries in the past, Yoruba people have been known to live in a number of states clustered round the centrally located mother city of Ife. The states share the same border to the north with the Niger people, on the east with the Edos, to the south by the Gulf of Guinea and on the west by Dahomey and Borgu. Yoruba people of this time had overwhelming respect for their mother-city

19

and this was why Ile-Ife was well protected against any foreign attack. The traditional ruler of Ile-Ife (Oni) too enjoyed considerable degree of respect from other Yoruba states in the Kingdom.

Oyo and Ketu were situated in the Savanna area of the Kingdom while the rest were within the tropical forests. In the 16th century Oyo was just coming up from its local level to occupy the stage of commercial prosperity with strong military powers that superseded all other Kingdoms and Empires along the coastal line. Its prosperity had two straight roads leading to it. One was its fertile soil that supported bountiful agricultural products and the other one was its position as the leading trade center in the south of Niger. Oyo being a manufacturing center of its time, its products were the pivots of triangular trading patterns throughout the region. Its major products of high quality cloth, leather, carving of quality objects and iron works were always in demand by the traders from Nupe and the Hausa states to the north, from sister Yoruba states to the east and south and yet its connection to the coastal ports on the Gulf of Guinea earned it more economic gains.

Coastal trade was the most important economic boom of this era and this was why Yorubaland became aggressively important to the traders from the north particularly the Jihadist group who was bent on fighting their ways through the Yorubaland to the coast of the Atlantic. If it were to be possible for them to reach the coast as proposed, then majority of the Yoruba city-states along the cavalry routes would have been put under the Fulani rulers just the same way that the city of Ilorin and its Yoruba inhabitants fell victim.

Oyo Empire would not have reached the height it reached during the 17th and 18th centuries if not because of the administrative skills of those that were then at the head of the government affairs of the Empire. On the other hand, if the prevailing situations of that time were to repeat itself now (I mean during this century), Yoruba people would have been sold into perpetual slavery to either the Fulanis or the foreigners. Reason being that most of the leaders we have today in Yorubaland are money grabbers who care less about the unity of the people, about their welfare, about the future of today's children and those who are greedy individuals that will always look for every opportunity to get rich quickly so as to become the greatest oppressors of their time and to the less privileged ones in the society. The Oyo leaders of this era including the Alafins that reigned in the two centuries did not acquire any formal education from any institution either at home or abroad yet they were able to manage the economy of the Empire effectively; they set up an independent standing army for the defense of their territory, they built roads and maintained fleet of horses that were being used for transportation and by the army.

Governments of lesser authorities were set up to take charge of the people in the villages and small towns, which we call local governments today. The courts of the land were free, dependable and functional and nothing went wrong with the finances of the Empire. Oyo Mesi was put in place to act as check upon the Alafin's powers. The members of this group were lineage appointed office holders and Alafin had little control over their appointment. The members of Oyo Mesi and Alafin held judicial powers in the capital while the former acted as mediators for provincial and vassal chiefs in their dealings with the King. They also act as a check upon the Ilaris while the army of the land was directly under their supervision and management. The appointment and promotion of the military personnel were equally the responsibility of this group. With the structure of the government in Oyo Empire in the 17th century, what are the significant changes that have been added to this type of government or removed out of it when the British people came to rule the country in the 20th century?

Edo (Benin) Kingdom.

Edo or Benin kingdom like its brother Kingdom of Oyo remained the most two powerful Kingdoms along the west coast of Africa up until the time that the British Protectorate was established towards the end of the 19th century. The inter-connection of the two kingdoms was obvious. *Oranmiyan*, the last grandson of *Oduduwa* who was sent to Benin to rule over them was equally the founder of the city of Oyo, which later in the years transformed into a powerful Kingdom. He was said to have left Benin in anger because of the disagreement between him and his high chiefs on matters of payment of annual tribute to the King and the chiefs by lesser communities in the Kingdom. On his ascending the throne of Benin, *Oranmiyan* cancelled the payment of annual tribute to him and the chiefs and instead he over

Omo N'Oba n'Edo –
Oba of Benin

21

ruled that the annual tributes should be used for the development of the communities that were supposed to pay the annual tribute to him and the chiefs. This was the main reason why the high chiefs planned to de-stabilize his royal regime at all cost. *Oranmiyan* when leaving Benin in anger left a cause behind that the Benin people will not see peace not until his only child named Eweka born to him by the Benin princess he married when he got to Benin was enthrone as the Oba of Benin. As a matter of fact, the people did not truly see peace as caused by *Oranmiyan* until this child named Eweka that was dump and deaf for many years before he was miraculously healed was enthroned as the Oba of Benin.

His other wife that was pregnant and expecting a baby by the time *Oranmiyan* left Benin and who was on the same trip with him back to Ile-Ife could not go further beyond the territory of the present Ado-Ekiti because of ante-natal pressure. The King had to deposit the woman with the people of this community for her care as he continued his journey back home to Ife. The story had it that the woman bore a baby boy and according to the tradition of this time, a message was sent to *Oranmiyan at Ile-Ife* concerning the birth of the new baby. Oranmiyan who had already had a dream concerning the name that the gods instructed him to give to the newborn baby sent back the emissaries with the name of *Ewi* literarily meaning that: "whatever is been asked for on earth shall be accepted in heaven". The baby grew up to become the King of Ado-Ekiti and ever since the name *Ewi has been retained as the Royal title of every Oba of Ado-Ekiti up-till today*. The success of these two Kingdoms could undoubtedly be linked to the spiritual supremacy of Oba *Oranmiyan* who was a great king, powerful warrior and skilled administrator.

The origin of the Edos according to tradition was close to that of the Yoruba people in mythology. They believed that the Edo Kingdom was founded and established by the youngest child of *Osanobua* (the High God). They also believed that the senior sons of the High God were the first kings of Ile-Ife and other Yoruba kingdoms including those of other countries in the universe. The oral history described it further that each of the children on their journey to the earth was asked to take with him whatever he liked. Some chose wealth, materials, magical powers and knowledge; but on the instruction of a bird, the youngest child chose a snail shell. When they all arrived into the world, they met it void and it was covered by water. They could not live either on water or in the void and something mysterious had to happen. The same bird that instructed the youngest child to choose snail shell appeared again and instructed him to over turn the shell and when he did so, earth dusts began to pour down of it to form the land where they could all stay to live. So the young child now became the owner of the land and his brothers had to become his tenants by bartering their belongings with him for a piece of land to stay and live. This made the young man to be richer and more prosperous that his brethren.

Oduduwa's mythical appearance into the Earth described it that he too was sent by Olodumare (High God) and on his way to the earth, he brought with him a cock (bird), some quantity of earth dusts, and a palm kernel.

When he arrived, he too met the world void and covered with water. He was instructed to throw the earth dusts upon the water and asked the cock to spread it over thereby the land was formed. The Biblical version of origin of the world too confirmed that at the beginning the earth was without form, and void; and darkness was upon the face of the deep. And God said, let the waters under the heaven be gathered together unto one place, and let the dry land appear: and it was so. Therefore every theory about the origin of the earth agreed that there was a particular time when the earth was void and covered with water and by whatever means, reasons or instructions the earth planet came into being and people were manufactured to occupy it. The rest of the story will be left to the scientists, historians and religious scholars of all religions in the land to shed more light unto this issue.

Edo people like their brothers from Yorubaland are industrious people of various economic disciplines. They are good farmers, craftsmen, traders, administrators, warriors and no-nonsense beings. Records showed that standard political structure and high administrative skills were already established in the Kingdom by the 14th century or even earlier before the Portuguese merchants visited the land for the first time. Its greatest sphere of influence in its territory and beyond occurred during the 15th and 16th centuries when its territory was

Edo People

expanded astronomically with strong political stability through the quality leadership skills of such Obas like *Ewuare, Ozolua, Esigie, Orhogba, and Ehengbuda* who reigned in the Kingdom of Benin during these two centuries. By the middle of the 17th century, it was revealed that the Oba of Benin ruled over an extensive territory from the region of Lagos down to Igbo-speaking areas of the present Delta state. Edo's influence on the east should naturally terminate at its own side of the bank of River Niger but according to Portuguese early maps of the time, its frontier extended as far as Bonny and Idah near the Nupe country.

Its contact with the Portuguese was dated back to 1485 when the kingdom was visited by the Portuguese Ambassador D'veiro, who returned to Portugal with the chief of Ughoton and who later became Benin's Ambassador to Portugal. This Ambassador was reported to be a man of eloquent speech coupled with natural wisdom. During his visit to Portugal, he was accorded state recognition and state banquet was given in his honor. On his way back home, the king of Portugal presented him with lots of rich material goods for himself, his wife and the Oba of Benin. He visited many historical places in Portugal and on behalf of the Oba and people of Benin he extended their hands of friendship to the king and people of Portugal. Based on this historical visit, the Portuguese people decided to establish Catholic missions with churches in Benin City. Their trading and diplomatic influence in the Kingdom were being noticed everywhere until say the second half of the 17th century when the English and Dutch traders began to un-seat them. Its trading posts and missions began to close down and in the 1660s their influence was extinguished completely in the Edo Kingdom's territory.

British Diplomacy in Benin.

The approach of the British to Benin was purely the mixture of force and persuasion, which caused serious rifts in the Oba's council. The first English men to reach the powerful Edo Kingdom as reported by Basil Davidson arrived at the port of Benin in 1553 during the reign of Oba Orhogbua. A Portuguese recorder that was with them at that time recorded that this Oba like Oba Esigie who ruled before him could read, write and speak Portuguese language very fluently. The British of the past were known for their hidden imperialistic agenda. They would present a different version of their intentions at first encounter but later come out with the original intention, which would lead the people at the other side of the negotiating table into their grave yards if care was not taken. History attested to this assertion in so many instances during their colonial days in Africa. This was the kind of diplomacy that they used to oust out their European brother – the Portuguese and which later culminated in the infamous punitive expedition against the Edo Kingdom in 1897.

The results of their military expedition were the burning of the capital, the wanton looting of the Oba's palace of Benin art works totaling about 2,500 pieces of its famous bronze treasures, which now adorn the British museum; the travesty of the jungle justice meted out to the nobles of the Empire, the marginalization of the ordinary people of the kingdom and finally the subsequent deportation of the reigning monarch of the Kingdom – Oba *Ovonramwen ne Ogbaisi* on September 13, 1897 on the orders of the British government at home through its agency in West Africa. British offered positions of importance to the chiefs who came out of their hidings and who indicated their willingness to co-operate with them. To this overture some chiefs responded but the throne was left vacant as it was and still against the Benin tradition to crown a new Oba while the old one still lived. All they could do was to rule the Empire by direct rule system through the African agents (the Benins) and after the manner of the French diplomacy.

Chapter –3–

The collapse of the First Yoruba Nation.

The first Yoruba nation was a powerful nation that comprised of Kingdoms, Empires, City-states and villages with similarities in the system of government derived from the mother-kingdom of Ife. There could only be slight differences here and there but the substance in the style of governance and mood of worship of their deities constituted significant similarities of the people as one indivisible entity. The ancient Yoruba states as well as the present are known to be cohesive in nature. This attitude may be related to the language that bounds them together or any other historical substances that glue them together as people. Historians and archeologists have learnt a lot about the developments that preceded the emergence of states in Africa and they have come into the open that the Africans developed their states and groups in response to local conditions and opportunities. For example, people because of protection to their trades and persons moved to south of the Sahara from the hot climate to more greener areas and thereby permanently settled to form city-states, empires and kingdoms.

Many theories have been postulated regarding the idea behind the state formation in Africa, which began among the Egyptians during the era of Pharaohs, and thereafter spread across to other parts of the continent. These explanations have led the historians to go deep into the era of "Pre-history" of African states and came out with the strong theory about the developments which led the African societies to create centralized political systems. They now say with authority that in most cases the development of states in Africa was as a result of conditions and opportunities, which sounds very logical and sensible as against the past theories of influence that spread either from Egypt, Europe or Asia.

Instead the reason they see involves African people living in a great variety of locations and they used their political skills and wisdom to create for themselves centralized systems of government, which others came to copy from them. Some of the natural primary conditions that were involved in state origins in Africa and elsewhere included fertile soils, abundance of rainfall for agricultural products, lakes or rivers for fish production, mineral resources for their technological developments and accessibility of trade routes with their neighbors. All these put together called for the success of the first Yoruba nation in which its people lived in a great variety of locations and which had productive economies and vibrant commercial systems that allowed their artists and craftsmen such freedom from scarcity, and provided for abundant metals, woods and other materials they needed for their living.

It was not a joke that the formula used in the creation of city-states, empires and kingdoms which formed the first and subsequent Yoruba nations created along with them sophisticated institutions of governments; and just like all other human societies of the world greed and love of power that had been planted into the system of human beings from the ages past sneaked in itself to cause political instability and social crisis in the growing society. Undoubtedly, Yoruba people began their journey from their mother-city of Ile-Ife and were heir apparent to an ancient and cultured civilization, which radiated in them from generation to generation and which we still see in them till today. Its culture is well known for sophisticated artistic triumphs, superior oral literature, complex pantheon of gods and urban lifestyle. Regrettably, its civilization saw the exodus of its millions of men, women and children into the Americas as slaves during this first republican era. The numbers of their men, women and children plus their cultural impact were so great that their religion and culture remained important today in modern Brazil, Cuba and in some cities of the United States. But unfortunately these virtues are gradually diminishing and becoming so unimportant in their home base land in the present Nigeria.

Historians have led some credence to Yoruba culture as being old indeed and that their language separated them from that of their nearest neighbors for at least more than 5000 years ago. They also analyzed that they separated from their most closely related neighbors, the Igalas in about 2000 years ago. This theory of linguistic relationship between Yoruba and Igala has led to some scholars to suggest that Yoruba nation may have been comprised by migrants who came from the region where the Igala people now live, near the confluence of the Niger and Benue Rivers. Clarity regarding all these theories would eventually surface one day through scientific discoveries in the future to put to rest everything about its postulations.

There is nothing wrong in postulating many theories surrounding a particular subject but as time goes on, the bits and pieces of facts from practical evidences from here and there would emerge to build up the pyramid of such subject. Clearer than in the past decades, archeological discoveries have now established the antiquity of Ife beyond any reasonable doubt. Artifacts from the mother-city have shown that the city has been enjoying uninterrupted way of life for at least since the 5th century and that from between 9th and 12th centuries it was already a big city with all attributable qualities of any city of its age in anywhere in the world. Some of the terracotta sculptures and bronze castings of this age that were found in other areas of the continent were synonymous with Ife craftsmanship and dated back to several centuries old. These sculptures attested to how important trade had been to Yoruba people from their day one.

One may ask a good question as to how the Ife craftsmen came about their source to copper, which was the main manufacturing material to their sculpture trade. It has been speculated that copper may have come to Ife through trade routes from the northwest of Africa, central Europe or from not too far away deposits in southern Nigeria. If these assertions were to be true, then Yoruba people must have grown high in trading activities among themselves and their neighbors especially in such commodities like cloth, kola-nuts and food items, which were abundantly cultivated on their land for an exchange of copper and iron from other neighborhoods.

In the development of a society or a nation, there is no period of complete cut-off but instead different levels of transformation may occur. The bronze-age in Yoruba economic development transformed itself into the rise of empires and various government systems in the land. Therefore trade was a crucial factor and one of the most important political developments in Yoruba history. Trading activities centrally dictated the migration of people from one geographical location to the other and as well changed their culture from one form into another. Under this centrifugal force, Oyo kingdom came into being and became prominence among all other Yoruba kingdoms of its first national republic. Oyo which is a city that was founded around 1100 AD by

Oba Oranmiyan, the last grandson of Oduduwa after he had vacated the throne of Benin in an annoyance with the Benin chiefs continued to grow and developing itself into a small kingdom with lesser powers and sizeable territorial land mass. As from the 16th into the 17th centuries, Oyo had become the dominant power in Yorubaland, establishing its influence in all the nooks and corners of the Yoruba kingdom and extended as far as to Dahomey, Bariba, Borgu and down to the Atlantic Ocean shores. Undoubtedly, the expansion program of Oyo Empire allowed it to trample on some little state-cities during this era and which could be associated with civil strife and demonstration of its military superiority over the rest of Yoruba empires.

The availability of horses to Oyo nobles and warriors from the north gave them tremendous edge over all other empires and kingdoms both in the war front and trade expansion within and outside their territory. This singular opportunity enhanced the Oyo warriors to force the powerful state of Dahomey to become their tributary between 1730 and 1748 and also to beat the Whydah and Badagry military forces and forced them to kiss the canvas at the orders of Oyo super warriors. The defeat of these two nations opened up trade routes for Oyo to have direct trade link with the European merchants along the seacoast. The major export commodity of the Oyo Empire was slave trade between them and the European merchants in return for cloth and other domestic goods like mirror, brass bangles and alcohols.

It was reported that between 1680 and 1730 exports of slaves from Oyo alone was averaged at 20,000 per year and for this period covering 50years, Oyo may have reached the staggering number of close to 1,000,000 (one million) slaves exported to the New World. Out of curiosity, if we are to go by statistical judgment and we allow for both natural and incidental deaths to occur for this period of 50years and we forego 20% of such figure for such calamity, it means that we shall still be left with the population of about 800,000 people to be remained within the Yoruba kingdom to work at various industries and expand the local economy that would be beneficial to the people and better their lives more than when they were exported to various foreign lands of no return. This was the major trade that elevated Oyo Empire from junior kingdom to world-class status of this period. Commercial wealth was actually very necessary to Oyo for it to maintain its military power that was built around a fast striking cavalry force. But for how long would this power last?

The Government of Oyo Empire.

Whenever reference is made to the first Yoruba Government, Oyo Empire played a key role because the standard of community politics in the empire was the role model for which the basic foundation for all other empires in Yoruba kingdom was built upon. Oyo political system was built on four strong pillars of who was who in the city with different levels of power assigned to each of them by the constitution of the empire. The four powerful figures were the Alafin who was considered as semi-divine personality and the monarch who holds all the authority of the empire, the Bashorun, the Oluwo and the Are Ona-Kakanfo. Alafin, the monarch and the head of the empire appointed three other lieutenants to head important divisions of his government; the Ona Efa

Current Alafin of Oyo

was the chief judge of the land dispensing the imperial justice, the Otun Efa was the head of Sango deity worshippers, the group that was in charge of the link with his ancestors, and the Osi Efa who controlled the palace finances. He was in charge of receiving all the tributes and tolls paid to Alafin by communities in the empire as well as the head of the intelligence service of the land. The administration of towns and villages under the empire was put under the Ilaris who may either act independently on their own or ask for the assistance of the chief priest of Shango shrine of the town or village they may be posted to administer, and who in most cases used both political and religious sanctions to enforce their judicial decisions. For the protection of the monarch, the wives of Alafin too had a role to play in the administration of their husband just the way the first ladies of any nation of today features in the administrative set up of the governments of their husbands. These women served the eyes and ears of the monarch within the women folk of the empire as they most of the time mixed with them freely the way secret service agents mix up with ordinary citizens to perfect their civic duties.

The Alafin of 12th to 15th centuries or probably beyond enjoyed the support and patronage of every member of their family the way and manner with which the Kings or Queens of any empire would enjoy the support of the members of their family during their reigns. In those days, Alafin used to associate his chosen son (possibly the elder son), the Aremo or heir apparent, with his rule in preparation for his succession. Kingship in Yorubaland is always a lineage issue and its baton passes from father to son and as such the father makes sure that the son he intends to succeed him is well prepared for the task ahead of him. In most of the cities and towns where kingship is regarded as being supreme in Yorubaland maintains this culture up till today except where the crown rotates among the families who have equal traditional rights to the throne.

Next to Alafin in the hierarchical order is the Bashorun, who leads the Oyo-Mesi Council that usually comprised of seven notable men of chieftaincy titles in the capital. This Council of men of high reputation and dignity often acted as a check on the activities and powers of the monarch. Their appointments were traditional in the sense that the Alafin had only minimal role to play when they were to be appointed. All that was needed from him after the selection or appointment of any of them had been made was only to give his blessings and ask for his cooperation in the smooth running of the empire's administration. The Council was so powerful that the Ilaris and the army were put under its authority and supervision. Even the fate of Alafin himself lies in the hands of the Oyo-Mesi should he act contrary to the public norms and principles that established him as the king. Large volume of power was given to Bashorun under the empire's Constitution as his decisions in most cases were final. He could proclaim that the ancestors and heaven had lost confidence in any Alafin that was found guilty of serious offense against the tradition of the people and their gods and he could as well order the beheading of such Alafin to appeace the gods. A case to note here was the judgment passed on Alafin Majeogbe who reigned at around the second half of the 18th century when Bashorun Gaa was the head of the then Oyo-Mesi Council.

The third in command in the Empire was the Oluwo who was the head of the Ogboni group. Oluwo by tradition in Yorubaland is the chief of Ifa Divinity whom the Empire or community consulted with in all matters affecting the progress and befalling calamities on their communities and his findings carries heavy weights. In his position as the chief priest who interpreted the intentions and opinions of the Supreme God (Olodumare) through Ifa oracle could accept or reject the Bashorun's decision to send any erring Alafin to his gallow. The

Constitution of the Empire was constructed in such a way that each group was given enough powers to check on the activities of the other group so as to minimize the abuse of power from any group or person. In this regard and in some instances when an Alafin had an immense influence in the Ogboni Council, he could use the provisions of this influence to check on the ambitious acts of Bashorun. This was the reason why Alafin's representative sat on the Ogboni Council not as an observer but as one whose opinion carries considerable weight in its decisions.

The next in line of authority was the Are Ona Kakanfo who was the Field Marshal of the army of the Empire. He had seventy other war chiefs called *Eso* whose decisions were very important in the War Council. For Kakanfo not to mingle with the politics of the empire, an army barrack was established for him, his war chiefs and his soldiers outside the capital city. This type of administrative arrangement was already on the ground in Yorubaland long before the colonial lords came to replicate it by building barracks for their security men in the 20th century to which they laid claim to as if it was their own invention. The only difference between these two systems was that the Kakanfo and his military men were loyal to the government of their time and he (Kakanfo) did not attempt to overthrow that government and install himself as the sole authority. But the foreign modern army introduced by the British had in their military training curriculum the instructions and methods of how to overthrow the constituted government of the people and install themselves as the government-in-power and at the same time the security agent protecting the people. The protection of the treasury of the land never meant anything to them because of their looting intentions and aspirations.

History reminded us that in the third quarter of the 18th century the political system of the Empire became very unstable and reached the level of civil war. During this period Bashorun Gaa was said to have raised five consecutive Alafins to the throne and destroyed four of them himself. He was known in the history of the Empire as the most cruel and non-volatile Bashorun Oyo would every produced. He and the members of his family particularly his son *Olayiotan* and his nephew *Obe* ruled Oyo despotically and unchecked until the Empire groaned under his iron hand. Oyo high chiefs such as *Jagunna, Ashipa, Samu, Alapinni and Agba-Akin* were just mere chiefs without any sound authority to err their views and opinions because of the excesses of Bashorun Gaa's power throughout the Empire.

When Alafin Abiodun became the monarch around 1770, he was so terrified of Bashorun Gaa to such an extent that he was determined to abdicate the throne voluntarily until his palace advisers advised him to go to Bashorun's courtyard every morning to prostrate for Bashorun as if he was the Alafin and he Abiodun was his mere representative on the throne. Bashorun Gaa reluctantly cherished this mark of respect as he knew that this attitude was wrong for an Alafin to prostrate for anyone under the heaven as from the day he was pronounced the king over his subjects in accordance to the traditions of Yoruba culture. Alafin Abiodun and his chiefs used this strategy to have enough time to plan for the extermination of Bashorun Gaa.

In the planning program, the King and his council members secretly invited Are-Ona-Kakanfo the Field Marshall to assemble his men to attack Bashorun Gaa's courtyard and destroyed all he had including the members of his family. The army led by Kakanfo himself entered the city of Oyo and massacred Gaa's family and everything belonging to him. In the end he was killed as a result of the iron hand he used in ruling the people. With the exit of Bashorun Gaa from the administration of the Empire, peace returned and Alafin Abiodun became a strong ruler and his period of reign was remembered as a golden age, but after his death, problems returned to the Empire.

The Collapse of Oyo Empire.

The collapse of Oyo Empire psychologically professed the collapse of the first Yoruba republic in the sense that the problems of the Empire sparked off lots of unrest and warfare throughout the Yorubaland. Immediately after the pass away of Alafin Abiodun, trouble started to re-surface itself in the Empire. Invasion assault on Nupe by Oyo was a disastrous defeat to Oyo side, and Dahomey no longer feared the strength of Oyo army anymore when they captured Ketu. The final stroke that broke the camel's back was in 1827 when Kakanfo Afonja, a slave-born child of the royal blood could not get the mandate for the throne and discovered a plot to exterminate him by the Alafin, raised a revolt in Ilorin, a town founded by his great grandfather. During this time Oyo Empire was already having so many problems at hand to solve and because of this the issue of Afonja was carelessly allowed to degenerate into a full blown crisis. He got the sympathy of some provincial chiefs especially from the Onikoyi of Ikoyi, a city that was then the largest provincial town in the Empire and as well as that of Mallam Alimi who was Afonja's Fulani advisor and the leader of the militant group from Dan Fodio's Jihadist armies from the north, and some Yoruba Muslims particularly Solagberu and others from within. Large numbers of Hausa and Fulani slaves in the empire fled to Ilorin to support the course of Afonja. The only surviving son of Bashorun Gaa named Ojo who was exiled in Borgu returned to Oyo with his own army to support Alafin to crush Afonja's revolt but his course was seen as revenge to purge those who had turned against his father in the civil war of the previous century.

The Onikoyi of Ikoyi at the on-set pitched his war-tent with Oyo and both of them were marching on Ilorin, but suddenly he changed sides in the battle to support the victory of Afonja in the battle. It was a clear victory for Afonja with the help of the ex-slaves but after the crisis, these ex-slaves became so notorious that they began to take vengeance on their former masters all about the place. Their excesses were now turning the Yoruba people against Afonja, and because of this Afonja ordered them to stop. Afonja was not a Muslim and to take advantage of this, religious interpretations were now being coined out of the situation. All sorts of meanings were being read into the whole scenario while some people were accusing him that he was hostile to the new Islamic religion coming from the north and as a result a plot was hatched to kill Afonja and truly they got him killed. The assassination of Afonja now opened the gate of authority to Abdul Salami and with the assistance of his Yoruba wife he mounted the throne of Ilorin as an Emir (an alien title in Yoruba kingdom) that gave his allegiance to the Sokoto Caliphate rather than to either the Alafin of Oyo or the Ooni of Ife. Alimi's sphere of influence among the Fulani led troops grew stronger to such a level that Afonja when he was around realized that he was no longer in control of his father's land. Equally Solagberu a Yoruba person and an accomplice of the Fulani's ploy to over-run Iloring, was as well eliminated in the conflict.

In 1826 when Clapperton visited Oyo-Ile during the reign of Alafin Majotu and during the reign of his successor Alafin Amodo, Oyo-Ile was captured by Ilorin and Alafin Amodo made a nominal submission to Islam. He was later killed in a counter-attack on Ilorin when Ilorin forces destroyed important towns in Ikoyi province as a result of the counter-attack. As a result of this devastation, Yoruba refugee had no alternative better than to move southwards to found a new place to stay. The last Alafin to reign at Oyo-Ile was Alafin Oluewu who reigned between 1833 and 1835. He too was killed in the attack he made on Ilorin with the help of the Bariba warriors around 1836 in an attempt to re-capture Ilorin from the Fulanis. When this attempt failed the capital was completely abandoned. The collapse of Oyo Empire could not be attributed to a singular factor, but to series of related military, economic and political problems, which it had increasing difficulty to resolve. In the late 18th century precisely in 1783, it suffered a terrible defeat at the hands of the Bariba and in 1790 the same fate befell it from the hands of Nupe warriors. Probably in the same year the Egbas revolted, while Dahomey in the south-west was increasingly becoming a powerful state.

Politically the conflict between Alafin and the council of Oyo-Mesi, which stretched over a long period of time and that remained unresolved, played a key role in the collapse of the Empire. Understandably, Alafin was unable to create a military force on his own in the capital and as such the control of the army was still largely rested on the shoulders of the Oyo-Mesi Council. The Constitution of the Empire did not give any Alafin the authority to raise fund for any project besides the ones that were in the known of the Council; therefore, Oyo-Mesi would still remained the boss to the military personnel. The same can be said concerning the loyalty of the provincial rulers. Their loyalty to the capital-city was already bearing diminished returns as most of them were now sniffing independence odor because of their growth and territorial expansion. After the decline in the slave trade business, the towns in the provinces that had earlier enjoyed adequate rewards from the spoils of the trade were nursing the idea of opting out of the union. They were now thinking that if participation in the Empire system could no longer provide them substantial rewards, there was no point sticking their heads to the course of the Empire anymore.

While the structures of Oyo Empire were falling apart in the north of the land, series of wars were being developed in the south, which involved Ife, Ijebu, Owu and Egba, and which led to the destruction of both Owu and Egba kingdoms. The decline of Oyo Empire and the conflict between Owu and Egba, set the stage for the long series of conflicts that engulfed Yorubaland for the rest of the century. The refugees that moved from Oyo down south formed the nucleus of the new states that sprang up in the first quarter of the 19th century.

Examples of such states were Abeokuta that was founded in the 1820s by the combination of Egba and the survivors from Owu, and Ibadan that was founded in 1826 on the site of an Egba Agura town by a mixture of Ife, Oyo and Ijebu. Yoruba historians made us to believe that Ijaye town too was established around the same period of time by a group from Ikoyi and led by their leader - Kurunmi.

Finally, Alafin Atiba Atobatele (the great - great grandfather of the author from mother side) who reigned between 1837 and 1859 founded the new town of Oyo after the destruction of Oyo-Ile in 1836. The political institutions of the old Oyo empire was replicated in the new capital city but Oyo's influence over towns like Ijaye and Ibadan was no longer there as it was in the past. But still yet Kurunmi of Ijaye was appointed Are-Ona-Kakanfo while Oluyole of Ibadan was given the title of Bashorun. Ijaye's sphere of influence extended to the north-west and that of Ibadan to the north-east, where it came into hot conflict with the original intentions of the Jihadists from Ilorin on their way to the Atlantic shores in Lagos. Despite their defeat by the gallant warriors of Ibadan in 1840 at the battle of Oshogbo, the rulers of Ilorin continued to agitate troubles and problems and were seriously involved in the wars that occurred between other Yoruba states towards the final quarter of the century.

With the eradication of Oyo-Ile as the capital of Oyo Empire and the establishment of new states of Abeokuta, Ibadan, Ijaye, there was significant shift in the development of new weaponry technology to fight the wars and the ways of living of the people. In the past, the importance of cavalry was necessary and paramount to the trade of the people and the security of their territory, but now with the closeness of the people to the Atlantic trade, European war technology and importation of arms were being learnt and purchased to fight the internal wars that were waged against the new states either from outside aggressors or those within. This actually increased the European penetration by the explorers, traders, missionaries that were later followed by foreign troops and instructors, and finally the administrators that were used to annex the whole territory.

The collapse of Oyo Empire significantly increased the population and the potentials of the small communities under the Old Empire. Examples were such places like Ogbomosho that was relatively small in the past and which now swelled into big city through the influx of refugees from the old Oyo area. Same could be said about Oshogbo that was originally a small outpost of the Ijesha kingdom, which now accepted many refugees and took on the character of an Oyo rather than Ijesha city. The position of Ibadan cannot be swept under the carpet in the new development.

The old Oyo military men formed the power group in the new environment because of their cavalry experience of the past. But unfortunately Ilorin had assumed a greater power that made it to control the northern routes and thereby monopolized the horse trade. Ibadan master warriors had no alternative other than to be quick enough to switch from cavalry war tactics to the new European military technique, which helped them to defeat the Ilorin cavalry at the battle of Oshogbo in 1840 with the aid of the long Dane guns that were superior to the bows and arrows. The collapse of the First Yoruba Republic caused us many drawbacks, as well as it opened new opportunity areas and new ways of life. It actually improved our thinking and trading abilities and provided us with many channels to the domain of our future problems as a people.

Chapter –4–
The Return of Yoruba Natives from Captivity.

The slave trader's activities along the West Africa coast antedate the discovery of America, but the trade received a big boost with the development of sugar plantation in Brazil in the 2nd half of the 16th century. The demand for this human commodity substantially increased in the 17th century in the Caribbean and South America, and during the 18th century it had spread to North America without limit. Many of these slaves would have passed through Oyo because of the super influence that Oyo had in the business. Initially the Yoruba themselves were not enslaved in large numbers not until the outbreak of the early 19th century wars that aggravated the search for slaves among the refugees that was brought about as a result of the displacement of the people from their original place of abode. Under this unavoidable situation, many Yoruba citizens fell victim and were taken captive along with other nationals.

The unfortunate ones were taken to the foreign land where they permanently lived and died in slavery while the few fortunate ones were rescued through the abolition of the slave trade program by the European powers that were originally the inventors of the business. It was in Exeter Hall in the city of London in June 1840, where the Prince Consort, the German born husband of Queen

Exeter Hall in London

Victoria made his first public appearance in England and also where he presided over the meeting for the abolition of the slave trade. This meeting produced positive results that saved the lives of many innocent African children and men that would have been bundled out of their domains and be made to suffer for the offence they did not commit. Before the historic meeting that ratified the abolition program, the British Naval force, man-O-war had started cruising off the West African coast on anti-slaving duties and put ashore at Freetown the captured vessels together with its cargo of rescued slaves. This action did not actually halt the trade immediately but it did put life back into the system of large numbers of emancipated slaves in Sierra Leone, out of which Yoruba descent constituted the bulk of it. On arrival at their new environment in Freetown, some of them became apprentice of many trades under the skilled European artisans in such areas as bricklaying, carpentry and joinery, tailoring and boatyard mechanics while some of them turned to farming in the suburb villages and traders in the cities of the colony. The younger ones including the children were sent to mission schools for instructions and the women turned to petty trading to supplement the meager income of their spouses.

The new environment turned many into the new religion of their masters, which was Christianity and those who were Moslems and traditional believers continued to adhere to their religious beliefs. It behooved on the people to learn the language and the culture of their rescuer hence they were at the mercy of the British organization in all forms at the colony. As time went by most of them became great in their professional and training callings. Those who sought to learn how to read and write English language became employee of the government of the colony, the missions, and the available commercial establishments as at then. Record showed that by 1840, after some of them had spent close to twenty years in the colony, they had become successful traders. One of them was Thomas Will who was the head of Yoruba Community in Freetown, who died and left in his estate the sum of two thousand pound sterling and a house in Walpole Street Freetown. Those in the employment of the missionary like Samuel Ajayi Crowther who arrived at the colony in June 1822 with others were rising steadily.

The life in the colony was not all that rosy for the liberated Africans because nearly everything that constituted essential living materials was scarce. The land to firm was restricted while trading activities were low and dull. This prompted the merchants and the traders to look for more favorable opportunities beyond the colony into the north of the region. In an attempt to expand his business activities, one John Langley who had been trading in the colony for many years and now trying to peep into the northern market place was almost sent to jail by Alkali of Port Lokko for selling gunpowder to his enemies; if not because of the timely intervention of the Governor of the colony in 1834 he would have gone to jail for this sort of trading offense.

Some years later, some group of liberated Africans collected money together and bought one of the condemned slave vessels confiscated from the slave traders to trade down to the coast as far as to Badagry and Lagos. It was this trip that offered some of the traders such opportunity to come in contact with their people they had lost contact with several years back. Some of them were able to meet with their parents, families, and people they knew as acquaintances and the moment was seen as a moment of miracle and joy. Two years later, Samuel Ajayi Crowther then a missionary teacher described the moment thus:

Samuel Ajayi Crowther

> *Some found their children, others their brothers and sisters, by who they were entreated not to return to Sierra Leone. One of the traders had brought to Sierra Leone two of his grandchildren from Badagry to receive instructions. Several of them had gone into the interior altogether.*
>
> *Others in this colony have messages sent to them by their parents and relations whom the traders met at Badagri.*

The trip sent vibrant signal to both the liberated Africans and the authorities in the colony. It was reported that in November 1839, that twenty three leading Yoruba merchants, led by Thomas Will, presented to Governor Doherty a petition regarding the establishment of similar colony like the one in Sierra Leone in Badagry where their people back home could enjoy the same Gospel facilities as they were in Freetown. The petitioners thanked the government and people of England for the hand of friendship and safety extended to the liberated Africans and the type of training they had acquired through their gestures and kindness. In the petition they requested that the Queen will graciously sympathized with them to establish the colony that the same may be under the Queen's Jurisdiction and also beg her to send along with them the missionaries so that the slave trade may be permanently extinguished in their country.

Administratively, Governor Doherty of the colony forwarded the petition to the Home Office through Lord John Russell who was then the Secretary with the following comment to the government:

> *If it should consist with the design of Her Majesty's government for the exterpation of the slave trade and the civilization of the continent to encourage the establishment of any settlements of this description, government's decision would be appreciated.*

The reply from the Secretary of State to Governor Russell went thus:

> *We cannot send them without giving them security and protection, which implies expenses. But they can go if they wish.*

The administrative saga on this subject matter went forth and backward until the Governor was certain that the twenty-three signatories to the petition who were mainly merchants with landed properties in the colony were not the ones intending to emigrate but rather those at the lower end of the ladder in the community who were not interested in the British government's colony project in Badagry but only to go back home at all cost. Based on the reply from the Home Office telling the Governor that whosoever wished to leave on his or her own could go, the Governor was able to issue passport to only forty-four men and seventeen women out of the two hundred people that applied. This marked the first official return of the re-captives from exile.

The yearning of the liberated Yoruba citizens to go back home did not received the total blessing of the missionaries in Sierra Leone because they assumed that once they allowed them to leave, they would return to heathenism while they settled back in their country. This opinion was later expressed at Abeokuta by Henry Townsend when he said that: "by leaving Sierra Leone, the emigrants had left the country where God was known for this where God was not known; thus turning their backs unto Him". Fortunately the emigrants proved the missionaries wrong in their thinking and assumption, which made the missionaries to adopt more conciliatory attitude in dealing with them. The proposed Niger Expedition was to be an exciting moment for everyone in the colony as soon as it was made possible because of many opportunities the Expedition would open to the African merchants in their urge to impact their people in the interior with European life-style.

The time was now coming to the missionaries to catch-up with the original ideas of Buxton regarding the evangelization in Africa by the Africans themselves. It was reported that it came to a stage when Governor Doherty no longer concerned himself on the poor people leaving the colony because of job scarcity, but of the merchants who wished to carry back among their countrymen the arts and improvements of Europe which they had acquired in the colony, with the fortunes which had been amassed by them. Samuel Crowther described the excitement in his forecast that: *the success of the Expedition would not just benefit only the Egbas and the Yoruba community but as well as the Kanuris, Hausas, Nupes and the Ibos who would want to emigrate to their countries.*

The hitch in the First Niger Expedition did not stop the emigrants for continuing their movements back into where they originally belonged to in the Yoruba country especially to Badagry and Egbaland. The missionaries too had no better alternative other than to follow the footsteps of the emigrants to wherever they wished to go because they too have a mission to accomplish. The Methodists, who played lesser role in the evangelical and rescue operations of the people from the slave traders than the Church Missionary Society were the first to reap from their labors, and to make the early use of the abundant opportunities that the emigrants had acquired over the years in the colony in terms of business knowledge and skills, exposure to European way of life and the knowledge of the new Christian religion.

On 24 September 1842, Rev. Thomas Birch Freeman, the Methodist Mission Superintendent at Cape Coast who on behalf of his organization had visited Ashanti twice was asked to take up the superintendence of Badagry as an out-station of Cape Coast in response to the request of the emigrants there in early June of 1841 through their petition to Rev. Dove, the Superintendent of the Methodist Mission in Sierra Leone. In their petition, the emigrants in Badagry invited the missionaries to visit them urgently in order to fulfill their desire of illuminating their country with the Gospel of God, building of schools and to provide instructions to their younger ones so that their country may rank among the civilized nations of the world.

The important factor that was amiss in the whole emigrant scenario was that Buxton's philosophy was not correctly addressed from the beginning. Trading capability skills or agricultural produce for feeding did only very little but did not go directly to the root of the issue. The missionaries initially forgot to find ways to develop Buxton's idea of "Africans for Africa" and by the time that their brains opened to this philosophy was when the idea of training the mind and head of the people was being discussed and planned. The beginning step to take towards this direction was when an appeal for funds to expand the work at Fourah Bay as a training institution and the improvement of secondary education in Freetown was lunched. Because the people were bent on returning home, they could no longer wait for the proposed training program or for the improvement of education that was forth coming from England as the urge to move back to their country was already deeply rooted in them. The missionaries had to be sent along with them immediately so that the investments on them both morally and financially would not be totally perished.

Rev. T.B. Freeman arrived Badagry on 24 September 1842 marking the official date when the missionaries landed on the soil of Yoruba country (now part of Nigeria) to begin evangelical works. On his trip to Badagry he was accompanied by William de Graft a native of Cape Coast and, who served him in the mission as an "assistant missionary". On his arrival at Badagry he bought a small piece of land for three hundred pounds sterling on which he immediately began to build a temporary chapel with bamboo and palm frond materials, and later started work on the mission house that was to accommodate himself, his assistant and other church staffs.

In fact when the house was completed it became a piece of an extraordinary object that attracted the natives who were often seen standing in groups very close to it to admire the structure because such was the first of its kind they had ever seen. He was holding prayer meetings on Sundays with the emigrants, obtaining lands for them to settle and sometime be their family judge to settle rifts among them, be there for them as their consultant in all matters relating to the growth of their personal life and that of the community. On Sunday 11

December 1842, Freeman Visited Abeokuta to link up with the Egba emigrants and there he was warmly received by Sodeke, his chiefs and the emigrants and he stayed in Abeokuta for 10 days holding prayer meetings, visiting the chiefs to discuss with them and going round the place to make sketches of the town. On the eve of his departure, he held a dinner party for the chiefs and the notables among the emigrants where chief Sodeke, a few of his family members and others were treated to European customs of eating and food.

According to record, Rev. Freeman returned to Badagry on 24th December 1842 on Christmas Eve to meet Henry Townsend who was sent from England by the CMS on missionary exploratory fact-finding of the country. The Church Missionary Society in London had already got the wind of the activities of the Methodists in the region and as they never wanted to be caught unawares, Townsend trip to Yoruba country became necessary particularly to Abeokuta where he had to collect information about the true picture of the interior of the country, the situation of the emigrants and the possibility of a missionary establishment there.

Rev. Freeman

On his arrival on 4 January 1843, he was warmly received the same way Freeman was received in the previous similar trip. He was equally impressed by the way and manner chief Sodeke and his people welcomed him to the town. The chief instantly offered him land space for his mission's use but he declined because he never wanted to commit the CMS in advance. What astonished him most about his trip to Abeokuta was the way the generality of the people received and accepted the emigrants as the same member of family without any proof of discrimination against them. He noticed that everyone of them were being treated as their blood brothers and sisters and they were never treated as ex-slaves but instead as honorable members of the society whose skills in the arts of writing, of building houses and sewing of clothes would enhance the further development of their community and the country at large. Chief Sodeke in his usual characteristic for extending hands of good gesture to people irrespective of where they may come from offered a whole quarter of the town to the missionary and their emigrant partners to do whatever they liked with it, but they refused because they wanted to remain proximately to their peers they had missed for a very long time. They thought that this would amount to segregating themselves from the mass of their people.

Townsend returned to England to report on his mission and to prepare himself for his pastoral ordination but left Andrew Wilhelm behind to look after the interests of the CMS at Abeokuta. At the same time the CMS, highly impressed by the report of Samuel Ajayi Crowther on the First Niger Expenditure also recalled him to England to spend some time at the Training College at Islington in preparation for his ordination too. Both of them were ordained in 1843 and Crowther was sent back to Sierra Leone to prepare himself for a mission to Abeokuta as the first native pastor of his people whose duties included the conduct of services in Yoruba language.

In January 1845 the CMS missionaries which comprised of Rev. C. A. Gollmer, Rev. Townsend, and Rev. Crowther, two school masters – Marsh and Phillips, one interpreter, four carpenters, three laborers and two servants set at their journey to Abeokuta via Badagry. On their reaching Badagry they were informed that the friendly chief of Abeokuta – Shodeke had died some eight days before their arrival and that they could not continue their journey until a new ruler was installed. The party was now stocked and at a cross- road. All that was to come to their mind was to find a way to utilize their time productively on all other viable projects that would complement their mission.

They began to establish a mission station at Badagry and by March of that year, they had built a Sanctuary, a school and work was in progress on the mission house. Delegation of responsibility was shared among the three senior men in the party. Townsend was put in charge of the school while Gollmer and Crowther were busy on the streets and the outlying villages around the town to preach the Gospel to the people and encouraging them to embrace the new religion for the good of themselves and the future of their children. It was really an exciting moment for the missionaries and the natives because the region was previously known as an outstanding idolatory area with different idol worshiping characteristics. With the activities of both Methodists and the CMS in Badagry the town thus became the first missionary settlement in Nigeria leaving behind there the relics of some of the structures of the time still standing till today. The first storey building to be built in Nigeria by the missionaries can still be seen on its original site as monument till today.

The tussle of the Obaship in Lagos between two ruling houses - that of Kosoko and Akintoye was raging on around this time. The English traders supported Akintoye, who had been made the Oba of Lagos and who was traditionally crowned by the Oba of Benin in 1841. His rival Kosoko was supported by the Brazilian and Portuguese traders who did not liked Akintoye's open-door policies. In the struggle for the stool of Lagos, Kosoko was able to oust Akintoye out of the throne through a general revolt in Lagos and Akintoye fled to Abeokuta where he was welcomed. From Abeokuta, he sent emissary to the English, both at Cape Coast and at Badagry for help. The English residents at Badagry promptly reacted to his petition under the protective security of the British interests and her subjects along the coast and sent urgent petition to any of H.M. Naval Officers on the West Coast of Africa against Kosoko.

In December 1845 Akintoye relocated to Badagry where he could conveniently plan for the invasion of Lagos and blocked Kosoko's link with his allies in Porto Novo. In March 1846, with the help of the native armies of Abeokuta and those that were stationed at Badagry by Akintoye lunched an attack on Lagos both on land and Lagoon; but unfortunately the expedition failed. It actually failed but at the same time the prevailing situation on the ground opened the door for the Egba chiefs to open the only road link between Abeokuta and Badagry to the CMS missionaries who had been waiting at Badagry for over a year for a safe passage.

In 1846, permission was granted to the party to move at once to Abeokuta and they asked Rev. Gollmer to stay behind on the coast to oversee the growth of the seed they had jointly planted at Badagry. Explaining the hurried arrangements made for the urgent move of the missionaries out of Badagry Professor J. F. Ade. Ajayi suggested that the most likely explanation was that Abeokuta chiefs intended to use missionary influence to secure the support of the British navy for a second attempt on Lagos. Reviewing Professor Ajayi's thinking, one would support and agree with his suggestions as his predictions on this issue came to past.

The continued report of missionary success both from Abeokuta and Badagry increased the influx of emigrants into the Yoruba country in hundreds and thousands. As they were coming in from Sierra Leone,

47

so also they were arriving from Brazil and Cuba. It even got to a stage when it was impossible for the Officer of the government in charge of emigrants to authenticate the accurate figures of those that emigrated to Lagos, Abeokuta or Badagry as the figures collated were conflicting and inaccurate. In 1844 Governor Ferguson gave an account of some between 600 and 800 emigrants that had got into Yorubaland. Likewise in 1851 a Naval Officer who received the emigrants at Abeokuta recorded 3000 of them in the town.

Many of the emigrants had now found their ways back to their hometowns of Lagos, Ibadan and Ijaye and as far to other places like Ede, Iragbiji and Ilorin. The role of the missionary began to change drastically towards the movement of the emigrants. They were now the one encouraging the emigrants especially the merchants among them who had earlier showed no interest to emigrate to begin their journey back home as they realized the important role they would play in the political and spiritual judgment of their people. Emigration was now made faster than in the past with the introduction of the mail boats by McGregor Laird who forecasted that his business venture would undoubtedly encouraged the traders in the development of their trades in Nigeria and equally speeded up the movement of the emigrants. His forecast worked as he predicted and it enhanced the trading activities along the coast- line.

From all over the places where the African slaves had been taken to, the urge in them to return home never extinguished. As far as to Brazil and Cuba from where Yoruba citizens constituted the bulk of slaves exported there and whose their remainders still lived in that part of the world up-till today maintained their original traditions there to the core. During the return of the exile, the vision of homecoming remained real among them too as they sought several ways of emancipating themselves. Sometime they would carry out their desire through the favor of a kind master, or through an organized escape means. Others would form themselves into club groups, which are usually found among the Yoruba people to contribute money together to buy out the freedom of one another or work under a leader for the liberation of all. With lots of obstacles in their ways, figures from the New World still trickled in to swell the overall numbers of emigrants in Lagos.

In 1859, Consul Campbell reported that there were 130 Brazilian families in Lagos. In 1863, a Catholic church had already been established and when Father Broghero conducted his first mass there about 400 people were present and when Father Bouche arrived in 1867 to superintend the church, he reported to have met about 500 Catholic members of the parish who were mainly emigrants either from Brazil or Cuba. It should not be taken for granted that these emigrants only converged in Lagos alone as they could as well be found either in Abeokuta or elsewhere in the Yoruba country.

There was no doubt about it that the impact of the Yoruba emigrants when they arrived was visible in all the areas of the future development of Nigeria and it would always go down into the memory lane of our country – Nigeria the contributions that the Yoruba emigrants and their off-shoots had made and still making in the realm of spiritual and physical aspects of the people. The missionary movements of the time that kept these emigrants together at local centers, who gave them scope and encouragement, who offered them new commercial opportunities, employments as teachers, catechists, clerks and who opened schools for them to train their children who later became the first good leaders the country would ever produced, and most importantly who provided opportunities for them to expand on the knowledge and training skills they had acquired during their sojourn in a foreign land should be saluted and give heroic recognition of their time.

Undoubtedly it was mostly the Yoruba emigrants who brought missionaries and developments into the country, and they must always be reckoned with as an essential and integral part of our development and always incorporate their fundamental principle of togetherness into our body politics and government. It would always be mentioned as truth whenever and wherever the problems of Yoruba people and nation surfaced that the slave trade had a profound economic, social, cultural and psychological impact on its society and people. This cankerworm disease really undermined our development than the colonialism that followed it and that through the trade Yoruba nation lost a large proportion of its young and able-bodied population that would have lifted up the glory of the community to a respectable height. But for the greed of the Yoruba rulers and traders of that time, this opportunity eluded us and the impact of their deeds drew back the hands of our clock as we are still suffering for the offense they committed against the nature till today.

PART 2
SOCIAL REVOLUTION.

–Chapter 5–

The Introduction and Side effect of Modern Economic and Industrial activities in Nigeria via Yorubaland and its people.

The suppression of slave trade along the West African coast opened up new economic advantages to the people of the region who had been closely associated with the obnoxious slave trading of the past. In the preceding centuries and precisely in the 18th century through to 19th century nearly every society of the world practiced some form of slavery that was even upheld by religious belief. Both Christianity and Islam accepted a phrase in the Old Testament where it was commanded that "thy bondsmen…. Shall be of the heathen… and ye shall take them as an inheritance for your children as being legitimate and ordained by God and sanctioned by his priests. This command was neither changed nor opposed to by the leaders of the two religious bodies that are being considered as old institutions of the world. Slavery could therefore come in different forms. They might come from political opponents or might be people of different religious beliefs as it happened in the days of Cromwell's Irish and Scottish Catholic prisoners that were sold to the West Indies or the non-Muslims who opposed the Sokoto Jihadists that were sold to North Africa.

In the past, the European laws favored execution of criminals but African laws would not but rather favored sales. As time went by when skilled or special talents were being discovered from the slaves, such slaves would be retained by their masters to supply them the special needs of the talents they had. For example, in Oyo Empire Hausa slaves were retained by their both military and noblemen masters to tend the cavalry horses that the transportation of men and goods and the military power of the Empire depended upon. Places like Wadai looked unto the skilled slave artisans, weavers and blacksmiths to boost its trading capabilities.

In those days the best way to get cheap labor in any community was through slavery and once the slave learned the language, and practiced the religion and custom of the new society, he or his children would eventually become one of the citizens of such society. In African kingdoms of the past, slaves had many privileges that were mainly assigned to them because of their degrading status but today, which earned their off-shoots greater places of honor in the community and high offices of recognition in the government. In Ashante, Oyo and Bornu, the slaves held important offices in the bureaucracy; serving in Oyo Empire as the Alafin's *Ilari* in the towns and villages; as Comptroller of the Treasury in Ashante, and as Waziri and army Commanders in Bornu. These positions today have become highly competitive when people would be scrambling to attain them.

When Britain abolished the slave trade in 1807, it did not only had to contend with the opposition of the white slave traders but also from the African rulers who had become so much attached to the wealth being accrued from the sales of slaves or from the taxes they would collect on slaves passing through their territories. The operators of the business both in Africa and in Europe were greatly distressed by the news that legislators in London Parliament had decided to end their source of livelihood. They contended that as long as there was demand for their commodities from the Americas, there would still be a way forward in their lucrative business and this made it possible for the business to continue in many parts of Africa for many decades after the abolition of the obnoxious trade. Every possible means was applied to block the total end of the trade but each time it met with stiff opposition from international slave traders and their collaborators both from Europe and America.

Time actually changes the status of events but events on its own may not endure forever. In the West Indies and America where the demand for slaves were so high, the traditional usage of slaves in the domestic areas were gradually been swept away to create a new field for their use in plantations. Originally both white and black slaves had been sold in America as "indentured servants" or debt slaves who were permitted to secure their freedom after a while. When large numbers of black slaves were brought from Africa, white slaves were been freed to become members of the society. As soon as this practice became effective, conditions worsened for the black slaves. The church pronounced that Christians could not be permanently enslaved, but laws were passed making it a crime to teach Christianity to the blacks, on the justification that Africans did not originate with Adam and Eve and for this reason they were not included in the Christ's plan of redemption.

It was even proclaimed by the Bishop of London when some slaves became Christians that "conversion to Christianity did not bring freedom". This is to flash back to some of the degradation meted out to the blacks of colored people of that generation in the hands of their fellow human beings. By the early 18th century, slave codes were created in the West Indies and southern states in the U.S.A. whereby African slaves and their children were condemned to eternal slavery. All the privileges that were granted to white slaves such as inter-racial marriages, manumission (the freeing of ones slave), rights to give evidence in court and others were being denied to their black counterparts. Their master's right to hold power of life and death over them was retained and if applied no one was powerful enough to challenge such master. Under the slave codes, Africans lost their status as persons and they became the master's property the way horses and domestic pets are to their owners. This was the slave situation in America in the 19th century.

Certainly if the British government had not initiated the abolition of the slave trade and if the economic trend of sugar market had not plummeted at the international market place thereby forcing the British merchants to look for other industrial commodities to support their new industrial technology, probably the African rulers and traders might still continue to embrace the trade to make their fortunes out of it. One could only imagined how more determinedly the African merchants and their partners would have clung on to the business as material goods coming from Europe and America became more attractive to them with the changes in western technology. It would have taken only the God of Africa to estimate correctly how many souls the African chiefs and their business collaborators would have been sold to the trade in exchange for colored television, cars or mobile telephone sets, which if "greed" is removed from the continent's dictionary of words, their indigenous scientists too are capable enough to set the basis of production of these material goods rolling from their laboratories.

The bulk of the profits from the trade undoubtedly went to the investors who were more knowledgeable and sharper in business technique and who were in control of the capital than the big for nothing rulers and merchants of Africa. The Europeans of this time used their profits to lay solid foundations of a powerful economic empire while the African Kings were contempt with wearing used caps, admiring themselves before the worthless mirrors and swigging adulterated gin and brandy bought with the freedom of their kinsmen.

The benefits of African consumers in the import trade immediately after when slave trade was abolished were things like spirits, guns and its powders to wage wars among the communities of the continent, salt, textiles, some house hold utensils like knives, china wares and buckets. Most of these items were of inferior quality while the spirit imported had no match in manufacturing quality and standard to the locally made gin called *Ogogoro* and which the British colonial government in the country labeled "*illicit*" and regarded as a prohibitive commodity under the laws made for us. Penalty for the production and distribution of the locally made spirit under the law carried long jail term of seven years maximum while drinking or finding it under the roof of ones building carried nothing less than three years behind the bars.

The British colonial administration in Nigeria promulgated the laws only to protect the sales of imported gin, brandy and wines into the country by European merchants. Regarding the previously existing manufacturing facilities in the continent, they were either destroyed or denied conditions for growth. Cheap European textiles replaced our gorgeous and heavily woven *Kente or Sanyan* clothes produced by local manufacturers as nearly everyone would like to put on three piece suits made out of petrol-chemical materials and under such scotching temperature. Samuel Johnson wrote in the late 19th century about Yorubaland thus: *Before the period of intercourse with the Europeans, all articles made of iron and steel, from weapons of wars to pins and needles, were of home manufacture; but the cheaper and more finished articles of European make, especially cutlery, though less durable are fast displacing home made wares.* Frankly speaking the predominance of the slave trade actually prevented the emergence of business classes that would have sat down to think deeply on how to spearhead the internal exploitation of the available resources of their society.

Everything was left into the hands of the Europeans to manage for the disadvantages of the Africans. The slave trade in fact drew African societies into the international economic play field but as fodder for western economic development and success. By the 19th century Africans were already made to loose confidence in themselves, their culture and their ability to develop and manage their own economy without the assistance and backing of the Europeans no matter at what level of their intelligence may be compared to that of their African counterparts.

Martin Luther King, the Afro-American civil rights leader was right to have commented that only few people could realize the extent that slavery had scarred the soul and wounded the spirit of the black man. His comment holds true not only with respect to the descendants of the Africans who were brought into the New World in chains but also to the descendants of the weakened ones left behind in the continent. This same assertion supported the thinking of the late Senegalese President Leopold Senghor when he said that the backwardness of black Africa has been caused less by colonialism than by the "slave Trade". It has been a serious discussion in the recent past that had cheap Africans not been available to work the land and mines of the "New World", what could have happened to the planters and the landowners of the New World? I presume the answer is simple. All they could have done was to turn their appetite of cheap labor to the use of either the native population or more to the continent of Europe as the practice in the past.

In the 17th and 18th centuries large numbers of poor whites were shipped in thousands to the New World, most involuntarily, to work on plantations and in the mines as servants just the way the black Africans were later subjugated. Around this time, indenture servants, convicts and deportees from Europe were being sold in the West Indies slave markets but as soon as the African cheap slave market was discovered, the European slave market dropped because of the special preference that the plantation owners had for the strength and the durable energy of an African man. This gave rise to what Afro-American writer William Dubois described as the replacement of "a caste of condition by a caste of race".

Nineteenth century witnessed the consolidation of French and British in West Africa and the reason this time around was no longer slavery business but its opposite, the campaign to end the obnoxious trade and substitute it with legitimate trading in legal commodities. Based on this program, the British established Freetown in Sierra Leone as a settlement for freed slaves and French adopted similar program and founded Liberville on the estuary of the Gabon River in the 1840s. With the opening of the British settlement in Sierra Leone, their merchants decided to press inland from the Gold Coast (now modern Ghana) and pushing up the Niger River to search for economic ventures that would replace the abolished slave trade. The merchant's expedition therefore called for the British involvement at an official level, which approved the First Niger Expedition in the 1840s in order to protect the interests of the legitimate traders and to stop the clandestine activities of the slave traders.

These events created the placing of the French and British players in the African football field as the two dominating teams that scored almost the same goals at the end of the game. When the scramble for colonies in Africa continent began after the great explorations of David Livingstone, Stanley and others, each of the two nations mentioned – British and French began to press inland from its own sections of the coast to stake out its colonial territories without no negotiation or approval from the landowners.

We all still remember who David Livingstone was. But if forgotten, David Livingstone was reared at Blantyre, Lanarkshire, in a Scottish poor industrial area and raised himself to the threshold of greatness with the aid of his Latin grammar in night school attendance after factory shift. He was the twenty-seven year old young man who was sitting quietly in the audience at Exeter Hall in the summer of 1840 when the First Niger Expedition's plans were hatched with such a fervent flourish. By this period, he was almost completing his medical training at the Charing Cross Hospital but decided to become a missionary, which he had long been attached to within himself. November of that year he was ordained a minister of religion at the Albion Chapel, London Wall with all others who were to serve the London Missionary Society in different and remarkable positions. Within a fortnight after his ordination, he was already on the ship bound for South Africa.

He was a great explorer, a man more sensitive than what others might think of him and a compassionate being. History would always remember the lecture he gave at the Cambridge Senate House where he spoke to a mass of people from the university. An eyewitness account of that occasion remarked that his speech made a great difference between the Christian explorer and the distinguished academics that shared the platform with him. In marked contrast to the academics, the audience saw a man who had been exposed to long continental weather of both sun and wind, and deep wrinkle of lines which spoke passionately of anxiety, hardship and disease, endured and overcome. He spoke about the various aspects of Africa; its physical features, its inhabitants, languages which he spoke very fluently and on the way to deal with the Africans.

The speech was heroic in nature and substance. The Zambezi Expedition and the Niger Expedition of 1841 had been set by the British government to achieve the same objective. Before the beginning of the expedition, David Livingstone had publicly solicited on his own idea and he had cried out loudly about it that the combination of commerce and Christianity both put together in one African basket would work out perfectly. This idea would have sounded strangely from a religious man whose job was to convert the idolaters to a belief in the Christian God, but he kept the modality of its working to himself and few of his confidants. By the time he would be ready to divulge his secret, only few of his friend and acquaintances would be able to catch up with him. One of this acquaintances in whom he confided was Professor Sedgwick, who acted as the chairman at the meeting in the Senate House of Cambridge and to whom he wrote before he traveled back to Africa.

In the letter he wrote to him, he said: "That you may have a clear idea of my objects that they have more in them than meets the eye. They are not merely exploratory, for I go with the intention of benefiting both the Africans and my own countrymen. I take a practical mining geologist to tell us of mineral resources of the country, an economic botanist to give a full report of the vegetable productions, an artist to give the scenery, a naval officer to tell of the capacity of river communications, and a moral agent to lay a Christian foundation for anything that may follow". He further said that all this machinery has for its ostensible object the development of African trade and the promotion of civilization; but what I can tell to none but such as you, in whom I have confidence is this: "*I hope it may result in an English colony in the healthy high lands of central Africa*". Consequently David Livingstone's idea of commerce and Christianity formed the corner stone pillar of colonialism in the entire continent of Africa.

The following statement was credited to Henry Townsend regarding the promotion of Abeokuta in his policy write-up in which he said: "If the power of Abeokuta could be increased and extended along the coast, and commercial prosperity brought in through the emigrant and European traders, then the influence of such a strengthened state would carry the Gospel further inland". In actual fact this policy statement ushered in variety of developments as envisaged by Rev. Townsend. It turned the period around for the training of an emigrant artillery force for the defense of the city against Dahomey, the installation of Mewu at Badagry and Oba Akintoye at Lagos and the establishment of the Abeokuta port. The first phase of the program was completed and the second phase was to get a British Consul appointed at Abeokuta to supervise the on-going activities between the natives and the missionaries on one hand and to monitor the social, political and economic conditions of the native tribes as well as to sell to them the idea of freedom in trading activities that would enhance the promotion of their civilization, social welfare and the principles of laws that would establish them as a great nation.

When Henry Venn talked to the Foreign office about this request, Clarendon the then Foreign Secretary refused the idea saying that the British Consul in Lagos could oversee the work at Abeokuta, which was less than 60 miles away until such a time the British trade there would grow to warrant the extra expenditure. Vein was not satisfied with the response of Clarendon and he continued on his own to look for someone capable of carrying out the assignment to the satisfaction of the Church Missionary Society and the government.

Going through the rank and file of the trusted Britons of the era, he finally picked on Dr. Edward Irving, a Surgeon and commissioned officer of the Royal Navy, who in 1852 accompanied Captain Foote to Abeokuta. He was instructed to choose an African "Under Secretary" who would in future take over his duties when he would be recalled back home. The agreement was that the Missionary would be responsible for his remunerations but he would have government recognition though not as a "Consul" but as "Lay Agent". In June 1853, the proposal was sent to the Foreign office for approval and Clarendon approved it with an instruction to Consul Campbell at Lagos that he should render all assistance he could give to Dr. Irving, in whose success Her Majesty's Government took great interest. When Dr. Irving was about setting out on his journey to Africa in December 1853, the C.M.S. committee added important details to his official duties at Abeokuta in the following order:

(1) He was to make an arrangement with the Vice-Consul Campbell in Lagos for securing the water frontage assigned to the Society as a free wharf that the native traders could use for their businesses.

(2) He was to study the resources of the country in commercial products like cotton, gums, indigo and dyewood and to invite the attention of the emigrants and the Christian converts towards them.

The reason behind this idea was to make the people to rise in social positions and influence and while they are receiving Christian instructions they would be competent enough to form themselves into a self-supporting Christian church that would give credence to the practical proof that godliness hath of the life for all those who believed and embraced it from generation to generation. In February 1855 Samuel Crowther Jr. who had been trained in London as a medical practitioner was appointed Irving's Secretary and assistant.

The people in England and the educated Africans at Abeokuta and Lagos plus the natives themselves had now realized that the promotion of legitimate commerce would be a platform of civilization in Africa. Hence the palm-oil business was gradually taking the position of the slave trading of the past. As if this was not enough, in the 1850s Henry Vein from Salisbury Square made frantic efforts into an increase in the production of cotton in Abeokuta, which he believed could promote the emergence of an African middle class. On his venture trail, he went to Manchester, where he met with the leading members of the Chambers of Commerce and finally hooked on to one of them – Thomas Clegg, and industrialist and a layman of the Church of England who agreed to cooperate with him in his adventure. Clegg agreed to provide a few saw gins and cotton presses, train some African youths on how to use them and prepare cotton for European market.

The business occupied the economic field only for sometime because the traders who were supposed to feed the industry were now willing to deal directly with the European traders rather than to be agents to someone else. And again the players in the business field envisaged that the new palm-oil trade just coming out would eventually surpass that of cotton in the very near future because of its urgent demand for the new technology in Europe. By October 1856, Venn changed his business program and strategy for Abeokuta country. He approved the foundation of an Industrial Institution at Abeokuta, which apart from teaching the people on how to make bricks, carpentry and joinery, cloth dyeing and domestic training, it would act as "a depot for receiving, preparing and sending cotton finished products to England". Henry Robin and Samuel Crowther Jr. were appointed managers of the Institution.

Henry Venn insisted that the primary objective of the Institution would not be a trading concern but only to transact the cotton business on commission for other parties. Some months later, Venn discovered some under-the-table business negotiations between Clegg and the managers in Abeokuta giving him the idea that Clegg was trying to hi-jack the Institute with the support of the two managers in the field. Based upon this assumption, Venn wrote a stirring appeal to Robbin telling him that the objective of the Industrial Institution would be defeated if he became direct agent of a European trader as the object was to enable Africans to act as principals in the commercial transactions and to take them out of the hands of European traders who might want to grind them to the lowest mark. He further noted in the letter that:

Henry Venn

We hope that by God's blessing on our plans, a large body of such Native Independent Growers of cotton and traders may spring up who may form an intelligent and influential class of society and become the founders of a Kingdom which shall render incalculable benefits to Africa and hold a position amongst the states of Europe.

While the African traders were being honest and transparent in their dealings with their European counterparts, the objects of the Europeans were at either variance or operating at opposite direction. They took the advantage of the fact that the Africans were not going to be the end user of their products and as such they could be beaten hands down as to the prices they would offer for their products. They preferred to deal with those they can cajole into exchanging their products with such useless goods like beads, rum, used clothes and other worn-out house hold items, rather than to deal with civilized and intelligent Africans who were competent enough to compete with them in the European market place. The strategically located place of Lagos could be a piece of discussion regarding the trade improvement in Nigeria in the 19th century and beyond. Lagos had been recognized as an important port-city from the time of slave trade where the European slave traders used as their final storage facilities for those that were to be taken to the New World on a journey of no return.

Although Henry Townsend's policy papers, which supported Abeokuta to be recognized as being superior to Lagos did not meet the support of the British government when it was tabled in the House of Commons. The Kosoko – Akintoye kingship tussle was another factor that could not be swept under the carpet. The purpose of "Abeokutan policy" was to convince the British government to use its resources to extend the Anti-slavery Treaty System to Abeokuta, thereby making the place virtually a British Protectorate or a colony. The policy proposed that Naval Squadron to be stationed at Abeokuta was to strengthen the defense of the town, and defend it against its slave trading enemies in Dahomey and Lagos. Kosoko, which the Egbas regarded as hostile ruler of Lagos was to be removed and replaced by his uncle and their friend Akintoye so that Lagos could be developed as Abeokuta's natural port and their outlet to the sea.

When Henry Townsend reached England and presented Abeokutan's policy papers, Venn forwarded the papers to the government for consideration and Hutt committee of the House of Commons was given the responsibility to examine its content and report back to the government. During the exercise, Venn lobbied laboriously with the members of the committee but could not make any supportive deal with them. At the end of it all, the report of the committee was out negatively. They based their findings upon the fact that the numbers of slaves and captives reaching Freetown compared with the numbers of slaves still being exported did not justify the budget to be used on men and materials for such additional development. Fortunately for Venn and his lobbyist group, the matter went to the House of Lords for deliberations. A committee of the House of Lords was put in place and they interviewed the same group of people that were previously interviewed by the House of Commons and at the end of the day, it concluded that an increase of the naval force would be necessary with the intensity in getting more treaties to be signed with states willing to give up slave trade, and to increase pressure on those that were yet to see the light. The House of Lords ratified those conclusions and when the case came back to the House of Commons, it rejected the conclusions of its own committee and adopted those of the House of Lords.

Lagos had at no time posed any problem of any kind that could warrant its bombardment by the British forces. The succession dispute in Lagos was an internal problem in nature and couldn't have been escalated to such a high proportion if not for the politics of the missionaries and the slave traders. The missionaries on their part strengthened their position by using diplomatic means to get what they wanted. As part of the diplomatic channel they used was the meeting of Bishop Samuel Crowther with the Queen Victoria of England through Lord Wriothsley Russell, series of lectures he delivered in England on the premises of his own life and other Africans in the same shoes with him, and the role that the British people played in the development of African people and their land.

The succession problem in Lagos divided the people into two factions as normally the case would be. Akintoye who was deposed by his nephew had the Egbas and the missionaries behind him as his ally while Kosoko, who deposed him, was an ally of Dahomey. Kosoko from his own part refused to sign any Treaty to end the slave trading but Akintoye who was exiled was willing to sign the Treaty with the British government to end the slave trade so long he was reinstalled back to the throne of Lagos. When Dahomey attacked Abeokuta in March 1851, the path to a drastic change, which the British government and the missionaries had been looking for now opened up itself. Lord Palmerton immediately issued instructions for the Naval Squadron to blockade Lagos and Dahomey, and take appropriate measures to save Abeokuta.

Apart from the succession problems, the British people including their Naval Officers stationed along the coast of West Africa particularly Commodore Bruce noticed that the potentials of Lagos went beyond being just an outlet of Abeokuta. He further advised that if government must intervene, it must be an outright annexation, and not of Lagos Island alone, but with the surrounding lands available around it to make it much easier for them to govern. Under the plan of an attack on Lagos, Beecroft concluded with Commander Forbes to force action. He took with him four warships to Lagos and invited Oba Kosoko to parley with him but he was defiant and attacked the British party thereby calling for a total war in Lagos. A month later, Commodore Bruce came back to Lagos and captured it on Boxing Day of 1851 for the loss of 16 men dead and 75 injured. Oba Akintoye was reinstalled while a trader was appointed as acting Consul to oversee the interests of the British there pending the arrival of Consul Benjamin Campbell.

Oba Kosoko and some of the leading traders in Lagos who were his supporters went with him on exile to Epe at the eastern side of the Lagoon. So also his supporters in Badagry were driven out of the town and they moved to Porto-Novo to live and continue with their various businesses. As time went by the Lagos traders began to see lots of inadequacies of making Lagos a subordinate of Abeokuta as the palm produce, ivory and shea-butter products coming from the interior yielded better profit to them than the agricultural goods produced by independent farmers. At this instance the traders began to protest through any means available to them to reverse the Abeokutan policy and make Lagos the commercial city of the Yoruba Kingdom.

The trade in spirits by the Europeans with West Africa was not a new thing in the 19th century especially during the slave trade days. Spirit had been regarded as one of the lucrative business commodities between the two parties. Immediately after the exit of slave trading, the market for spirit became boisterous along the coastline and the business was mostly handled by the English manufacturers and agents whose, specialty was to import Jamaican rum into the continent. The question of rigid custom laws and restrictions on importation were just not there around this time and as such other European nations like Germany and France took advantage of the loopholes to supplant the English manufacturers with an inferior and cheaper spirit to compete with the English traders. By the end of the century, it was recorded that all the gin exported to Nigeria was the production of concoction of potato spirit, which was prepared in the cheapest form possible to satisfy every mass production standard.

Interestingly, much of the products were manufactured in either Germany or Holland while the bulk of the products were carried into the continent by British vessels to the order of the British merchants. The trade along the West African coast especially from Lagos down to the Niger Delta was so vibrant that the profits accrued from the sales and the quantity consumed in the region could not in any form be compared to the statistics of both sales and consumption in Europe and America put together for this period. During this time spirit obviously displaced the native palm wine and native kolanut entertainment, which was the usual custom of the people in every household of Yorubaland. People now preferred it for use in marriages, burial ceremonies and native religious rites in the land and for those who could not afford to provide it in any social ceremonies became object of ridicule and classified as pauper in the society. It was gradually creating class among the people and between those who lived on the coastline cities and those from the interior of the Yoruba country.

Top African elites and some of the educated ones among them who had the opportunity and privilege to either work in the government service or trade with the Europeans began to form themselves into class-clubs segregating themselves from the people below the ladder. It was this class of Nigerian people that had the privilege of drinking the chemically controlled spirits as allowed by law in Britain, France or Germany while the heavily diluted ones of poor quality were meant for the ordinary street men and women of the society all in the good name of profit making venture. It was in fact the trade in liquor that actually increased the establishment and extension of British Administration in Nigeria and elsewhere along the Atlantic coastline.

Because of the government interest in the trade regarding the revenue accrued, it became impossible for the administration to adequately examine the pros and cons of the trade and even blind folded it not to look into how it could be controlled. Secondly the profits ploughed back to Europe by the European merchants plus the intoxicating role the product was playing in the destruction of the lives of the ordinary African people on the streets to the advantage of the white man's hidden agenda on how they were to annex the land pre-occupied the minds of the planners in London, Paris and Bonn. The rate with which the commodity was being rolled out of the factory became alarming and the consumption level in West African territory too became higher than before.

The Europeans who were formally found only on the coastline cities were gradually penetrating into the interior to actualize their hidden agenda of annexation. The construction of rail line and motorways accelerated the movement of the products into the interior of the continent and when it became a thing of national problem the Christian organizations began to openly discussed the issue of spirit consumption by Nigerians as disgraceful attitude, which prompted them to start organizing lectures and campaigns on how to wage war against the deadly trade. Even some of the British administrators in the Colonial government of Nigeria and ordinary native observers in the country were unanimous that the traffic was doing a great deal of harm to the Nigeria population. R. Burton officially remarked at a point in time that this traffic was worse than the slave trade for the Yoruba people

66

while Joseph Thompson was horrified at the effects of liquor in Lagos and the Niger Delta areas making him to comment in strongest term that if serious action was not taken, the imported disease would drive the people to "a tenfold deeper slough of moral depravity".

The effect of the poison water (liquor) as it was generally referred to during this time reached the level that any foreigner coming into the country for the first time would clearly see the damage it had done to the people by the helpless and uncontrollable drinking attitude of both alcohol and spirit in the society. Major F.D. Luggard in1895, after traveling extensively within Yoruba country remarked in the letter he wrote to his friend Nikki concerning the drinking habit of the people thus:

> "The Yorubas amongst whom the poison [liquor] is distributed are a singularly industrious people, eager to engage in trade of all kinds – a people who should long ago have reaped the benefit of their energy and industry in an increase in comfort, and in improvement in social and agricultural appliances, had it not been for the sterilizing and strangling influence of the liquor traffic on all forms of legitimate trade".

With all honesty, the British people back home opposed to the liquor traffic that occupied the trading field of this era but the scrupulous merchants amongst them that colluded with similar merchants from other European countries were the perpetrators of this crime and possibly with the aid of some government officials in both London and Lagos. Britain had long been seen at the forefront of an international anti-liquor crusade as from 1884 onwards. The role played by its chief delegate – Sir Edward Malet to the Berlin West African Conference was excellent and outstanding, but the intention of other European countries that attended this conference was to bombard African continent with such commodity until their aims and objectives were achieved.

The issue became a great concern to Salisbury Square and Goldie who was by then already trading and making in-road into the interior of the continent. In 1886 the C.M.S. rallied the support of other missionaries like Wesleyan Missionary Society and United Presbyterian Mission to form a united front that would pressure the British government to check on the flow of the traffic into Nigeria. Not only had the British subjects alone that were greatly concerned with the trade but so also the educated Nigerians in the missionaries. People like Bishop

Samuel Ajayi Crowther, Bishop Johnson, R. Blaize and others threw in their heavy weights on the matter to see that the tempo of the trade was reduced drastically or vanished out completely from the surface of Yoruba territory.

The efforts and skills of all the progressives of the time saw the scaling down of the trade to its barest minimum level that everyone appreciated. Sir George Goldie was extremely happy at the success of his skills and diplomatic approach he gave to the issue during its struggling days. On 3 May 1895, Goldie was invited by the anti-liquor crusaders to address them at Grosvenor Square in London where he made use of the occasion to blast the Lagos government and the Niger Protectorate about their roles on the importation of liquor into the country all in the picture frame of robust revenue. From the missionary side in Lagos, the liquor issue became controversial between Governor Carter of Lagos and Bishop Tugwell of the C.M.S. in the Times. Words of bricks were hauled at each other until when the people's judgment prevailed. Governor Carter and his administration were not only condemned by the British press but by the Colonial office in London, who reproved him for so indiscreetly supporting a pro-liquor views and stance.

The liquor campaign was so effective that every native organizations in Yoruba country joined hands together to fight the war of the "Fire Water". Also from the interior, the Emir of Bida, HRH Maliki appealed to Bishop Ajayi Crowther to help him petition Queen Victoria of England to put stop to liquor importation, which he said had ruined his people so much and made them became mad. The Aborigines Protection Society also joined hands with the Native Races and Liquor Traffic Committee to distribute posters against what they called "poison of Africa" and demanded for a stop to the flow of the "fire water" into the country. It was reported that never in the history of Lagos had African opinion been so strong and unanimous as in the period when anti-liquor hysteria saw the Moslems concerting with educated Africans and Lagos chiefs at a rally on 15 August 1895 in which James Johnson, Chief Taiwo, J.S. Leigh and others spoke very strongly against the traffic of liquor trade. It was in this meeting that James Johnson (later Bishop) moved the motion which was used as an important truncheon to whip the ass of the trade and that was unanimously adopted.

The adopted motion was thus constructed:

That this meeting recognizing that the Traffic in spirits,

*that is, Gin, Rum and poisonous liquors, introduced into
Western Equatorial Africa, is working immense harm,
physically, morally and spiritually against every section of
its communities, and further recognizing that the time has
come when a decisive blow should be dealt with against the
Traffic, pledges itself to support every effort which may be
made in Africa or Europe to suppress it.*

It was reported that in Abeokuta alone 8,207 signatures of Christians, Muslims and Native people were collected and sent to Britain on almost 250 sheets of paper. Similar signatures were as well collected in Lagos, Oyo and Ogbomosho.

The role played by one of the most devoted ecclesiastics British subject of his time ever to be sent to West African territory – Bishop Herbert Tugwell would ever be remembered in the history book of the "War against Water Fire". His primary thinking from the beginning about the genuineness of the British government was that every hand would be on the deck to build up Nigeria with the Christian moral and social values that were entrenched in the government of the then Britain and other countries of Europe. He believed that it was the divine moral obligations of the British newly introduced government in Nigeria to aid the church in promoting purity and righteousness and to guide the people to the path of industrialization as it was in Britain; but his thinking and believe worked opposite direction to the aims and objectives of those in the then government.

Bishop Tugwell was reported to be a tough man in nature who never compromised stupid ideas and never cared to spare anyone, either black or white in his judgment. He would treat and bullied on any erring officers of the administration the way an elderly person would deal decisively with children whenever they are out of their ways. At a point in time, it was said that when he was horrified by the rate at which veneral disease was spreading in Lagos among the Europeans, he forced the managers of those factories that employed the services of Africa women to stop employing them because of sexual proximity.

Having noticed that the usual practice of the seamen who frequently anchored in Lagos was to run after women and spirit, he decided to borrow one thousand pounds to erect the Sailors Institute where morals were being thought to close the gap of this contagious disease. Bishop Tugwell was so much enraged with the way the Yoruba people were being destroyed by alcoholic products that he saw everything around the country in the spectacle of liquor traffic. He was of the opinion that instead of destroying the people with liquor trade, there were such things like railway lines, motorways, and roads to construct to connect towns and villages and better trades that could be introduced to lift them up rather than the horrible liquor trade that continued to ruin the lives of the people on daily bases. It was then not a mistake on the part of the Bishop when he scolded Mary Kingsley who was the arch defender of the merchants and the liquor traffic when he described her and her cohorts in the administration as *"a set of wild emotional, vain, cruel, and shocking creatures".*

The defense of the administration was that the tax revenue on liquor had every advantage as it was regarded to be one of the pillars of the nation's wealth and that without it there would not be sufficient fund to run the government. But for Bishop Tugwell such ratiocination was the crudest form of nonsense. He argued that how could evil beget good? And that an administration built on liquor revenue was absolutely a dishonest one because the trade was the greatest obstacle and hindrance not only to the religious and social progress of the people but as well as to the development of the nation. He therefore described the whole scenario as scandalous, disgraceful and a dark blot on the administration of the then colonial government. The Fire Water crusade was fought seriously with the mobilization of the opinions of all well-meaning Nigerians including the Christians, Moslems, Native Chiefs and Nobles of Yorubaland and beyond. Speeches at conferences, symposia and synods throughout the country and speeches at Grossvenor House in London and articles in the *Times,* which became a convert to the course of the crusade in 1895, all lend their voices and strength to the capitulation of the trade.

Following an article that Bishop Tugwell posted in the Times of 27 March 1899 about what he saw, heard and witnessed during his 1000miles Episcopal tour of Yorubaland on foot concerning the alarming increase of drunkenness of the people, the merchants with the support of their God-fathers in the administration prosecuted the Bishop for libel. He was humiliated openly and secretly only just to silence him but he remained undaunted. His English people in the colonial government misunderstood him because they could not foresee that this man was delighted at an event that God Himself had ordained from heaven. Bishop Tugwell's fighting actions in the crusade sent crucial messages to move the humanitarian pulse of British people, the chiefs and people of Lagos particularly when he was charged to court for libel. Never would the Lagos colonial government forget the degree of embarrassment it incurred by the actions of the merchants in the libel suit.

In Britain, the public scandal on liquor traffic was seriously pulling down the moral and religious tower the people and the missionaries had been erecting in West Africa over the years. If things were allowed to go the way the scrupulous merchants and their co-conspirators in Europe and Nigeria wanted, then the investment of the moralists and the pennies of the people of England towards the success of the project would suddenly collapsed and be swept down the drains. For this reason, Chamberlain, the Secretary of the State for the Colonies, found himself besieged by anti-liquor crusaders with facts and figures regarding the issue. Under the prevailing circumstances, Chamberlain had to make an announcement that the new Governor of Lagos Sir William Macgregor, who was just transferred from New Guinea, would abolish the nefarious traffic as he had done at where he was coming from. For the rest of the story that followed the "Fire Water" crusade in Yorubaland, the brains behind the crusade, their contributions and participations, our readers are advised to read all of its full details from the book of Professor E.A.Ayandele on the Missionary Impact on Modern Nigeria 1842 – 1914 and other relevant literatures on similar topic in the libraries of the African History all over the world.

The economic products of Yorubaland immediately after the exit of the slave trade and the numerous inter-tribal wars of 19th century were at variance in different sectors. Migration from one location to the other for some obvious reasons dictated the strength of the economy. Predominantly, Yoruba people are known from the beginning of creation as experienced farmers that dwell both in the rural and urban areas of the land. Those that are living in the cities are either traders or artisans of various trades. To work on the land, people had to move out of the cities and traveled some distances away to till the land for both permanent and seasonal crops that would be sufficient enough to feed and maintain their families and cater for other responsibilities like building of houses or educating their children. The growth of cash crop economy in the 19th century began through the European demand of palm oil for the lubrication of their newly invented machines in Europe especially in England and for some other technological discoveries. The trade in

71

palm oil led to re-organization of production in the interior through the development of slave estates mostly owned by the powerful warlords. The trade also re-organized the development of African educated traders in Lagos who were the only group of enlightened Nigerians that could handle importation and exportation of goods business as at the time.

The return of slaves especially from Brazil brought with them via the Spanish and Portuguese African colonies cocoa pods, which was adopted quickly in Ibadan and Abeokuta. The successful spread of cocoa crop in Yorubaland owed its stay in the economy to the experimental planters of the seed at Agege and Otta, including prominent members of the C.M.S. and African churches. The rapid growth of the industry in such places like Ife, who had adopted the planting of the seed in the 1920s, was joined in the following decade by farmers from Ondo, Akure, Ekiti and some other parts of Yorubaland. It later became a strong pillar in the economic fortress of both the colonial, regional and national governments of Nigeria.

The construction of railway lines between Lagos and Ibadan, which was completed in 1900 and extended to Kano in 1912 - was a major achievement of the colonial government in Nigeria during the 19th century. The expert knowledge acquired by the Yoruba artisans and technicians when the railway lines in their country were being constructed gave them the good job opportunities they had when Ghana's railway lines were under construction as most of them now worked as supervisors and engineers in their new location at Gold Coast. This alone accounted for the starting point for the large-scale migration of Yoruba people to Ghana and the neighboring countries. The people have a high reputation for their skills in whatever trade they found themselves both at home and abroad. For hundreds of years back, Yoruba people have had very thriving records in craft industry and a complex division of labor.

The development of urban centers within the Yoruba Kingdoms and Empires produced such marketing system in which their agricultural produce, craft goods plus imported goods from all over the world changed hands through their women folks who are primarily the petty-traders. Market segment is not new to Yoruba traders because the produce that is abundantly produced in any particular locality always dictates the model of supply and demand of such commodity. For example, in the Savanna land area of the Yoruba country where labor in farm land is not as intensive as what is expected in the forest land, agricultural produce such as yams, coco-yams beans, cassava roots and others are mainly produced in large quantities for distribution to other areas that have shortages of such produce.

Yoruba people are risk takers, great travelers and explorers in their own rights. They are abundantly found in all the countries of the world including the countries of the West Africa as permanent settlers especially after the partitioning of Africa in the 19th century. They had established their trading presence in Ghana since the middle of the 19th century and at the turn of the century they were already a force to be reckoned with in Accra, Kumasi and the cities of northern Ghana. Their immense contributions to the economy of their sister nations along the West coast of Atlantic and the entire African continent, Europe, America and Asia has been huge and it would continue to rise because of the high level of expert knowledge they have acquired over the years through learning and skills from all over the world.

Chapter –6–

Introduction of Western Education and European culture into the Territory of West African Coast.

The Africans are known to adore God's Holy name in every situation they found themselves but yet they are always found to be disappointed at the end of every transactions or dealings they have with others. But their story will not end there, because their God has perfect plans that He will use for them to glorify Him. The introduction of western education in Africa at the late 18th to early 19th centuries was the design of the Supreme Being Himself and not that of any one or by any scientific approach of any nation. The colony of Sierra Leone came to existence through the agitations of the humanitarian opposition group to slavery nurtured by the British determination to stop the obnoxious slave trading from its major source in West Africa. The Sierra Leone Colony was founded by three groups of African slaves from England, Nova Scotia Province (Canada) and Jamaica from the New World. During the American War of Independence, those black loyalists to the course of the British in the feud and the white compatriots, after the British had been defeated fled to either England or Nova Scotia in Canada as refugees who ran for being persecuted by the American authority.

By the time these two groups settled at their new locations, they found that life was too harsh for them to bear especially the black groups because of the race they originally came from. The unwillingness of the white population to accept them into their society or recognized in practice the freedom and equality which the British law granted them when they were fighting the war on their side in the USA became a

75

huge problem to them. They now saw them as nuisance on the streets of London, Manchester and other cities until when Granville Sharp in association with the British government decided to send 400 of the unwanted blacks of England to establish a colony in Africa.

In 1787, the first set of colonists arrived Sierra Leone peninsula and named their pioneer camp there – Granville Town, to honor the name of their mentor. In those days, it was too burdensome for only one person to cater for the welfare of 400 people who were just planted in a new environment, which was totally against their wish. This was the situation that Granville found himself. To resolve the issue, a group of merchant humanitarians came to his aid by forming the Sierra Leone Company of which Granville and Wilberforce were directors. Immediately the news reached Nova Scotia, they sent one of their black members to England to meet with the directors of the new company to discuss the logistics and modalities about how their members too could benefit from the scheme.

The delegate sent to England was Thomas Peters, an Egba man who had been sold into slavery in America, and who escaped to join the British army during the American War of Independence and later fled with the loyalists to Canada at the wake of persecution. His meeting in England with the directors of Sierra Leone Company promised freedom from discrimination and free land in the New Colony for the blacks from Nova Scotia. On his arrival back to Canada, arrangements were made for the passage of about 1000 black loyalists for the journey to the new colony and they arrived there in the month of June 1792, which was at the peak of the raining season in the tropics.

The third group of the early settlers was the Maroons, those who were the free Negro slaves from Jamaica and who revolted slavery at about 100 years before to maintain their independence in the mountains, until they were defeated in 1796 by the British who immediately deported a large number of them to Nova Scotia. Through the harsh condition of living for them in this new location at Nova Scotia, they voluntarily requested for passage to Africa and they arrived Sierra Leone in 1800. Problem of survival would always be the first face of difficulties to appear to any first settler in any new location at anywhere on the surface of the earth and as such the case of the Sierra Leone early settlers was not an exception. According to record some of the colonists arrived at the start of the rains; some died of malaria while some of them did not know how to farm in the African way because of lack of farm implementations they had been used to from where they were coming from. African foods also became problem in a way for them for they did not know how to eat the crops that are being planted in Africa anymore.

The space of land allotted to each of them to till was not large enough as those spaces available to them in America because the Temne land owners would not part with large tracts of land nor could large labor men be found without recourse to estate slavery, which the colonists abhorred. Temne people actually feared the colonists and because of this, they refused to sell their land to them permanently but allowed the use of the land only on temporary basis. As such they were being regarded as tenants under the laws of the community. When the arrival of more people into the colony was increasing so also the fear of the Temne people too was becoming alarming and the next move for them was to try and uproot the colony completely from their soil.

The settlers too had many internal complaints regarding the administrative rules of the Sierra Leone Company as they began to smell the bad odor of discrimination between the whites and black colonists. Those from the Yankee group were able to compare things very quickly and resolved to conclude that they had hardly suffered so much in America when they were there than now when they allowed themselves to be treated in a master – servant relationship in the land of their own continent by the British subjects. The company's appointed governor to administer the colony was an autocratic ruler who failed to provide the land promised to every family of the colonists and who tried to impose land rents as against the free tenancy of the land promised. Based on these factual points made against the administration, the colonists rebelled and put up public placards declaring a new code of laws that would usher in a new independent government.

The governor and his few supporters were in a great trouble and distress and the government faced imminent overthrow. But the governor was so lucky that the timely arrival of the Maroons and their escort of soldiers helped him to over power the rebels. In the end Sierra Leone Company came to realize that hence it was not looking for profit on the project, it therefore welcomed the British government's action in taking over the camp as British colony in 1807. By this time close to 3000 or a little more black settlers had been taken to the colony but unfortunately only about half of them were alive in 1807 because the rest numbers had died as victims of pioneer life.

By the time the British Navy came to patrol the West African coast to put an end to the slave trade, Freetown obviously became their headquarters from where they operated. The colony at Sierra Leone was then the only available settlement place along the coast where they could bring the captured ships on the high sea with their human cargoes thereby increasing the population of the colony steadily. Sierra Leone colony was becoming popular with great attention as the report was reaching England as to its size because of the constant arrival of the captured slaves numbering sometime in hundreds and sometime in thousands depending on the number of slave ships the navy could catch or pounced upon at every given time.

Between 1807 and 1850 the population of the colony had grown from its 2000 number in 1807 to 11,000 in 1825 and to 40,000 in 1850. With the diverse ethnic or national population, Sierra Leone now became the cultural melting pot of the world that was able to blend peoples of different culture, religion and languages originating from every region in West Africa from Senegal down to Angola. The administration of the colony was gradually becoming complex to manage both in nature and reality.

In 1814, the British government appointed Charles Macarthy as the governor of the colony and one of his primary objectives was to spread the opportunity of western education and Christianity among the re-captives who were now being uprooted and cut off from their original societies by circumstances that were beyond their capabilities and defensive logistics.

The plan was that the British government would provide the fund while the missionaries would be put in-charge of the cultural and religious changes that were expected to turn them into the role model of African Christians. To begin the implementation of this plan Governor Macarthy began to settle the re-captives in the villages where Schools and Churches had been established. Those that were not sent to the villages remained in towns and were recruited to serve either in the army, the Royal African Corps or be made to learn one trade or the other under the tutorship of the original settlers who would educate them and give them their own surnames that they gladly took

Charles MaCarthy

in appreciation for the training and the upkeep facilities they provided them during their apprenticeship.

Initially superiority complex arose between the early settlers and the re-captives because the settlers looked down on them as being crude and illiterate heathens. Is it possible to address this issue as being discriminative among people of the same race or can we call it nature-made hatred? Your line of reasoning here is welcomed without any bias of any sort. However the re-captives remained undaunted and took to education and Christianity with zeal and passion. Most of them began to move out of the villages to settle in Freetown for better job opportunities and city interactions. When they got to the city, they were ready to learn or take up any new trades that would open them up to the path of competing with the whites and the black traders in Freetown; and to solve their accommodation problems they used communion efforts to build their mud houses alongside the elegant storyed houses of the settlers.

As time went by they systematically graduated to be recognized as peddlers, hawkers, tailors, barbers, carpenters, bricklayers and other menial trades until they began to trade and operating big stores that offered them the large income to buy storeyed houses like the settlers. It was on record that by 1839, two of the re-captives were so prosperous in their businesses that they were able to purchase auctioned slave ships for their trading activities along the Coast of Africa. The group was now being noticed as hard working people who lived modestly and cooperated with one and another to buy goods in wholesale purchases to be re-distributed to the petty traders among them for larger profits. Gradually and through this system they were out-selling both the Europeans and the black merchants in the region.

The re-captives knew one thing from the on-set that if they failed to compete favorably with the European and the black settlers of the colony, their chances of having a place in the community government would be difficult and as such, they used every bit of their income to send their children to secondary schools in Freetown and as well as to universities in England. By the time their first generation graduated from colleges and universities where they were well interacted with the children of the colonists and, which later resulted into inter-racial marriages, the distinction between the two groups began to disappear. Through this generational mix, a distinguished national clan identity of *Creole* was apportioned to them. They now developed their own language, which is a mixture of English with Yoruba language enriched by Portuguese, Spanish and French vocabularies that contained some elements of Temne, Madinka, Ibo, Susu and Arabic that has a melodious liquid tongue that eliminates the harshness of English.

In 1845, a secondary school for boys was established in Freetown and after two years in 1847, the Grammar school for girls and a Teacher's Training College, Fourah Bay were also established. In 1876, Fourah Bay College acquired the status of a University.

The educational system began to turn out black teachers, clergymen, doctors, lawyers and writers who were the "first" of the professional class of West Africa. By 1860, it was reported that greater percentage of children were attending schools in Sierra Leone than in England. The following African personalities were the "first" in their professional class of the time that rose to the highest pinnacle of their profession; John Thorpe was the first African lawyer in 1850, J.B. Horton, the first doctor – 1859, S.A. Crowther, the first bishop – 1864, Samuel Lewis, the first knight- 1896, as well as the first newspaper editor and owner and he was the first to obtain double degree from the universities of Oxford and Cambridge.

Crowther at Fourah Bay

In both the church and government, the Creoles pioneered a very good path to which future generations of West Africans would follow. When the Anglicans in 1861 withdrew their missionaries from Sierra Leone, the entire evangelical works there were being taken over by the Creole clergymen under the semi-independence Native Pastorate Church. In 1872 there were already enough qualified Creoles to replace the entire European staff of the government and they had already secured seats in the Governor's Council. In 1893 when Freetown became municipality with its own Mayor, the council was run by the Creole and towards the end of the century the Creoles had formed an educated society that was proud of their achievements in every area of development and who can now voice out their opinions vigorously in the press and featured prominently in both religious and secular government. By the 1880s, Creoles were already operating different businesses in Bathurst, Monrovia, Cape Coast, Lome, Porto Novo, Lagos, Niger Delta and the Cameroons.

The time for the Yoruba re-captives to return back home from Sierra Leone presented itself when the traders from its group found their trading ways to Badagry and Lagos in a ship that probably carried some of them away from their original home place for an undisclosed destination and now purchased at an auction market by the wealthy merchants of their tribe for the benefits of mankind. Their first appearance on their native land after so many years in exile was when the vessel of their tribesmen sailed down the waters to anchor at Badagry in one of the beautiful sunny and warm days of 1834. This time around the aim of the ship was not to carry human cargoes but to load legal trading commodities, its merchants and traders of mainly Yoruba extraction. The vessel traded down the coast of the Sea to as far as to Badagry and Lagos where some of the traders found sizeable number of their lost families, friends and relatives.

Bishop Crowther in his diary described the meeting moment as an extraordinary joyous time for both the traders and their relatives. It was

like a miracle to all because the belief of this people was that once they had been severed from each other every hope of meeting one and another for life had been lost. The re-captive traders were once again relaxed on the arms of their loved relations and told them the stories of the ordeal they went through both in the slave dungeon and their new environment where they now lived. Some

Bishop Crowther in full regalia of the re-captives were still able to recognize their children, blood brothers and sisters, who tried in vain to persuade them not to return to Freetown again.

When the ship returned to its base in Freetown and the whole story was told to their people in the colony, the urge for every one of them to travel back home was rapidly been built naturally in them. This urge prompted a highly political move made by twenty-three leading Yoruba merchants in the colony when they petitioned Governor Doherty for the passage of the interested Yoruba citizens wishing to return back home. In the petition of these merchants that was led by Thomas Will (the Yoruba leader), they requested as follows that:

We feel much thankful to Almighty God and the Queen of England, who had secured us from being in a state of slavery, and has brought us to this colony and set us at liberty and thanks be to the God of all mercy who has sent his servants to declare unto us poor creatures the way of salvation, which illuminates our understanding so we are brought to know we have a soul to save......, so we take upon ourselves to direct this humble petition to your Excellency that the Queen will graciously to sympathize with her humble petitioners to establish a colony to Badagry that the same may be under the Queen's jurisdiction and also beg of her Royal Majesty to send missionaries with us and by so doing the slave trade can be abolished totally.

Their major reason for asking for this request was that if a colony is established at Badagry, the people would be able to establish all the modern facilities they had seen and enjoyed at Sierra Leone colony to the advantage of their people and thereby providing adequate protection and freedom to them. They envisaged that under such condition, their lives would be better programmed than when they were under the siege of unnecessary frequent wars against each other. As previously mentioned in the last chapter, this request was not approved by the British government but the people on their own decided to start moving back home. Their movement back home became huge problem for both the missionary and the government in England about which way to follow. But at the end of the day, the will of the people triumphed and the missionaries had no alternative than to find their ways to follow the people's path because they did not want to loose so many years of their investments on them both morally and financially to unknown religious hawkers. The emigration of the Yoruba re-captives to Badagry and Abeokuta regions continued without break.

The failure of the 1841 Niger Expedition, which the government in England hoped would open up ways for its people to get into the interior of Africa, was a big blow on them in terms of human and financial losses. The question of planning another expedition, which they thought would be a waste of money and loss of people's live, was never come to mind, but still the people remained stubborn and the exodus tempo was increasing beyond anyone's imagination. Those that were already back home in Badagry continued to press on Freetown to send to them the missionaries that would light the candle of the Gospel to their people.

In June 1841, the Rev. Thomas Dove, who was the Superintendent of the Methodist Mission in Sierra Leone reported that he received request petition from the emigrants at Badagry in which they specifically asked for the Gospel of God to be preached unto their people, the establishment of schools to train the young minds and the flag of the British to be hoisted as protection to the lives and properties of their people. Rev. Thomas did not waste anytime to take action by forwarding their request with strong recommendations to their Mission's Headquarters in England. Based on the fast track movement that the Methodist Mission took, their representative, Rev. Thomas Birch Freeman arrived Badagry on 24 September 1842 to mark the effective date for the beginning of missionary establishment in both Yorubaland and Nigeria and the work began in earnest.

On Sunday 11 December 1842, Freeman traveled to Abeokuta where he was warmly received by the chiefs, the emigrants and the Egba people. His journey lasted him ten days during which he interacted closely with the town and its people. Possibly the Salisbury Square might have heard of the move already made by the Methodist Mission that this missionary competitor had begun to reap from the farmland where their labor was significantly scanty. To counter their efforts the Salisbury Square horridly bundled out one of their officials into the ship sailing to the West Coast of Africa on fact- finding mission about what was going on in the interior of Yoruba country. This official was Henry Townsend who was then a young man of 26 years old, frail looking but intelligent, determined and ambitious. He arrived Abeokuta via Badagry on 4 January 1843 and was welcomed very warmly by chief Sodeke and the Egba people, the same manner with which Rev. Thomas Freeman had been received the other time when he visited Abeokuta.

The bulk of the job both along the coastline and the interior of Africa lied on the shoulders of the native people themselves who were to be the beneficiaries of the project when it succeeded. This was why all eyes were focused on Samuel Ajayi Crowther as a leader to be trusted by both C.M.S. and the British government. Much have been said and written about this illustrious son of Yoruba extraction who was the "first" African Bishop in the Anglican church and a gentle Yoruba boy that was captured by the Muslim slavers during the slave trade business, sold into slavery but rescued when the British cruiser of anti-slavery patrol seized the ship in which he was to be taken to the New World and released its human cargoes in Freetown, Sierra Leone. In the already established colony for the returned slaves in Sierra Leone, he entered a school ran by the C.M.S organization and was later baptized in 1825 with the name of *Samuel Crowther.*

After graduation from the school, he was sent to England for a year's course program that qualified him to become the "first" African to graduate from the new college, Fourah Bay Institute. On his return to the colony, he was working as a tutor in the college and became an evangelist and again returned to England to be ordained in 1841 as pastor. The Church Missionary Society saw the qualities of responsibility they were looking for in Samuel Crowther and without wasting time he was chosen as their ideal candidate to deliver their indigenous African church programs and ideology. Undoubtedly Crowther was an intelligent, reliable, a devoted Christian, Victorian in his manners but African to the core in his outward look. In 1843, Crowther was posted to Abeokuta where he diligently worked as a teacher, missionary and a trusted leader of his native people.

In a surprised moment while working at Abeokuta, he stumbled into his maternal mother and his sister whom had been forcefully severed from him by the slave traders 25 years ago when his hometown *Oshogun* was raided by the slavers. This accidental re-union was great to his family and he used the opportunity to baptize his mother in 1848. His personality was pointing the right way to a higher office in the missionary and the administration of his native people. His dignified humility commended him to both missionaries in England and the planners of the first Niger Expedition of 1841. The same character trait brought him before Queen Victoria of England and her husband in a warm and healthy atmosphere where he explained the situation in Africa to the greatest amusement of the Royal family. The intention of the mission was to serve as a precursor to a larger program, through which the humanitarians expected the Trinity of Christianity, commerce and civilization to wipe out the slave trade in the Region of Niger River and to be followed by peace, piety and prosperity which would be nourished by healthy and legal trading activities.

Although the first Niger Expedition was a failure because of the villainous-ness of malaria attack that killed 40 people and incapacitated 15 others out of the 145 Europeans that were put on the mission. Yet the recorded success of the Expedition went mostly to Samuel

Crowther and his Sierra Leonian liberated Africans on the trip that never succumbed to the threat of the killer fever. His published journal about the Expedition became the corn for grinding in the mill of the policy makers in England. Crowther was the sort of man who would never ventured to revenge what humanity did to him and other Africans that were brutally treated in the hands of their slave captors but instead he was busy finding ways about how the conditions of life of these people could be improved and how they could totally become a free creature.

Crowther set himself to do three things. He began with a book on Yoruba vocabulary, which was the first time that a native person had written about his own language. Secondly, he continued with the translations of several books of the Bible by himself in some instances and by the help of others at some other instances. Thirdly, he was a sensitive sage translator. When he was working on the translation of the Bible into his mother tongue, he researched into the words used by specialists of the traditional religion or Muslim expounders of the Koran. He collected Yoruba proverbs because he was deeply aware that much of African wisdom was distilled out of them. He was much fascinated by the tribal myths and legends from the storehouses of African theology and he brought all these to bear in the Yoruba translation of the Bible that lasted him and others forty-five years in making to become a genuinely Herculean achievement.

Crowther was loved and respected by the man at the center of decision- making at the Salisbury Square in person of the strategically minded General Secretary of the Church Missionary Society, Henry Venn. When Abeokuta was under siege from the warriors of Dahomey, Crowther traveled to London to present Abeokuta's case before the

Henry Venn

British government through his organization the C.M.S. The General Secretary – Henry Venn threw his weight behind the demands of Crowther and his people because of the trust he has for his only friend in the continent of Africa by rallying the support of the British people for immediate action to save Abeokuta. Shortly after Crowther had left London, the British government bolstered the defense of Abeokuta with the dispatch of gunboats and alas! Abeokuta was saved from the hands of the Dahomey slave-trading regime.

In England this African man was found compelling by the British cabinet ministers, the Queen of England, and her husband Prince Albert and the large audience of the British people he had every opportunity to address. They were all impressed by his engaging eloquence, his gravity and stateliness, his skills and tact in presenting his case. In 1854 and 1857, Crowther accompanied the second and the third Niger Expedition when he focused his missionary attention on the liberation of the people of the Niger Basin. Crowther's aim was to plant a chain of missionary centers and built schools along the region of Niger River and deep into the country's interior among the Igbo, Nupe and Hausa people, which he successfully achieved with the mark of great honor.

With all the outstanding qualities of a man that Crowther carried with him and with the close observation of his boss at Salisbury Square, the time had now come for the General Secretary to blow out loudly his silent trumpet regarding the C.M.S. program for Africa. Henry Venn, skillful as a politician and extraordinary as a visionary, had envisaged a self-supporting and self-propagating church in Africa for a long time but was waiting until God Himself would open the doors for the materialization of this noble program. He had seen in Crowther the making of a bishop out of him, which was good enough to carry out the mission in Africa. For this purpose and the time created by God, Henry Venn flunk the doors open when in 1864, Samuel Ajayi Crowther was consecrated as the "first" African Bishop in the fountainhead of the Anglican denomination at the Canterbury Cathedral in England. His consecration day was a blessed day throughout the English land as the event was regarded as a major break through in the English church history, which was witnessed by a capacity of congregation from across the country and that was given one of the most publicity in the news papers of the day. The philosophy of Henry Venn that "an African church would not be complete without an African born Bishop" can no longer be swayed by the actions and arguments of the white C.M.S. missionaries in the field who were against Samuel Ajayi Crowther becoming a Bishop in his continent of origin.

Bishop Crowther's Episcopal territory was an expansive one because of its geographical size. He was the Bishop of the countries of West Africa beyond the limits of the Queen's dominions, which consisted of Sierra Leone, the coastal areas of Ghana and the Island of Lagos. This was a very big challenge for one man who had no mobility, telephone connections and other administrative facilities that could easy be the tension of the burden as we have them today. Yet the Bishop undertook this challenge with zeal and passion and sustained the ups and downs of the exhaustive position from 1864 to his last day on 31 December 1889.

During his Bishopric tenure of office, he established the numerous missionary stations in the Niger Basin that still stand till today and which included the stations in Igboland and in the Niger Delta region. He knew the problems of the people of the coastal line more than anyone of his time and he actively participated in the solutions to those problems. He was deeply respected by his people including those whose religion differs from his own especially the Muslim potentates of the Upper Niger region because of his wisdom to dialog with them rather than denigrating their religion. As his weapon to deal successfully with the Muslims, he was very knowledgeable in the book of Koran the way he was with his Bible. Each time he was to dialogue with the Muslim leaders, he did not need any Koran interpreter to help him dove his point home. In every diocese that he worked, establishment of schools was his pre-occupation and principal starting point for the students to learn both the words of God and other basic professional skills that would earn them a good living in their future developments.

Bishop Crowther laid the solid concrete foundation for our nation to dwell upon. Based on the type of foundation he and his colleagues laid in the Christian faith, commerce, transportation infrastructure and political development, all came to present themselves in the clear mirror of the continent where people clearly understand and feel very proudly to say and identify where they belong to in the committee of Nations of the world. In the area of evangelism, it can be proudly said that Bishop Crowther and his immediate followers built a strong stone foundation for the church in Nigeria and he actually carried the program of his mentor – Henry Venn to letters. He envisioned a church that was deeply African in governance and spirituality, and richly Anglican in doctrine and worship. Today the church of Nigeria is one of the fastest growing, and dynamic churches of the Anglican Communion with over 90 Diocese and with more than 20 million solid members.

The rapid expansion of trade after the third Niger Expedition of 1857 ushered in legitimate trade in commodities that attracted a number of British merchants thereby creating cultural changes in those areas where the trade flourished. The merchants were first attracted to the areas with large water tributaries that were having outlets to the Sea. During these ages, the only fastest means of transportation connecting the world together was through the Sea as air technology was yet on the drawing board and not developed. In this wise, Lagos and the towns along the Niger River were the only ones that enjoyed the benefits of the trade of the Sea. The legitimate trade of household needs set aside the slave trading after its death and positioned itself at the center of commercial field.

The large companies that were big enough to open deports in the Delta Basin and in Lagos brought into the country assorted goods ranging from European clothes, shoes, housing materials and utensils, European foods and home furniture. Initially it was the people of these towns that had first hand access to these goods but later when the motorways and railway lines were constructed to connect the cities to the interior, the interior people too began to enjoy similar opportunities. The Industrial Revolution in Europe especially in England contributed immensely to the cultural changes that happened in Africa and elsewhere in the world. The British trading merchants used this opportunity to introduce their commodities into their areas of influence both in Africa and other areas in the world.

To legally address this issue, companies had to be formed and chartered under the British Company Registration Laws. The first of such company that came to trade in Nigeria was the United African Company (UAC) founded by George Goldie in 1879. In 1886, Goldie's Consortium was chartered by the British government as the Royal Niger Company and granted broad concessionary powers in all the territories of the Niger Basin. The company established its' Corporate

George Goldie

office/headquarter far inland at Lokoja from where it was managing the affairs of the country as its bona fide property. The company began to interfere in the political and social issues in the territories along the Niger and Benue rivers, sometimes engaged in serious conflicts with the natives when its British-led native constabulary (police) intercepted slave raids in return for the payment of annual tribute. Gradually the taste for European goods and materials crept into our society and these goods including foods, drinks, furniture and other materials derailed the African home made goods and materials.

It reached that point when the goods made either in England or elsewhere across the Atlantic Ocean were considered the best or of high quality while the home made goods were of inferior type. This negative cultural thinking was being passed from generation to generation until its persistence still remained with us till the present day.

Chapter –7–

The defeat of the old African Culture through Slavery, Trade and Social Reforms:

The study of the old and new African culture put together in the same basket would enable the social scientists of the continent to move further in their study of African social, cultural and psychological characteristics which would go a long way in solving such knowledge that can help to solve our socioeconomic problems. Reinventing the study of the African social and cultural characteristics that had long been lost due to neglect and religious domination of some groups will surely be a lasting solution to Africa's socioeconomic impasse. The Europeans whose culture and economic characteristic patterns we follow today developed their socio economic standard to meet with their culture for the attainment of the developments in their continent. For any meaningful socioeconomic advancement of any nation or group of people to be noticed, the lifting ladder of such program must be tied to the apron of the culture of the people of such nation or group. The marriage between the two is permanent and cannot be dissolved.

An example of such discussion is the case of Africans that survived the harsh forces, which transported them away from their homeland to other continents, and yet they still practice traditions and cultures that are traceable only to their continent of origin – Africa. This attitude actually justifies the fact that these people apart from the long distances of where they now settled to their original homeland, the sense of belonging to their original ancestral source, which had endured for many years, will continue to survive from generation to generation. The age-old culture, traditions and their variants will continue to manifest themselves remarkably as long as the reproductive system of the people practicing them still remained functioning. Today, we can see that African traditions and culture are remarkably manifested in the oral and written literatures of the African-American groups in the US as against what we see very many decades ago.

The African tradition in African-American set-up and in literature is a literary creation which embodies many ways in which the African-American writers explores what Africa is, what it means and how it relates to him/her, and what it portrays to the whole world. The little they could grasp about the continent and its people, which came down to them through generational history baton continues to expand in schools, colleges and universities in America. Whereas the schools and universities in African continent get themselves busy by directing their efforts and energies towards the European history, culture and traditions. The belief of the people of the 18th and 19th centuries in America regarding the African continent was that the place called Africa was a lost homeland that its image could be remembered vividly; but in the 20th century, Africa was regained and its people in America began to examine chronologically its lost glory in tradition, culture and history.

The African tradition in African-American literature, which began as a fading memory of a lost native land, has now progressed to an intensive fascination, and culminated into a cultural reunion. In Henry Louis Gates, Jr's book - *The signifying Monkey 1988*, the author particularly referenced the relationship between the people of Africa and their gods in their cultural heritage when he said:

> *The black Africans who survived the dreaded "Middle Passage" from the West coast of Africa to the New World did not sail alone......violently and radically abstracted from their civilizations, these Africans nevertheless carried within them to the Western hemisphere aspects of their cultures that were meaningful, that could not be obliterated and that they chose, by acts of will, not to forget their music (mnemonic device from Bantu and Kwa [Yoruba] tonal languages), their metaphysical systems of order, and their forms of performance.*

All these attributes he poured on the first generation of Africans in the New World have many things to do in the development of the continent if they are properly addressed and articulated. Exploration of these words to their roots could serve as an essential catalyst for a meaningful order of socioeconomic program of African people.

The tradition of a people is too difficult to extinguish no matter under what condition such people may found themselves or subjected to. This was what happened to many Africans that were forcefully taken out of their original places during the slavery era to different locations in the New World. Notably among these people was one Olaudah Equiano who was kidnapped from the eastern Nigeria and taken to West Indies, and was finally brought to slavery in Virginia, US. In his autobiography he detailed his remembrance of his native culture and his experience of slavery when he wrote thus:

> I hope the reader will not think I have trespassed on his patience in introducing myself to him, with some account of the manners and customs of my country. They had been implanted in me with great care, and made an impression on my mind, which time could not erase, and which all the diversity and variety of fortune I have experienced, served only to rivet and record: for, whether the love of one's country be real or imaginary, or a lesson of reason, or an instinct of nature, I still look back with pleasure on the first scenes of my life, though that pleasure has been for the most part mingled with sorrow.

The statement of Equiano narrated above strengthened the sensibilities that later appeared in African-American writing. Immediately after the 18th century, Equiano's cultural sentiment began drumming its melodious rhythm unto the ears of the African-American writers such as Alice Walker, author of *The color purple;* Toni Morrison – *Song of Solomon,* and Alex Harley of the famous *Roots,* all of which echo the sentiment of Equiano about what Africa meant to the souls of the African-American writers. The interest of the African-American writers concerning the African traditions and culture in the US has been referenced in this text in appreciation to the good work they have been doing and which they will continue to do in many more years to come. The power in the art of their profession is substantially sending messages of good tiding to the African-Americans of the United States about their continent of origin.

It is not of recent years that the American writers have been looking forward towards Africa for inspirational ideas about the continent and its people. In the 1920s, the migration of many black people from the tobacco fields of the south to New York City contributed immensely to the cultural development we see today in the African- American history and which later transformed itself into the popular Harlem Renaissance. Through this transformation, the African-American writers that lend their hands of support for the noble job included one amongst all – Alain Locke (1886 – 1954), who was recognized as a brilliant scholar and cultural critic of his time. He once remarked that: "If the Negro is interested in Africa, he should be interested in the whole Africa; if he is to link himself up again with his past and his kin, he must link himself up with all of the African peoples".

One thing we failed to realize and recognize after all said and done is that in some respects we do not learn how to find out what Africa has in stock to offer or give to us but instead, we all look towards what we have for it forgetting that Africa is a long-aged mother who is well experienced, who had witnessed and absorbed many tribulations, persecutions and had lived with many ill-fated dramas through many generations. On the rock that African culture stands today, it was not without the aid of tribulations of different characters and events, out of which the World War II played some key roles. The World War II brought together the Africans and African-American soldiers that were fighting fascist racism and dying for Europe, which in the real sense did not belong to them in any form other than to exploit their talents, energies and mineral potentialities. When these two family members met at the war front, they came to realized that they themselves were being subjected to injustice in colonial Africa and the segregated United States of America by the same family member that rushed them onto the war front to fight on their behalf.

Gently and gradually, the Black students and the African-American expatriates in European cities, especially in France, began to find brotherhood and solidarity, which was expressed in the poems of Sedar Senghor of Senegal, Aime Cessaire of Martinique, and Leone Damas of French Guiana and coined by Jean-Paul Sartre as the Negritude ideology. From here various ideas about how a link could be formed between the two separated family members was coming to existence. The African-Americans in particular and for identity with the mother Africa began to change their slavery names to real African names. One of such big names was that of Le Roi Jones who for this purpose turned in this former name to where it belonged and took a more suitable and prestigious African name of Amiri Baraka, which actually fitted into his race, color and creed.

The artistic creation in the black community of the sixties mingled with the popular culture, termed "Black is beautiful" that gained much more ground to support the African ideology of the time and which implored the Africans in the Diaspora to associate himself or herself with the continent and its people, and to seek with them in their struggle for independence and economic development. One way to actualize this program was for the Africans living in foreign lands to travel back home to look for answers to the numerous problems facing the continent. Fortunately many of the African-Americans of the feminist writer's guild of the 70s and 80s took the bull by the horn to set some of their plots in Africa. They were able to make commitments to an exploration of self to mother Africa and ever since then Africa is no longer viewed to anyone from a distance as it used to be for the writers and singers of the 18th century.

The trade association between the people of Europe and Africa, which re-invented itself during the 20th century rushed the clever party into the association's pact with the idea of subjugating the other lesser party and this was what eventually happened in the case of the African partners in the play field of the continental economy. Undoubtedly, African land mass which can comfortably contain all of the US, China, India, New Zealand, Europe and little more; the cradle of human evolution and where civilization began in the universe suddenly changed position to become the most problematic continent in the world. This is a continent that has a history, which had been established before the arrival of the two religions (Christianity and Islam) into the land, and which was able to maintain its cultural heritage including the very old civilizations in Egypt and Nubia, the Great Zimbabwe, Ashanti and Oyo Kingdoms and Ile Ife dynasty, the Dogon people, Hausa/Fulani heritage with trading and warrior excellence, the Yoruba city building culture and agricultural expertise and which had the first university (university of Timbuktu) in the world. Apart from the millions of its citizens that were either forcefully taken into slavery or died on the voyage while crossing the Atlantic Ocean into the New World or got killed in many internal strives organized by the imperialists among the member nations of the Great Continent, today around 800 million people are currently living in Africa.

It is a matter of common sense that if a community or a nation is to be destroyed, the first place to attack is the culture of its people. Once the culture is destroyed all other logistics would fall into place and this was the case of African people in the hands of the imperialists. What they did was to loot the whole continent in every possible ways of their history and cultural goods. For example, if one visits London Museum today, he/she would find some displayed African artifacts, which are conspicuously displayed in the showcases and which some of them represented the treasures looted from the Palace of Benin Kingdom and some other places during the European raids of the early 20th century in Africa. Today these artifacts are making daily income for the looters without any compensatory recourse to the original owners of these stolen goods.

The last two centuries had marked periods of deceit about the true position of Africa and its history and this is why it is hard for the people to see with the spectacle of future because it was not possible for them to know the truth of their past. When the modern economic trade that was to silence the slave trading came, it came with motives and intentions that were even worse than the slave trading in some instances. First of all, the west coast of the continent was bombarded with European liquor of different brands that later turned the people into alcoholic citizens everywhere.

European merchants and the colonial officials stationed at either in Lagos or Porto Novo and which approved this sort of liquor trade knew very well that when a person is fully charged with the power of intoxication from alcoholic products, the focus of such person is automatically tilted while his orientation diminishes or dropped thereby causing him/her not be his/her very self not until he/she returns from the journey of alcoholism. 99% of what he does when such person is under the influence of the spirit may not reflect his/her true intentions but being forced to do them by the actions of the alcohol he/she takes. At first, the towns and villages along the coast of the Atlantic were the first citizens of Africa to taste this type of drunken habit but as time went by when, the cities and towns in the interior were connected by rail and motorways, European culture now became a thing of essential and competitive commodity.

It became competitive among the elites of the time who were of

Christian group and who saw themselves as the inventors of the new order. Gradually people of lower status too began to abandon their airy native dresses, which provided them enough clean air to the body when walking along the streets under the scourging sun for the tight-neck European dresses that wrapped-up every part of their body from their shoes to the hats. They now turned themselves into rats in the mole-hole that could hardly come out during the daylight.

The Christian missionaries and their native followers that brought European life-style to the continent, when observed that the liquor trade was not part of the bargain to evangelize the continent began to kick against it with the strongest language possible. All they could not comprehend was that there is always a big difference between politics and evangelism as the two are only to complement each other's efforts but each of them would always remain in its parallel line as it is found in geometry. Gradually and through force in some cases, western and missionary proselytization, the colonialists subordinated traditional African authority, and the values and norms of African communalism in the minds of the Africans. Nyasani was correct in his write-up when he argues about the new anti-African script that was deeply imbedded in the minds of contemporary Africans to the point that they have adopted and assimilated wholesale whatever the west has to offer.

He also pointed out correctly that the end result is not just a cultural betrayal, but also a serious case of self-dehumanization and outright self-subversion both in terms of dignity and self-esteem. Indeed, there is no race on the surface of the Earth which abhors or abdicates its own culture to flirt with another under experimental ideas, which promise nothing more than vanity and to large extent was the game played by the African race with the European imperialists. The overwhelming attitude that went into the heads of the Africans of that generation, which allowed them to submerge a whole race in the ocean of never receding tide of the imperialist culture, would ever remain a mythical puzzle to deal with by the generations of this day and in the future. Africans would ever express their dissatisfaction about what happened during this period of the continent's history as a time when they were painfully crucified on the cross of the blackmailers, arm-twisters and gunrunners.

The impact of western civilization and cultural dependency of Africans on European life-style broke the chain of command that existed in the African community and family set-up of the past time.

The new system introduced the act of individualism in our society and not only for those who practiced the new culture but as well extended to the people in the rural areas who now operated in isolation. The communal help that was been offered in the past from one family to the other vanished unexpectedly and where it existed, it was only within the immediate family groups. The larger family courts where family disputes were being settled between husbands and wives or between blood brothers and sisters no longer existed because of the introduction of new administration of the foreigners.

I quite agree that a community cannot remain stagnant without undergoing certain changes as the philosophical events of time dictates, but what I am saying and support is that if any part of our culture will have to undergo some refinement and pruning so that they can become harmonious with the spirit of modern culture and practice, the fundamental structures of our culture should not be destroyed and thrown into the garbage bin. What is missing in other cultures that plunged their citizens into the deep sea we see today is the non-availability or the total rejection of some basic principles that built up the pyramid of those cultures.

If we observe it very closely, we can see that the rate with which crime is committed today in both Europe and America among the teenagers (both male and female) was just not there some decades back. Why? Because of the importation of culture from one place to the other, this is much easier and faster today than say about three decades ago. In Africa today, we can see variety of European or Asian foods that have found their ways into the food racks of many stores and households while that of African foods can only be found in the communities where African people lives in either America, Europe or Asia. The native languages of the land are gradually being eroded away giving chances to either English or French languages to take their places. The market economy of all the nations of Africa is either tie to Dollar, British pound sterling or to French Francs. In Nigeria for example, the local market women prefer to take the Dollar currency in some cases to the Naira, which is the country's legal currency and they are even more efficient and current than some of the Bureau de Change offices about the conversion of foreign currencies into Naira.

In China or India, the moral order upon which their nation's economy and development is predicted was based on their cultural foundation. But today you will find African people and their governments rushing to Asia for economic aide and activities while leaving behind unattended to the endowed beautiful land that is always ready to produce bountiful economic produce that other nations of the world cherish and envy. It is undoubtedly sure that numerous core values of African culture had been neglected, abandoned or carelessly sent parking so as to allow the entry of dangerous and killing cultures of other people to come into their societies. In America today, a day would hardly pass without reporting on the national TV one form of criminal act or the other and such cases are no longer a matter of concern to the American citizens because they have adapted their mental thinking towards viewing such incidents on their TV sets.

Transfer of culture through modern technology has its merits and de-merits and if care is not taken, the effect of its disadvantages will out-weigh that of the advantages that it is suppose to provide responsible human race. People can easily get out of control through what they learn on the Internet on daily basis. Sometime it sounds stupid to a right thinking fellow when a girl of between thirteen and fifteen years of age would come on the national television with her mother by her side telling the whole world that she is prepared to carry pregnancy and that she is already of the age to take care of a baby. So many times various programs of cultural degradation are aired on the national TV here in America where ladies would come on the TV in search of the fathers to their born children among numerous boys that had slept with them. Sometime this type of search would be extended to the same members of family between father and son who had slept with the same lady or between the same blood brothers. Ladies who are suppose to be in the school would come on the TV to narrate to their viewers how a day could hardly pass without having sex with numerous boys in their mother's bed, at abandoned houses, in the school buildings or in the church premises. This is the new type of culture that is spreading out of the advanced nations of the world and who knows the extent of damage it would have done or will do to the innocent people of the less privileged nations that are still struggling with what its people will eat for the day.

Frankly speaking, the imperialists could be blamed for the atrocities they committed in Africa during and after the colonial rule in the continent. At de-colonization there were not enough university graduates to run the fledging new states and in some areas not even enough secondary school leavers to work in government offices. The legacy left by the imperialists was very weak democracies, concentration of power in the hands of those with the most access to weapons and the instability of ethnic and religious conflicts within the European-imposed borders. It was a matter of an open game that after the exit of the imperialists, they still continued to supply weapons of destruction and destructive national guidelines as an integral part of their policy of pre-colonial influence to the new states of Africa. What followed their exit were the history of conflicts, military coups and corrupt dictatorships everywhere. The control of mineral resources of the continent that were meant for the development of the countries where they are seated was directly in the hands of the business lords either in London, Paris or Lisbon.

From the economic gains they accumulated from every resources coming out of the continent, very minimal percentage out of them would be re-allocated back to the countries where these resources are being taken away as either loans or the so called aids which would attract huge interests that would role-back into their accounts in their home countries. Instead of teaching the Africans about how to catch fish, they keep on giving us fish to eat under their own terms. When the Africans realized the game of hide and seek that the imperialists were playing, the game was slowed down and another program of debt relief to African countries was introduced knowing fully well that over 1000% of interests on the loans they granted them at the independence dates have rolled back into their accounts undetected. Who is to blame for whatever problems we face in Africa today?

The Africans themselves are equally guilty of the offences we tried to rope unto the necks of the imperialists. Just like what I use to tell some of my African-American friends that the hues and cries of the black man in America about discrimination is no longer an issue to attach much interest to, as it may not be tenable again. Discrimination happens everywhere in the world because there is greatness in the power of skin color. The existence of black people in the continent of America could be dated back to over 200 years and hence the black color in them since all these days cannot change from its original black color to either pink or brown to reflect age-long skin changes, then where is the rationale behind color discrimination? What I am saying here is that the African-Americans in the US should stop crying about color discrimination and face the real music of life because America has been designed to be a land of opportunity for those who can work very hard to earn good living. It is also a land of competition where anyone from anywhere can succeed irrespective of color or creed.

The same thing is applicable to Africans who still seat somewhere in the continent to apportion blames rather than to take action about how corruption among their leaders could be dealt with decisively and eradicated to the barest minimum in the governments of each nation of the continent. No government in Africa is excused from this deadly disease that has eaten very deeply into every fabric of our body system and that has destroyed our economy to its taproot. Slavery and colonial era had come and gone. It will not be proper or adequate for us to still sit down halfway at this age nursing the wounds afflicted on us by either slavery of colonialism while those who afflicted us inhumanly continues to grow from strength to strength everyday. The reward of our labor is on this planet earth and we should try to catch up with it here on the earth and not sitting back to aim at meeting our reward elsewhere than where its fullest usage is not certain.

Chapter –8–

The Role Played by Bishop Ajayi Crowther and other Early Nationalists of Yoruba Extraction in the Political and Economic Development of Nigeria.

From the study of history, the founders of our great nation – Nigeria had learned of the travails of a strong and powerful nation in Africa knowing fully well how the institutional orders of the past had, in time, been destroyed by convulsions and upheavals, by vices and decadence. Also from their study of human nature, they became acutely aware of man's self-interestedness and his selfishness, his arrogance to flout the orders of the constitutional instructions lay down by the law and authority, yet they designed our political institutions to take all these into account. In doing this, they concluded that while our political institutional supports were absolutely necessary and could as time goes on re-channel and curb individual excesses in their individual selfishness and discourage political convulsions, something much more would be needed if the nation was to survive. Through the search light of their philosophical thinking, they summed up that the gritty and noble work of securing the nation would in the final analysis have to be done by individuals of study character. They believed that only a people who possess the right dispositions of managerial skills and abilities, and strong but tempered religious beliefs would be able to keep what they the founders would bequeath to them through their struggles from the end of the 19th century through to 20th century.

The thinking of our Founding Fathers must have been correctly in line with the thinking of John Adams (1732 – 1799), the second President of America when he said in one of his speeches that: "Human passions unbridled by morality and religion….. would break the strongest cords of American Constitution as a whale goes through a net". Therefore the arduous task of sustaining the Nigeria nation would fall upon every citizen of the nation including you and me, and the millions yet unborn. This calls for the sort of people we must be able to trust and the role we must play in the building of the nation.

The arduous task of building a virile and responsible society depends largely upon how the members of such society perceives its internal problems and how strive it struggles to find solutions to their relief. It is for this reason that I chose to offer to the Africans particularly the Nigerian public in my writings the visions of our Founding Fathers on the virtues they believed that were necessary for the sustenance of the young governments, which were put in place for us by the colonial imperialists of the 20th century. In every nation of the continent, I feel obliged to ask this question. How can Nigerians, Ghanaians, Namibians, Zimbabweans or Congolese fully know their countries and themselves without knowing at least a little bit about the men and women of courageous minds who pledged and risked their own "lives", "fortunes" and "sacred honor", for the blessings of liberty and growth we enjoy today? For this purpose I chose to reflect on the ideas and opinions of our past leaders about how to make our society great. In my other books especially *The journey of the First Black Bishop – Bishop Samuel Ajayi Crowther,* I explored the travails of slavery that ruined the early developmental play field of our continent and which subjected our people into second hand citizens wherever they may find themselves.

I also addressed the introduction of western education into our communities and the side effect of the new trading technology that suited the purpose of our European partners and reduced the status of the African partners to the lowest ebb of the business ladder. All these were to rekindle some facts that were lost in transit in many premises of our history and in the art of moral education of our young and as well as the adults of our communities. The great deeds and virtues of our Founding Fathers are growing more and more dim by the lapse of time but if we are to survive as a people, it is not too late for us to retrace back our steps to pick up the gloves on the post where they hung them very many years back for a renewed fight. There is a question mark as to the saying that we constantly refer to when we intend to please ourselves for our failures that "we are winning?" Are we really winning?

I may not want to go into the larger play field of the African

Founding Fathers but limit my exploration to the confines of my country – Nigeria and to my people – the Yoruba race to whose participations in the building of our nation are eulogized in this book. The virtue I refer to here is what the Yoruba Founding Fathers of our nation thought would be essential for the success of the nation's new experiment. These virtues are, of course, not the exclusive property of the Yoruba race, but for other cultures and people who may wish to share them or may aspire to embrace them for their own benefits. One thing I would like to emphasize upon here is that there is something that the Yoruba race all over the world cherished and honor about these virtues. They believed that God gave our nation a name and a great position among the nations of the world. Their hope and prayers are that the gratitude of their hearts may be expressed by proper use of those inestimable blessings of both human and natural resources, by the greatest exertions of patriotism, by forming and supporting institutions that are willing to cultivate the human understanding, and for the speedy progress of the Arts and Sciences, which would establish laws for the support of piety, religion and morality.

The hope of their virtues is to exhibit on the great theaters of the world that social, public and private character, which will give more dignity to a people who will possess their own sovereignty that the crowns and diadems afford to sovereign princes and imperialist dictators who are ready to suck the people into their marrows. These sorts of virtues would equally be peculiar to that of a free people who will chart a new course in Africa and the world at large and who will represent the eyes of mankind and show the right path in moral and political assemblage of the people. What is now the result of the capacious vision of our Founding Fathers, their bold ambitions for the emancipation of their people and the integration of their lofty ideas about how we can live together to make Nigeria truly an exceptional nation?

Do we really excel to the satisfaction of their spirits in heaven, the private and public virtues of their intent? What is our present source of discontent as a people? Is it the economy or cultural decline that is our chief malady or have we been fallen short of our duties and aspirations to move the wheels of the nation forward as expected of us by those looking at us from distance? Don't we need to restore this nation's sense of greatness, to learn one more time again about the great works of our great men and women of the past so that we may be able to move more faster on the right track of the level ground rather than the mark we are presently making on the undulating steeps in a rugged terrain.

Before I move on let me say this that our Founding Fathers were not perfect human beings neither were they saints. They too had their own flaws, whether great or small, but these could hardly disqualify them as our guides to use today. Their struggles and sufferings should always remind us only that the perfect is the enemy of the good. If therefore any of us should fall short in any form or the other, there is no reason to despair, but such would only present a reason to try harder until we succeed. This brings to mind how John Adams (Past American President) urged the Americans of his time to *"read and recollect and impress upon our souls the views and ends of our own immediate forefathers and recollect their amazing fortitudes"*, so I urge the same recollection today. At the dawn of our independence in 1960, we had various ethnical differences that would have barred the noble course that our leaders immensely suffered for if not for the fact that our nation has been destined to become a free state as at that day and year - 1 October 1960. The colonial lords with their imperialist tendencies had that doubt in their minds about how we are to forge ahead and reach the promise land without calling back on them for expertise skills and knowledge. But today our nation is ranked as one of the greatest nations of the world, which has the excellent administrative skills and knowledge to successfully steer the wheels of a nation – to God be the Glory.

I may not be able to catalogue all the names of our past Founding Fathers that contributed in one way or the other to the goals and achievements of our nation but I want my readers to pardon me for this mistake, which may not be my inability to do so but which may be due to space availability in this book. I am sure and positive that other future writers from our community would eventually reference their names and their contributions in a much better and bigger form than what is expected from me. There is always a two- way action to double edge sword and this was what slavery and the introduction of Christianity doctrine did in our past. The slave trade carried many away from us to unknown destinations and made them remained there for life. But Christianity doctrine changed the course of the past and introduced new culture that ushered in the art of reading and writing of letters, new trading patterns, new ways of life that put permanent stop to old characters and behaviors and opened up the closed gap that existed among the people of the ancient time.

The first to be referenced in order of preference among the beneficiaries of this new order would be our beloved son of all ages and generation – Bishop Samuel Ajayi Crowther, whose efforts and his love for his people excelled that of anyone of his time and beyond. Much have been written and said about this illustrious son of Oduduwa in theatre halls, classrooms, podia of amphitheatre arena in colleges and universities, Church-pulpits and in town meetings in Yoruba land. But one thing that has never been mentioned about him was that "for when exactly are we going to stop mentioning the good works he did among us and when shall we remove his name from our book of honor?"

This past summer of 2006, I was at the Canterbury Cathedral where Bishop Ajayi Crowther was consecrated in 1864, and the week I was there coincided with the week when Bishop Crowther's works in Evangelical movement in Africa was remembered by the British people. This glorious occasion gave me the opportunity to interact with many people from the Church of England that journeyed to Canterbury from various places to participate in the weeklong ceremony. It also afforded me that opportunity to speak with the staffs of the Chancellor of the church and the library staffs who gave me some valuable materials for my research works. What an awesome and prestigious occasion it was?

Canterbury Cathedral (Bishop Ajayi Crowther was Consecrated in 1864)

Bishop Ajayi Crowther must always be seen as an extraordinary person among us whose time must also be cherished and remembered from generation to generation. Although he was captured at the age of 15 years by Foula slave traders, but for a purpose and that purpose was actually fulfilled to its entirety. His tenure of office as the Bishop of his people (1864 – 1891) marked the period when Christianity movement in our country was re-established following the failure of the early Catholic missions – the Capuchins in Benin and Warri in the 16th century and also a period of when things had not "fallen apart" between the merchants of the sea and the Salisbury Square. Personality such as Henry Buxton who was a stunt leader of the anti-slavery movement and an evangelical crusader from Salisbury Square shed a lot of light on how the obnoxious trade of human slavery that was the glorious commercial commodity of the people of the coastal cities of West Africa of the time could be rooted out completely when he proposed thus: "That the efforts of Britain to stop the slave trade through diplomacy in Europe and naval patrols on the Atlantic had not reduced the number of slaves that were being taken out of the continent and that the best remedy was to move to its source of supply which was in the interior."

He then suggested that the British must elevate the minds of the African people and call forth the resources of her soil. That the missionaries and the school masters, the plough and the spade, must go together to make agriculture flourish and not until when this was done that the venues to legitimate commerce will be opened whilst civilization will advance as the natural effect, and Christianity will operate as the proximate cause of this happy change. Boxton's proposals to the British government opened up the preparation for the First Niger Expedition of 1841, which the government spent close to one hundred thousand (100,000) pound sterling in budget.

In the exploration journey, there were three steam boats, four commissioners of the government who were authorized to make treaties with the local chiefs and who were to explore the chance for a consul to be stationed anywhere along the route of Niger waterways; scientists who were equipped with the scientific instruments that were available as at then, with which they could study the climate, the plants, the animals, the soil, the people of the land including their social and political institutions, their culture and the traffic on the rivers. Also in the party were a chaplain and two C.M.S. missionaries out of which Samuel Crowther was one of them and who were to report on future establishment of missionary works along the banks of the river.

Although the Expedition failed but yet the little result that came out of it marked a good beginning of an in-road into the interior of Africa. Treaties were signed with the Obi of Aboh and the Attah of Igala while land was acquired at Lokoja for the model farm to begin. Forty five out of the 150 European members of the Expedition died of malaria attack and the model farm could not function because of lack of supervision by the experts and it was wounded up; no consulate post was established and the treaties signed were not ratified, yet the journey was capped as a success. The Expedition afforded Crowther to know more about his people, their welfare and the structures of their political institutions as well as how to approach their tons of problems. He made good record of every notable event and places of interest and resolved within himself that the arduous task about their freedom was imperative to him and his team.

Though he became worried as a person but remained undaunted as a leader. In 1843, the African Civilization Society and the Agricultural Society, both that were the baby projects of Henry Buxton were disbanded and after two years of both calamities, Buxton died of heart broken possibly because of the failure of the First Niger Expedition, which he single handedly initiated. But fortunately for him, his influence and ideas about Africa did not go down with him into his grave. Those ideas he left behind set in motion a non-disposable publicity jingle in the government of Britain from which the failure of 1841 Expedition could not hold sway. The Second Niger Expedition that was approved by the government took off with Samuel Crowther and more missionaries on board the ship.

The project was more successful than the first time and with less human casualties. The government now began to encourage the signing of slave trade treaties with the local chiefs through their Naval Officers patrolling the sea to strengthen the activities of its naval squadron and the protection of the missionaries along the banks of the Niger. The wide publicity about the success of the Expedition in Freetown sent signal to the Liberated Africans in the colony among which request had been made for passages back to their towns in Yoruba country. With the favorable news about their country now circulating around them, the urge to intensify their request from the government increased. The same news in turn led to the extension of the work of the Wesleyan Methodists and the C.M.S. from Gold Coast and Sierra Leone to Badagri.

The appearance of Samuel Ajayi Crowther on the scene of Yoruba play field was not without history and some obstacles. The boy Ajayi who hailed from the town of Oshogun, a few miles south of Iseyin was around 15 years when his home town was sacked by the Foulas and the Oyo Muslim slave raiders and was captured and made prisoner in the dry season of 1821. He changed hands until he was finally sold unto the Portuguese slave merchants who put him on board the *Esperanza Felix* on 7 April 1822. On the same day that the ship was to begin its journey to the Americas it was captured by the British Navy Squadron patrolling the sea in search of the slave merchant's ship carrying slaves to the New World. As destiny would begin its course on this boy Ajayi, he was fortunate to be one of those rescued and he arrived Sierra Leone in

June 1822 with others into the waiting hands of the missionaries there, who immediately began to re-model his life and getting him ready for the career he had chosen in the spiritual realm.

He was one of the early Yoruba victims of slavery to settle in the colony of Freetown. While in the destined new land, he was growing in wisdom and knowledge plus in obedience to his trainers especially Mr and Mrs Week who later became the Bishop of Sierra Leone at a later period. Ajayi was founded by this family teacher as a bright and promising child at the C.M.S. School in Sierra Leone that he had to send him to England for a year's education at the C.M.S. School in Islington, London. At the completion of the one-year advance course in England, he came back to Sierra Leone to take appointment as a teacher for the government. Crowther was noticed by everyone in the position of authority at the colony as a hard working and diligent young man who was in no way a disappointment to both the missionaries and the government of the colony.

When another opportunity presented itself for the missionary to send a native to England for special training as a catechist who would eventually work among his people, Crowther was the obvious choice. His old teacher in recommending him thus wrote about him that: *He would, I have reason to believe, prove a very useful instrument for carrying on the work in West Africa. He has abilities far surpassing any that I have met with before and added to this he appears to be truly pious.* Based on his abilities and the opinions of those he was working with, he went back to London the second time to acquire more knowledge in his chosen and ordained career.

It was when he came back from London the second time that the Fowel Boxton's plan for the civilization of Africa was to come to fruition and when the First Niger Expedition program of 1841 was to be hatched. Under this program, the British government gave the C.M.S a chance to send some of its native men with the three exploring vessels for the project, and Crowther was obviously the most qualified candidate among the native African Christians of the colony. His role in the Expedition was remarkable and very important as the link between the African people of the interior and the white foreigners which in no way might have been possible as at then became a plan of possibility through his influence and capabilities. The overall assessment of the Expedition was a failure but the remainders of the men who survived the malaria ordeal after recuperating for a while at Fernando Po, staggered back to England and Crowther was left behind in Freetown to continue his teaching job and move on with his evangelical life style.

A few years later, the C.M.S. after acting on the recommendations of J.F. Schon that the African missionaries would be suited for the spread of the evangelical works in the interior based on the assumption that they would survive the malaria climate better then the Europeans began to experiment the scheme. Again Crowther was considered the most suitable candidate to lead this pious scheme and for this purpose, he was ordained and sent to go and establish mission among his people in the region of Abeokuta. This scheme was really an opener to everyone both in the missionary and the circular world that Samuel Crowther was up to a great task of emancipating his people and that he was capable of being their touch bearer and their leader.

While at Abeokuta, Crowther was lucky enough to meet his aged paternal mother, sister and his half brother all of whom he had lost intimate contact with for almost 25 years because of the hardship toll of slavery that happened in his country at the beginning of the first quarter of the 19th century. He used his evangelical position to baptize his mother and gave her a new name of Hannah on 5th of February 1848. The people and the chiefs of Abeokuta were highly impressed by the transformation wrought in the land by Crowther and his evangelical team. At a point in time, Chief Sodeke himself who was never a Christian once declared that in ten years of the arrival of the missionaries into their midst, the people had been turned from

Queen Victoria and Prince Albert of England

war to peace. As if these achievements were not enough for only one person, someone in a distant land heard of Samuel Crowther and this was Lord Palmerton in London who had been anxious to meet and know him at all cost.

This time too coincided with the time that the British government was to consider a plan for the Second Niger Expedition and it needed a first class advice especially from someone who knew much about the area of River Niger and its people very well so that a repeat of what happened during the First Expedition will be avoided. Samuel Crowther was once again invited to London for a serious talk with the government on the project. When in London, he impressed Lord Palmerton so much so that he had to arrange for him to visit Windsor Castle to meet the Queen and Prince Albert where he again impressed the Royal family about the situation of things going-on in Africa, its landscape and the devastating life-style that the slave trade had left behind for its people. Samuel Crowther was always a copious diarist and a revealing one for that matter. He recorded about how astonished he was when he was at the Castle with Lord Wriothesly Russel to meet the Queen.

At a certain moment in the Palace according to him, he remarked that he was unable to distinguish between the Queen and her Lady-in-waiting because of the type of dress that both of them put on. The dress of the Lady-in-waiting was much more elegant than what the Queen herself was wearing and this obviously brought confusion to Crowther as to who was the real Queen amongst the two. He wrote that he was in blissful ignorance of the Great Majesty before whom he stood, conversing freely and answering every question put to him about the way slaves were entrapped in their homes or caught as captives in war. Among the interesting topics that Crowther talked about during his meeting with the Queen and Prince Albert (her Husband) included the position of the Port of Lagos, the city of Abeokuta, the meeting he had with Sir H. Leeke who rescued him and other slaves from the slave ship many years ago and his recitation of the Lord's prayers in his own Yoruba native language, which the Queen commented that it was a soft and melodious language. The meeting ended with a marked farewell gesture from the Queen and the Prince. Samuel Crowther was during this trip invited to Cambridge University to address the undergraduates there, where he appealed to them for more missionaries to come to Africa to lend their hands of help for the preaching of the Gospel.

Samuel Crowther now became a paragon of the virtues to be recovered in a fallen man as long as he was ready to submit his heart and soul to the course of the missionary process and to which he gladly did. The growth of African catechists working in the missionary was getting higher and the evangelical works in the interior was now becoming very stimulating and challenging. Salisbury Square in London was keeping pace with the development of things in Africa and the General Secretary of the C.M.S, Henry Venn was determined to initiate the African church at the earliest time possible. To complete this equation,

Crowther was again brought back to London and this time he was to be consecrated as the first black Bishop in the Church of England. His nomination to the episcopate did not go down well with many in the missionary enterprise of Africa and more so those who saw themselves as the princes of the African missionary, but as faith and destiny would determine this issue, Crowther was unanimously agreed upon to be elevated to this high office ever to be occupied by native African.

On St Peter's Day, which was the 29th of June in the year 1864, all roads leading to the city of Canterbury were opened to every available transportation means of the time. The Church of England produced all the pomp and circumstances at its command for this occasion. It was recorded as a very great event that called for special train to run from London and elsewhere taking the participants and well-wishers to Canterbury Cathedral. Dignitaries of the Church and state were invited. So also in attendance were Admiral Leeke who rescued the boy Ajayi many years back from the jaws of the slave merchants and the widow of Bishop Week who thought him how to read and write English alphabet from his day one at the colony in Freetown and who tailored and molded his life just the way his own mother would have done and cared for him.

The lady was now old and fragile but she still maintained her posture and alertness. When she entered the Cathedral, she found her way to a front seat, where she might easily see and hear everything about the program of the day. Interestingly one of the churchwardens came to beg for the vacation of the seat where she sat because that seat was reserved for a distinguished lady who had a ticket. She turned around and quietly said that: *"I think I have a right equally to this seat, because that black minister to be consecrated Bishop this morning was thought the alphabet by me."* What a moving and powerful statement? The Dean and the churchwarden on hearing this at once apologized and asked her to remain on the seat.

The Archbishop of England himself led the congregation, the Bishop of Lincoln read the Epistle, Bishop of Winchester read the Gospel and the sermon was delivered by a Professor of Philosophy from Oxford University – Rev. H. Longueville Mansel from the first Book of Peters verses 2 & 3. And thus someone who was once a totally obscured Yoruba child was now transformed and elevated by Divine Permission, into the high office as a Bishop in West Africa. The University of Oxford in recognizing his achievements conferred on him immediately after

113

this occasion an honorary degree of Doctor of Divinity. Within three weeks of his consecration and on 24ᵗʰ July 1864, the new Bishop was on the boat for Lagos to begin his new role and face the fire of life awaiting him in his own country.

Space may not allow me to enunciate into details the numerous ordeals of life that the Bishop went through from the hands of both his people and the foreign friends who would sometime collude with the Africans to frustrate the good efforts of the Bishop. But as destiny would write about him, Bishop Crowther was a defender of his people's rights until his last days on 31 December 1891 at a very ripe age. His record of achievements in both his official and private capacities as the man of his people and honorable leader of his time were well documented for every generation that followed him to browse. He left an indelible mark of honor on our sand of history that would always be a guiding touch-light for every Yoruba sons and daughters in whatever line of discipline they may choose for themselves.

The Church Missionary Society raised many African dignitaries of the 20ᵗʰ century especially from the tiny colony of Sierra Leone which was inspired by the philanthropic company as a home for repatriated slaves and which was nurtured by the British determination to end the slave trade in West Africa. The organization of the Church Missionary Society was founded in 1799 by those who had been active in the Sierra Leone Company and this was why the issues at the colony was not a new thing to the directors of the Sierra Leone Company who now transformed into the leadership of the C.M.S. The colony after it had received the blessings of the British Crown through the abolition of slave trade Act of 1807 and the physical patrol of the British navy along the West Coast of Africa intercepting slave ships and forcing them to berth at Freetown to discharge their human cargoes, the missionaries now began to organize the colony into parishes and provided education which culminated in the establishment of training colleges for boys (Fourah Bay College) and for girls (Annie Walsh Training Institution).

Among the beneficiaries of this gainful project were Bishop Ajayi Crowther and host of other Yoruba dignitaries that started the project which later metamorphosed into a nucleus that gave birth to what we know as Nigeria of today. Train the mind first and then leave the rest to the body to support the head that would carry everything in a human being to its destination. This was the case of the Sierra Leonian trained slaves and their offshoots born in the colony. Before the slave trade was completely exterminated, many of the slaves of Freetown had in the 1840s began to find their ways back to their various places of origin along the coast from Gambia to Calabar. Some of them who were lucky enough returned to their tribes and were able to find their relatives while some that could not settled in other places for the sake of the then available trading opportunities that took over the race from slave trading.

The largest group of people that migrated out of the colony was of the Yoruba extraction. Some of them found their ways back to Badagri, Lagos, Abeokuta and later to Ibadan, Oyo and some other cities of Yoruba country in the interior. In 1864, the missionaries began its exploratory journey to Abeokuta, which was then the capital of Yoruba Egba Kingdom and in 1851, when the British government terminated the slave trade markets in Lagos and established a consul there to prevent illicit smuggling of slaves, the road was wide open for the missionaries to come into Lagos. Lagos being an advantaged location because of its access to the sea attracted a large number of the returning slaves and this made Lagos to be rapidly developed than other areas of the country in terms of commerce, government organizational logistics and church developments.

The structural pattern of Sierra Leone both in Christianity organization and government placement were brought unchanged to Lagos. The city was divided into parishes, each with its own church. St Paul was for Breadfruit Parish, St John for Aroloya, Holy Trinity for Ebute Ero, St Peters for Ita Faji and St Judes for Ebute Metta. The educational system in Sierra Leone that poured out a stream of teachers, clergymen, doctors, lawyers and writers, which then produced many of the "firsts" of the professional class of West Africa, was repeated in Lagos for the furtherance of African development and self-supporting ideas of people like Henry Venn and his committee members at Salisbury Square in London.

Among the "firsts" of this kind was Macaulay Thomas Babinton, who was the founder and the first principal of the historic C.M.S Grammar School in Lagos. He was of Yoruba extraction from both Ore-Aganju in Ikirun district, and Oyo Township. His father was Ojo Oriare, a receptive who was among the rescued slaves that resettled and lived in Sierra Leone colony where he trained his children to the level of prominence in the African society.

T.B.Macaulay married to the second daughter of Bishop Ajayi

Crowther named Abigael and bore to him many children out of which Herbert Macaulay who later became a famous politician and the "father" of the modern politics in Nigeria was one of them. He attended Fourah Bay College, which was then under the C.M.S, and after graduating he was sent to the Church Missionary College at Islington for his technical training, which was in preparation for the industrial take-off in West Africa.

When he returned from abroad, he worked as a tutor at the C.M.S Grammar School Freetown from 1849 to 1851. In 1852, he was transferred to the Yoruba mission in Abeokuta and put in charge of the Christian Institution, a school set up for industrial and practical training for students. In 1854, he was ordained a pastor and continued with his teaching appointment until 1859 when he founded the new C.M.S Grammar School in Lagos with the

TB Macaulay
(Father of Herbert Macaulay)

support of his father-in-law, Bishop Ajayi Crowther and the Sierra Leonian community in Lagos. The school continued to grow in strength and popularity as many of the C.M.S trained personalities in the Yoruba country and in Freetown lend their hands of help to the Institution. T.B. Macaulay was greatly remembered for his immense contributions to the translation of the Bible into Yoruba language. Unfortunately his life was consumed on 17 January 1878 by the deadly disease that emanated from the small pox epidemic of 1877 through to 1878.

Holy Johnson James

On 19th July, 1892 in his speech delivered to his audience he said that: "there are times when it is more helpful that a people should be called upon to take up their responsibilities, struggle with and conquer their difficulties than that they should be in the position of vessels taken in tow, and that for West African Christianity, this is the time.

"This statement was made by the popular "Holy Johnson James", whom I would have given the native name of

"Akinlolu" if I were to be alive during his time, the great personality of his era throughout the length and breadth of the West African coast. He was born into a Yoruba family of the re-captives in the village of Waterloo in the Sierra Leone colony around 1836 as twins. He owed his survival solely to the fact that he was born under the British flag otherwise both himself and his twin brother/sister would have been killed at birth in accordance with the African custom of the period.

In 1847, Johnson entered the C.M.S School in St Mathew's Parish, Waterloo where he showed remarkable traits of responsibilities to the amazement of his teachers and the colony leaders of the Parish in hymn singing, Scripture and catechism memory passages. Some years later he entered the C.M.S. Grammar School to obtain his secondary education where the school curriculum was basically the replica of those Grammar Schools in England. In 1854, he entered the Fourah Bay Institution and in December 1858, he graduated from the Institution and took up appointment as catechist at Kent.

His appointment to Kent and to the Grammar School, where he was a tutor for two to three years developed his intense Christian devoutness and puritan propensities, which added a nickname of "Bishop" to his appellation by his friends and colleagues when they noticed in him how he would not miss his three time prayers in a day and when he would withheld some of the students dinner when they would neglect their class works for other social attendances. In March 1863, he was ordained deacon and took up curacy of the Pademba Road Church under the European missionary superintendent and in December 1866, Johnson was elevated to the position of priesthood. He belonged to the first experimental generation of Henry Venn's idea of native African church organization with the tag of "the settlement of a native church, under the native pastors, and upon a self-supporting system." Although the Sierra Leone experiment was noticed to be painful and perplexing in its process because of the beginning stage hardships but it inspired the native aspirations that irrevocably clashed with European missionary ethnocentrism. But notwithstanding the problems of the initial hurdles, the difficulties met were successfully pinned down by the few Africans that were in the front line of the educated West Africans of the time who were ready for the development of Africa by the Africans.

The ultimate goal of this experiment was to land it on the premises of political self-determination, but its rhetoric primarily focused on racial equality and ecclesiastical independence. The experimental period coincidentally fell into the time when an incipient African nationalism in the colony, spawning "Ethiopianism" ideology was being advocated. The Ethiopian movement extolled African identity, it defended African capability to run their own affairs, and anticipated the conversion of the entire African continent to Christianity and Johnson became one of the earliest and most aggressive advocates of its ideology.

In fact he became the apostle of the movement and for Johnson, the native pastorate experiment represented a unique opportunity for the glorification of the "Negro race"; he saw it as a cynosure of African Christianity that would allow the continent to take its rightful place with the most Christian, civilized and intelligent nations of the world. He was inspired to write and sum up the whole situation of the time thus: *"We see nothing around us which we can call our own in the true sense of the term; nothing that shows an independent native capacity excepting this infant Native Pastorate Institution.* He further asserted in strong terms that the desire to have an independent African church *"closely follows the fact that we are a distinct race, existing under peculiar circumstances and possessing peculiar characteristics..... and that the arrangement of foreign churches made to suit their own local circumstances can hardly be expected to suit our own in all the details.* He then predicted rightly that: *"the use of our own liturgy and cannons is a mere question of time".*

The race controversy that lasted from 1868 to 1873 witnessed a lot of ups and downs especially in the circle of Johnson's Ethiopian organization, which animated clergy and laity alike and crossed denominational barriers. Ethiopian movement was bolstered by Edward Blyden, an African nationalist with whom Johnson struck an alliance when he was transferred to Lagos and who developed considerable interest and influence from Johnson's line of thinking. Although Johnson remained the undisputed champion of the native pastors and the leading figure in the agitation for ecclesiastical independence but what hampered the smooth running of the movement was lack of sufficient fund and well devoted and dedicated people who could buy the wholesale stocks of the movement and resale them to the consumers who were the African natives. During this time, the churches in West Africa depended solely on the C.M.S and foreign aids for the emoluments of its staffs in the field and for the movement of same from point A to B and as such its loud voice was always suppressed or silenced half way.

Notwithstanding, Johnson's Ethiopian movement was able to challenge the entrenched European structures and attitude and drew inspiration from the African heritage, and called for the establishment of an authentic African ministry. The good work of Johnson and his movement evoked sympathetic response from the C.M.S Headquarters at Salisbury Square in London and he was invited to London in 1873 for dialogue and discussions. His ideas when tabled were thoroughly looked into because they contained far-reaching consequences and if they were to be ignored, things would fall apart in African region. As a result, the C.M.S resolved that Africans should join the staff at Fourah Bay College, which was to be elevated to a fee-paying university and where "any well recommended Christian Africans" could be trained for other vocations other than pastoral education which was the original plan for the establishment of the Institution. Furthermore this move eventually led to affiliating the college to Durham University in 1876.

Johnson was transferred to Lagos in June 1874 and his Ethiopian movement moved along with him to this more hospitable environment than Freetown. Before he came to Lagos a vigorous, if incipient, nationalist movement was already on the ground and instead of him sticking to his own ideas alone to multiply the same principle, he immediately identified himself with the group. He became its leading and most outspoken figure who would never take "NO" for an answer. Incidentally the Parish he was to work – Breadfruit parish was the home base for the most ardent nationalists among the population, the wealthiest and most important church in Lagos. From 1886 to 1894, he served as a member of the Legislative Council and with this resume in his kitty he enjoyed greater pre-eminence among Nigerian Christians, a status that would have been too difficult for him to enjoy had he remained in Freetown. Around this time, it was only Bishop Ajayi Crowther that was more popular than Johnson.

His ideology of "Africa for the Africans" became a rallying point of focus for the educated Africans, the White Cap Chiefs and the natives of his Parish and beyond. The prayers for the Queen of England in the prayer book of the church was changed and substituted with that of the Kings of the land and this alarmed the European missionaries who thought that sooner of later secession through Johnson's militancy was inevitable and could come un-noticed. Amid the entire trauma, the C.M.S of the time in 1876 made Johnson the Superintendent of all its stations in the interior of Yoruba land. This was a position pointing to his elevation to the Bishopric chair, which he would have used to exercise his powers in the jurisdiction of Abeokuta and the rest of

Yoruba country. But Johnson's superintendence lasted for only four years and the period generated lots of controversies, and which resulted in his removal.

There was no doubt about it that Johnson was a good material stuff for Bishopric position and as the period of 1880s progressed, increasing calls for such position in both Sierra Leone and Nigeria became very obvious. The C.M.S from its own part favored the appointment of a native Bishop to take charge of the Yorubaland, which had long been overdue. In pursuit of this demand, Johnson visited England again in 1887 to set forth the views on native self-government in a powerful statement entitled "A memorandum on the West African Native Churches and Missions and Native Episcopacy", which was described as "an impassioned and coherent argument for a native Bishop". His eloquence impressed his audience but the CMS decided to pursue the Yoruba option to that of Sierra Leone whose argument he advanced and focused in his paper.

In short Johnson's candidacy for this position met with stiff opposition from the European missionaries possibly because of his revolutionary tendencies towards the establishment of Native African Episcopacy. Instead of bagging the Bishopric position, he was appointed a member of the Lagos based C.M.S Finance Committee, which they knew that he would do very well as a good fundraiser. As soon as he left England for home, the European missionaries through their counterparts in Sierra Leone especially the young Bishop Ingham denounced the native pastorate scheme as ill conceived, unsound and untenable. Various games were played to tumble the demands of the Africans but thanks to the uprightness of Ethiopian movement who remained undaunted, vibrant and unceasingly fueled by the burning flame of the nationalistic fervor.

Johnson fought gallantly for the planting of the Native Church in Africa and his labor would be very difficult to be kept under the carpet. He was a good soldier of his company and a leader to reckon with among his people. The fight that his movement put up against those who were ready to ride on the backs of the natives to achieve their aims was fought by only few soldiers among the educated Africans of this time, but the result of the battle was encouraging for those who were to take the sword and the shield from them for more vicious battles lying ahead. Johnson was never a Saint as he had his own flaws like any of us but these flaws may not be enough for anyone to judge his characters and abilities as either a good or a bad soldier.

His remaining years were spent as Assistant Bishop of Western Equatorial Africa and were filled with different missionary activities while the light of his legacy and leadership traits and characteristics lived unquenched in the African church movement, which continued to challenge the missionary Christianity till today. His spirit of African nationalism, which grew naturally out of Christian mission paved the ways for those who were to take the mantle of political advancement in Africa and especially from his beloved country – Yoruba Nation whom he defended with everything he had in his possession until he answered the call of his Master on May 18 1917 while still at the war front fighting as a gallant soldier.

A question that was asked many centuries back and asked many years ago is still the same question being asked today about the position of Africa in relationship to the kind of friendship between us and our good old friends in European countries. Precisely on 16 February 1885 at St Paul's classroom in Lagos, a debate was held on the following topic:

"Are the present efforts of European countries to acquire and increase their possessions in Africa and to develop their commercial interests therein, calculated to be an advantage to Africa and the African race generally?"
Without any side talk, it was the same statement that aroused the intellectual abilities of our first and subsequent generations of educated Africans in Nigeria who came out openly to discuss, and attack the problems of the continent from its roots. One of such vocal and dedicated African of the struggling time was Herbert Macaulay, born on 14th of November 1864 at Broad Street, Lagos and grandson of Bishop Ajayi Crowther and son to Thomas Babinton Macaulay, the founder and the first Principal of the first Grammar School in Nigeria. He was truly the father of Nigeria nationalism and also the heir apparent to the throne of Nigeria modern politics. Herbert Macaulay's first appearance on the public scene was the time he exposed the European corruption in the railway project finances of 1908, which the colonial administrators saw as an extraordinary attack on the government and the European race. As if this was to end his attack on the colonial administration of the country, he engaged himself in defending the Royal lineage of Lagos. In 1919, the colonial government forcefully took some parcels of land in Lagos without going through the proper acquisition process. Macaulay, acting on behalf of the Lagos chiefs took the case to the Privy Council in London and he won with compensatory amount of Twenty-two

thousand and five hundred pounds sterling to be paid by the government to the chiefs who were the rightful and legal custodians of the land.

As a result of the Privy Council's decision on this case, the colonial government in Lagos retaliated by deposing the Oba of Lagos and appointed another in his place. Macaulay went back again to the court to challenge the actions of the government relating to this unruly sack of a traditional ruler by an imposed government of a foreign land. The case dragged for 10 years, which time he was jailed twice on trumped-up cases against him until again by another Privy Council decision, the Oba was restored to his throne in 1931. In 1922, Macaulay founded the first political party in Nigeria and he called it Nigeria National Democratic Party (N.N.D.P). The political party made national appeal to the people of Nigeria to rise up and kick against the attitude of the colonial government that was brutal to the survival of African people.

His political platform called for economic and educational development, the Africanization of the civil service and self-government for Lagos. The party had its footings properly entrenched in Lagos and by 1938 another movement called National Youth Movement, which had more national outlook than N.N.D.P sprang up to put more pressure on the government regarding the previous requests of the N.N.D.P. By 1944, the Nigerian first political party that embraced ideas from all walks of life throughout the country was born and named the National Council of Nigeria and Cameroon (N.C.N.C), which later transgressed into National Council of Nigeria Citizens after when Cameroon which was formally part of us went away through plebiscite to form their own country. The aged Macaulay was made its president while the then young and articulate Nnamdi Azikwe who later became the first black Governor-General and the first President of Nigeria emerged as its Secretary-General. The formation of the party included the amalgamation of labor unions, social clubs, political clubs, professional associations and more than 100 ethnic organizations in the country.

There is no way that one mentioned the contributions of our past leaders that the name of personality such as that of Dr. Nnamdi Azikwe could either be taken for granted or be swept under the carpet. In fact the highest number he scored in his political and social achievements throughout his life time was recorded for him through his association with Yorubaland and its people and for this reason he was always accepted and will continue to be accepted as part of Yoruba race till eternity. The Great Zik of Africa as we grew to know him was born on 16 November 1904 and was the founder of the modern Nigerian Nationalism. He attended Storer College at Harpers Ferry in West Virginia US but later enrolled and graduated from Lincoln University Pennsylvania in 1930. As a brilliant and academically fit student, he became a member of Phi Beta Sigma Fraternity – an academic award to brilliant students in American colleges and universities.

On his return to Africa, he stationed in Accra where he became the founding editor of the West African Pilot to show how interested he was to the problems facing the people of his continent especially the rude attendance of foreign colonialists to matters affecting the native Africans. He later relocated back to his country of origin – Nigeria with a view to establish his media industry. His unbridled success in the business promoted him to the larger field of politics in Nigeria. He co-founded the N.C.N.C alongside with Herbert Macaulay in 1944 and in 1954 he became the Premier of Eastern Region of Nigeria after he had represented Lagos in the Western House of Assembly. Nigeria at Independence in 1960, while recognized the valuable work that uncle Benjamin rendered for the freedom and development of his people asked him to be their first native appointed Governor-General and when the country attained the status of "Republican" in 1963, he was equally asked to be their "First Native President".

His name would always be remembered each time we pass through such places like Nnamdi Azikwe International Airport in Abuja, Nnamdi Azikwe University in Awka, Anambra or when we look at his portrait on the face of Nigeria's five-hundred Naira currency denominations. All these are the legacies of the good works done by a good, dedicated and devoted citizen of a nation.

Other titans of this era which space would not allow me to reference into details include the followings: Sir Adeyemo Alakija, the grand father of my beloved wife and who was born in 1884 and called to Bar in 1913 with the original name of Placcido Adeyemo born to the family of Ribeiro and Maximiliana from Brazillian Lagos and Abeokuta family axis. In 1923 and 1926 he represented Lagos twice in the Legislative Council before he later emerged the first President of Egbe

Chief Olabode Thomas

123

Omo Oduduwa. Also onto the list was our beloved doyen, Chief Olabode Thomas- the Balogun of Oyo who was born into the family of a well-known Lagos aristocrat. He was the founding Secretary-General of the Action Group following his active participation in Egbe Omo Oduduwa; Dr. Crispan Curtis Adeniyi Jones; Mr. Eric Moore and Egerton Shygle all who were members of the Legislative Council of Nigeria of their time. Sir Kitoyi Ajasa, Christopher Sapara Williams (the first Nigeria Lawyer) and Dr. Obadiah Johnson (the first Nigeria medical doctor); Sir Kofo Abayomi – founding member of the Nigerian Youth Movement and who later became its President all lend their credible hands of participation to the building of our nation. How can we forget Mazi Mbonu Ojike,

Sir Adetokunbo Ademola

the apostle of boycott of products from Britain and who was the deputy mayor of the Lagos Town Council or Chief Rotimi Williams who was in the 50s the chairman of the Lagos Town Council or Dr. Olorunnimbe the famous Mayor of Lagos or Sir Adetokunbo Ademola the respected Chief Justice of Nigeria or the late Oba Akinsanya the Odemo of Ishara in Ijebu land or Adegoke Adelabu alias Penkelemesi from the city of Ibadan, Chief Obafemi Awolowo the greatest political tactician of our age, Chief Anthony Enahoro of the fugitive offenders fame and a great politician of our time, Chief Samuel Ladoke Akintola the controversial premier of Western Region and his deputy Chief Fani-Kayode the " Fani power" and a brilliant lawyer from Oxford, Chief Akinyemi Obe from Iddo Ani, Chief Akinfosile, the late Oni of Ife – Sir Adesoji Aderemi, Sir Odeleye Fadahunsi and host of others.

We shall continue to remember all of you and the good role you played as our past leaders and our heroes who led us to the promise land where we are today. We shall from time to time look unto the tears of struggle rolling down your cheeks and the blood which continually dropping down from your bodies all just for the salvation of our souls and the sustenance of our bodies. To all their sufferings and courage I say bravo to all of you and your enduring patience when all of you faced imprisonment terms and imminent death sentences from the captors of your people.

Chapter –9–

The Sum Total Period of Imperial Government in Nigeria

The political activities of both British and French regarding the subjugation of West African people from the coast line unto the inland of Africa was not without reason. The successful exploration of the Senegal and Niger Rivers contributed immensely towards the idea of partitioning and scramble for territories in Africa, and which later invited the imperialists of Europe through the first hand information they got from their traders who moved up and down these Great Rivers of Africa. This assertion reflected the general opinion of the planners of the Exploration especially when one of them Laird wrote in his memoir on hearing of the solution to the Niger problem through the discovery of quinine that: [The long sought for highway into central Africa was at last found. The long trip to the interior of Africa also offered a boundless field for commercial enterprise, an extensive market for the goods manufactured in Europe and the forceful control of the colonists through guns and other weapons of destruction.] Fortunately the period when imperialist tendencies were being hatched coincided with the time when the slave trading was being suppressed and abolished in the West coast of Africa. The barons of the slave trade business especially those at the coast cities and towns had no other alternative but to change gear in search of new commodities and new markets that would replace the old one. Naturally, all efforts were being made by them to push European commerce along the trails left by the explorers of the two rivers.

For example, between 1817 and 1840 the French made an attempt to establish plantations and built forts on the River Senegal at Bakel,

Dagone and Richard-Toll. Likewise in 1832 the British and the Americans sent out an expedition up the Niger and set up trading stations on its banks. From 1836 to 1841, the British government tried all it could to establish trade posts along the banks of the Niger River and set up experimental farm project in Lokoja as a means to overthrowing the slave trade. But unfortunately all the efforts by the trio – America, British and French to push up the Niger and Senegal Rivers failed because of the low support they got from the African rulers and its middlemen plus the white mortalities from the wicked hands of malaria fever. The African climate at one point became so dreadful to the British government that they almost abandoned the West African exploration project and turned their attentions and efforts towards the Sahara where they established two vice-consular posts. Richardson-Barth Expedition from Tripoli to Bornu and Timbuktu in 1849 were the success of this intention. Though the project of the West Africa was not totally abandoned by the imperialists and for this reason both the British and the French in the 1850s resumed their drive from the Guinea Coast inland up the Senegal and the Niger rivers.

By 1865, French had gained full control of the Senegal River through the efforts of General Louis Faidherbe who was the governor of Senegal from 1854 to 1861 and who again came back to govern the territory between 1863 to 1865. The use of force by the French armies on the natives enabled the French merchants who followed the footsteps of their armies to establish their trading posts northwards from the region of Timbuktu down the Senegal to the coast. The defeat of French by the Germans in 1870 temporarily halted French political expansion inland; but it resumed back in 1879. In 1883 they had occupied Bamako on the Niger and from there they moved to Timbuktu, which they finally occupied in 1894.

In the case of Nigeria, the British resumed its exploration of the Niger after the discovery of quinine that tremendously reduced the high rate of mortality among the Europeans in 1854. After three years into the project, the British did not only agreed to subsidized the trade development on the Niger, but as well sent their warships along with the European merchants to suppress any opposition from the African natives who may when necessary asked for their legitimate rights in the development of the new trade coming to their areas. As from 1857, the British merchants had already established trading posts up the Niger, and by 1859, they had reached Lokoja - the confluence of the Niger and Benue where they established their first model farm and built their trade station. The trade along the Niger banks was so well flourished that by the late 1860s as many as five British companies had already been established and successfully operating on the banks of the Niger River. What could have been accepted today as healthy competition was what caused problem among the companies of the 19th century, which was then called "dangerous rivalry" that nearly tore down the walls of the trading companies of the time along the Niger banks. But in 1879 Goldie Taubman who later became Sir George Goldie came to rescue the split-away companies when he amalgamated all of them into one big company called the United African Company. In 1886, the company was granted charter by the British government under the new name of the Royal Niger Company. It was this new company that the imperialists used to lay the foundation of the annexation of the whole country, which later came under the term called "amalgamation".

The same company's activities under the guise of commodity trading won Northern Nigeria for Britain during the scramble for Africa at the end of the century. By the time the European goods began to reach the markets of Hausaland in large quantities with cheaper price tags, the caravan trade of the past fell drastically and in years later it collapsed totally because the loading capacity of camels could not be equated or matched for that of a steam vessel. Interestingly, it was this method of goods penetration through the waterways into the interior of Africa especially as from the 1850s and the occupation of the entire Western Sudan and the Sahara by the British and the French that finally collapsed the caravan trade between the West and the North of Africa, which had been in existence for over 2000 years.

The commercial rivalry of the earlier period that existed among the trading companies on the Niger River before the companies were amalgamated into one single unit by George Goldie now turned into commercial warfare between the Royal Niger Company and the competing native groups that entered the palm-oil trade especially those from Brass and Opobo. The Brass traders of the past were known to be notorious and ardent slave traders with records far exceeding anyone from anywhere in the region but the Anglo-Brass treaty of 1856 made them to soft-pedal and promised to stop the dangerous trade and opted to divert their potentials to the new palm-oil trade which was introduced to them in place of slave trading. Following the treaty, the Brass merchants began to explore the palm-oil market up the Engenni

River to Oguta and from Aboh to Onitsha. In search of palm-oil market potentialities around this region among the natives, the British firms broke through the Delta and established themselves on the middle Niger at Aboh, Onitsha and Lokoja. The British merchant Macgregor Laird, who enjoyed the British government patronage, opened his trading posts in those areas; but the Brass merchants did not take kindly to this move and in their reply, they fortified the river and encouraged the destruction of Laird's factory at Aboh and Onitsha. In support of Laird, the British government had to intervene and came to the assistance of Laird by providing naval escorts to laird's ships through the Delta and at the same time bombarded Aboh and Onitsha in retaliation and punishment for their attacks on Lairds factories.

The British efforts to take over the trade on the Niger River was masterminded by their fellow countryman George Goldie who in 1879 was able to bring all the British firms operating along the banks of the River into one entity – United African Company. The company grew very rapidly and in years later, it had established up to one hundred trading posts along the banks with the British government support of twenty gunboats to suppress any would-be rivals. It offered high prices for oil in order to push the French competing firms into closure and bankruptcy. The one good news about what was going-on around this period was the resistance of the traders from both Lagos and Brass, who reluctantly remained a hardened bone in the flesh of the United African Company despite all the gunboats pointed at them.

In 1886 when Goldie had a Royal charter for his company and it now became Royal Niger Company, his wings grew larger and stronger as the company now automatically became the government of the Niger region. On assuming this new position plus the backing it got from his home government in England, the company began to eliminate its competitors one after the other until it succeeded to eliminate its last opposition from Lagos and Brass by imposing heavy license fees and taxes on the Lagosians and the Creoles, and by disallowing the Brass and the Kalabari traders to enter its area of operations. Those who flouted the company's marine orders would have their canoes confiscated and the traders found in them charged for smuggling. This action strangled the economy of the Kingdom of Brass while the natives suffered the worst humiliation of their lives in the hands of this self imposed government of an ordinary foreign trading company on the soil of Africa.

The Royal Niger Company with George Goldie at its head became supper power of the greatest dimension in the region of the Niger Delta and in 1893 Goldie brazened the belt of his customs so tightly that the Brass smuggling trade was totally stopped. When the Brass merchants petitioned the consul, Clande Macdonald, who repeatedly asked the British government to stop supporting the Royal Niger Company, did not received any favorable result because of the position of influence of Goldie among the government circle in England. It was revealed that some prominent members of both British political parties – Labor and Conservative held reasonable share in his company, which was at this time the most profitable British charter company in Africa.

Another point that supported the non-withdrawal of the government patronage and support for the company was that this time coincided with the time when scrambling for territories in Africa by the European imperialists was at its highest peak. In this regard, Goldie held the balance of power for the British because he was in a position to decide the faith of the British government in either way. If his monopoly was broken in the region, he could conveniently withdraw his business activities in the region and allowed the whole Niger region fell into the waiting hands of either the Germans or the French. In the end of it all Consul Macdonald was forced to admit in 1894 that there was not much he could do to help the situation of the Brass traders.

The height of the powers that the Royal Niger Company artificially assigned to itself included the establishment of its own constabulary (police) force and the courts where cases were decided and in most cases the verdicts of those courts offended the integrity and natural position of the natives. In 1895, King Koko and the people of Brass revolted against the inhuman treatment meted out to them by the officials of the company and they set up an army of 1000 strong men in 30 war canoes to destroy the Royal Niger Company's headquarters and port at Akassa. In retaliation to this action, the Royal Navy and the company's troops blew up Nembe and Twon, which were the local towns where the port was seating and confiscated all the Brass war canoes. The King was tried and fined 500 pounds while his people were driven into the swamps, where many of them died of hunger and smallpox epidemic. It was estimated that the number of the natives consumed through this means were larger than the number killed by the British bullets. The Royal Niger Company had no other equal as far as trading was concerned in the region of the Niger River of this time be it either white or native traders. As powerful and great as it was, it could close any market at will and offer any price to run down its competitors anytime.

As a result of the trade atrocities committed by the company coupled with the outcry of the natives that was reaching the ears of the government in England plus the arbitrary bombardment of Akassa, the British government forced Goldie to give up the charter of his company in 1900.

The trade war in the Delta area among the traders particularly between the British and the French firms on one hand and the natives on the other clearly showed that the imperialist government back home in Europe supported one team against the other in the battle. From the perspective of the British traders, the British government was ready to back them up on any move concerning the expansion of British trade and interests with military precisions and force. They made sure that the middlemen who were mainly the natives were forcefully taken out of the business scene and planted their own men in their place. Goldie's amalgamation of the British firms, his skillful use of economic and political weapons to set the stage ready for the colonists to climb, and the steady support and responses he got each time he needed such from the government, marked the entry of the colonial administration in Nigeria.

Unfortunately a person who was called the father of Nigeria in the British circle was the one who excluded the people from his own family clan in the key areas of the economy of his beloved country, in which the profits were large, where capital could be accumulated and from where the economic development of the country he fathered could be stimulated. Through his business and political actions, the people of the Delta region sank into dismal subsistence-level of poverty where they remained throughout the colonial days and which up till today the influence of his regime along the banks of River Niger still maintained negative impact on the lives of the people of the region.

Period of Colonial Rule in Nigeria 1900 – 1960.

The period of colonial rule in Nigeria was marked by the time when the imperialists came to assert their foreign authorities on the subjects of the nation without consulting their opinions on how best they could be governed but how best the British system of government could be imposed on the people with force. As the slave trade declined, it carried away with it the powers and popularity of the coastal city nobilities and as palm-oil trade took over the reign of the day from its predecessor, it carried the new men from the interior to wealth, power and prominence. Like in all other places where the palm-oil trade thrived there was social upheaval of revolutionary proportions as the lower classes, led by the few educated ones amongst them struggled to rear their heads above the waters and began to kick against the prejudices and oppressions of the nobilities, which had been raging on for decades.

The British rule over the territory of Nigeria was very systematic in nature and well planned from its beginning. Collaboration of the British government with the missionaries, the traders of their own blood and the use of military precisions to harass and intimidate the natives played key role in the achievement of their goals for ruling the country for upwards of sixty solid years. The intended purpose of the Niger Expedition was first and foremost about how Britain could expand its trade and maintained status quo with the people around the regions of the Great River. To achieve this program of penetration, they had to diffuse the minds of the people and gave them another heart in form of robot, which could be remote controlled from any obscured corner of the earth. At the start of the program, the obnoxious slave trade that was marketed to the people by the Europeans particularly the Portuguese and supported by others in the 18th century after it had gainfully benefited them in labor productivity, financial reward and economic development suddenly decided to kill the business and began to parade the waters of African coast with gunboats to subdue the powers of both the European and the native slave traders. A tiny portion of the land of the Temne people on the coastline of Africa called Freetown was selected as save heaven for those who were rescued from the jaws of human wale whose intention was to take them to the labor sugar plantations in the Americas.

After settling down in the land of Freetown in Sierra Leone, life began to change into a new model for the slaves that were rescued on the waters of the Atlantic Ocean and who came from different African nations. The philanthropists from some countries of Europe particularly from Britain donated their pennies and shillings to maintain these people that were put together in the same place under the same condition. After a very long time of stay here, some of them through destiny were fortunate enough to have the opportunity to travel back to their homes of origin. Many of them died sojourners in the land keeping with them to their graveyards only the memories of their kith, kin and places of birth that they never saw the beauties of its land again. Their offshoots had no alternative other than to resign to faith and to learn the new culture, which now bounded them together as one people.

The missionary ideas and philosophy introduced by their saviors began to spring up and occupied the minds of some of them while some remained adamant to the traditional religion of their ancestors. Those who embraced the new religion did so in appreciation to what the white man did in rescuing their lives from the hands of their captors. At the colony, those that were still young to be molded were put into the schools and thought how to read and write the letters of the Whiteman's language and through this knowledge they mastered their trading patterns and way of life, which helped them to see clearly the difference between their past and their new life-style. The thought that immediately came to their minds was the terrible conditions under which their kiths and kin were still living and how they could be rescued and transformed. With the little they had acquired from the colony, they thought they could do better to change the life-style of their people no matter how small it could be. For this purpose they began to struggle for their ways back home. Those who came from Yorubaland found their ways back to Badagry where they had the warm feelings and love of their people they had not seen for many years of absence.

Some of them remained in Badagry while some traveled by land to Lagos and Abeokuta where they settled and began another new life, which was the replica of the type they were living at the colony in Freetown. Their people were happy to learn a lot from them and tried to emulate their new life-style particularly the new religion that they whole-heartedly embraced. Years later their rescuer from the hands of the slave traders began to change color like chameleon and began to issue harsh and tough instructions on how the people should now leave their lives. As this was not enough, directions from afar off across the Atlantic Ocean on how they could trade, how the percentage of the profits from their labor could be shared and how the mineral resources of their land could be controlled were pouring in unabated. The same gunboats that were pointed at their enemies on the high sea the other day during the second quarter of the 19th century were now being used to suppress and oppress the same people in the 20th century.

Both Africans and their European missionary counterparts were given almost the same kind of treatment at the start of their religious introduction to the people especially those who began the work in the interior. In Abeokuta, Rev. Townsend, a missionary that was highly rated amongst his professional colleagues was like a son of the soil because of the great work he did among the Egba people for the progress of the community. In fact he was a Yoruba man to the core because of his ability to speak and write Yoruba language very fluently even more than some of those that were born into the language. He was the first person to open newspaper industry in Nigeria where the news of the country and the advancement of religious faith were being disseminated among the elites of the time. It was reported of him that when the campaign against the Hutt Committee was taken to the House of the Lords in England, Townsend who happened to be in England on holidays at the time was asked by Henry Venn to put up a memoranda for him to be presented to Lord Palmerston concerning the true situation of things at Abeokuta, which its picture had already been painted as a land full of promise for the future evengelization and civilization of the country and as the gateway to an overland route to the north with as much potential economic value as the Niger waterway.

Rev. Townsend in his usual character of the love he had for Abeokuta prepared a very meaningful and clearly expressed document, setting out the aims and objectives of the missionary at Abeokuta, the level of success attained so far, the menace of Kosoko and that of Dahomey, the huge economic potentialities of the region through River Ogun, the friendly disposition of the chiefs and the loyalty of the emigrants. All he was aiming at was that Abeokuta must receive a special privileged consideration from the government as to the rapid development and protection of the town in preference to other areas of the country.

Based on the paper prepared by Townsend, the C.M.S drew up an official memorandum, which set out a new policy to the government in which part of it read thus: Most of the advantages which were proposed by the Expedition of the Niger in 1842 are now within reach of the British Government by securing the navigation of Ogun River. Traders from the banks of the Niger visit the principal markets of Abeokuta and there is little doubt that the road to Egga and Rabbah, the former of which towns was the highest point reached by the Niger Expedition, might be opened for trade through the channel.

When Townsend's paper and the C.M.S. memorandum were presented to Lord Palmerston on 4 December 1849, Lord Palmerston decided to send Beecroft, who was home on leave, on a diplomatic mission to Abeokuta to enquire more facts about what was said concerning the town and furthermore to find out the wishes and dispositions of the

Yoruba people including the succession dispute in Lagos between Kosoko and his nephew Akintoye. On his way to Abeokuta, he was asked to visit all the Obas along the coast to put across to them the decision of the British government to stamp out the slave trade business and put in its place the legitimate trade that would make the people become free and independent and to urge on them to sign the prepared treaty concerning the issue. He was to explain to them that the purpose for the new trade was to promote legitimate trade under peaceful atmosphere whereby the rulers and their people will enjoy the exchange for the products of their country those European commodities that they may need for their own enjoyment and that the great natural resources of their country may be developed for the general development of the entire community; and that the practice of stealing, buying and selling of men, women, and children may end.

Beecroft arrived Badagry on 2 January 1851 and on the 7 January, he proceeded to Abeokuta where he was warmly received by both Townsend and the chiefs of the city. He had an ample chance to discuss freely with the prominent chiefs on matters concerning the political situation of Abeokuta and it's environ, the issue of Akintoye/Kosoko and Lagos, and the economic development of the town. On 18 January, the war chiefs (Baloguns) as a body called on him to pledge their loyalty and acceptance of the peace treaty that the British government asked them to sign. Beecroft was glad and impressed by what he saw on the ground at Abeokuta. On his getting back to Badagry, the petition he asked Akintoye to prepare for him before he traveled to Abeokuta regarding his own side of the succession rift in Lagos, which he would take with him to England, was already done on his behalf by Gollmer. In the petition he wrote in part that: My humble prayer to you is that you would take Lagos under your protection, that you would plant the English flag there and that you would re-establish me on my rightful throne at Lagos and protect me under my flag; and with your help I promise to enter into a treaty with England to abolish the slave trade at Lagos and to establish and carry on lawful trade especially with the English merchants.

The succession dispute in Lagos divided the people of the region into two warring factions; the missionaries and the Egba people including half of Egun natives of Badagry were solidly behind Akintoye while the slave trade barons of Dahomey, Badagry and Lagos supported Kosoko. Based on the intelligent report reaching Beecroft when he got back to

Badagry, he decided for the safety of Akintoye's life to take him with him to Fernando Po, which was then his official town of residence as the British consul for West African coast. Although Akintoye refused his offer to go with him because he never wanted to be stigmatized as a deserter of his supporters and friends who stood behind him through thick and thin; but the consul insisted and he agreed to relocate to Fernando Po from Badagry on a short stay. As soon as he left Badagry, the tension became heightened and later prompted the two parties to consolidate their efforts at each other's throat.

Chief Mewu led the Akintoye's supporting group, which included the missionaries, traders, emigrants and other native supporters; while Possu led Kosoko's group with other leading Badagry chiefs and some native supporters. On 11 June 1851, the looming civil war that had been raging for a long time finally touched down when a group of women traders from Lagos sang some inciting war songs at Badagry market place pointing to the cowardice action of the flee away Akintoye and the poverty ridden of the group following him in sharp contrast to the manliness and the wealthy position of Kosoko of Lagos and his supporters everywhere and who were ready to stand the test of all odds. The British people in the region met at once to decide on the next line of action to take and in five days later, Commander L. G. Heath in H.M.S. arrived Badagry to take in the vessel for protection all the British subjects living in Badagry. But Gollmer rejected the offer on the ground that they were not willing to abandon their friends and instead Commander Heath decided to issue out arms, which the emigrants could use to defend themselves in case of an attack.

Mewu's native group was also given twenty guns, twenty kegs of powder, twenty iron bars for shot and quantity of rum while one thousand pistol balls and two thousand musket ball cartridges were issued to the emigrants. In the ensuing battle, Possu and his Badagry supporting chiefs and natives were defeated and all of them fled to either Lagos or Porto Novo. Their come back attempt to re-surface at Badagry was repelled and this subjected Badagry to a state of siege for the rest of the year. The menace of this incessant attack on Badagry made the British authority to decide to station permanently one of their warships around the region of Badagry to patrol the waters on regular basis.

In March 1851, Abeokuta's territory was attacked by Gezo, the King of Dahomey and his army and marched up to its gates, but due to the resistance and gallant fight of the Egba warriors, they failed to take the city by storm and they were defeated but with heavy losses from both sides. Gezo's action was widely publicized in England and aroused the sympathy of the British citizens from all walks of life. In support of Abeokuta's existence, donation of money, clothes, and other useful items were sent by the people of England to Abeokuta for the course and gallantry efforts of the Egba people.

Exploiting this emotional situation, Henry Venn increased pressure on the government to issue direct order for action in Lagos and to issue more ammunition for the defense of Abeokuta. By this time under review, Lagos was peaceful under the rule of Oba Kosoko and for this reason there was not enough excuse for an attack on Lagos but notwithstanding there could always be a way to rope him in for one trouble or the other. All Palmerston could do was to send Beecroft to Lagos and urged on him to sign a treaty, which its primary objective was to stop the slave trade of which Oba Kosoko himself was its chief baron. Beecroft was asked to tell him that: Lawful commerce is more advantageous to the nations of Africa than the slave trade and substituting it with lawful commerce, is conferring a benefit upon the people and chiefs of Africa. That Great Britain is a strong power both by sea and by land and that her friendship is worth having but her displeasure it is well to avoid. All diplomatic channels were threaded by Venn to see that Kosoko was removed forcefully from Lagos because of his inability to drop the slave trade gin in his blood veins.

As part of his plans, he used both father and son – the Crowthers to drive his point home before the Queen and Lord Palmerston as Vein confessed himself that it was Samuel Crowther's visit to London that finally moved the government into action. When Crowther was ready to travel back home on his trip to England, Lord Palmerston wrote to thank him for the important and useful information he provided the British authority regarding Abeokuta and the tribes adjoining it. In the letter he said that: I request that you will assure your countrymen that Her Majesty's Government takes a lively interest in the welfare of the Egba nation, and for the community settled at Abeokuta, which town seems destined to be a center from which the lights of Christianity and civilization may spread over the neighboring countries.

In September of that year, Lord Palmerston drew up a new memorandum for the Admiralty saying that the government could no longer permit the accomplishment of the "great purpose" of abolition to be thwarted by Kosoko and Gezo his accomplice; and that the attack of Gezo on Abeokuta in spite of the solemn warning he was given was a possible act of invasion. He therefore asked the Lords of Admiralty to order the blockade of the ports of Dahomey till the King signed the treaty and ordered the restoration of Akintoye based on the assurance of Captain Denhan, Crowther and Beecroft that there would not be much problem by the time the order was to be carried out. The Admiralty then issued instructions to Commodore Bruce to carry out the government orders to letters. Lagos and Abeokuta now became two areas of attention to the British government and they had to be protected because of how significant and important the two locations would be in future to the intentions of the government. On 17 November Beecroft arrived Badagry to consult with Commander T.G. Forbes, the Naval Officer in charge of that area of the coast and both of them proceeded to Lagos with four warships. On arriving Lagos, they invited Kosoko to a meeting and told him about the new intentions of the British government concerning the end to slave trade and pressed on him to sign the treaty abrogating the trade but he declined using an excuse that Lagos was under the Oba of Benin and it was he who should be asked to sign such treaty.

Based on the rejection of Kosoko to sign the document; that which was envisaged from the beginning of the plan now opened up an avenue for the British government to strike Lagos and its first attempt failed possibly due to some tactical error or military logistic inadequacies. Commander Bruce arrived back in Lagos on Christmas Eve and attacked the city on Boxing Day. It was reported that on the second day of the battle the superior war techniques of the British side prevailed when rockets from one of their gun boats blew up the Royal arsenal of Oba Kosoko, which caused a great damage to them. The next chance left for Kosoko and his leading supporters was to flee to Epe and Lagos was captured with the minimal loss of sixteen men killed and twenty-five wounded on the British side. On New Year Day Oba Akintoye signed the slave trade treaty, and on January 5, 1852 similar treaty document was signed by the chiefs of Abeokuta while Possu in Badagry appended his signature on the document on behalf of his people at a later date.

Now that Lagos was captured, the doors for both the missionaries and the state officials including the British traders were flunk opened for everyone to come to Lagos, which had hitherto been too dangerous a place in the past years. An opportunity they had been looking for now walked into them without much hassle or strain. In March 1852,

Gollmer came to Lagos to demand and obtained from Oba Akintoye for the C.M.S. five pieces of land on the Island of Lagos free from real estate imbroglios. The exodus of the emigrants from Badagry followed almost immediately and four months after Gollmer had moved to Lagos, Louis Frazer, a trader who succeeded Duncan as Vice-Consul at Whydah, arrived Lagos to act as Consul until the arrival of Benjamin Campbell in August 1853 as the first official Consul of Lagos.

The program of stopping the slave trade business in Africa at all cost played a significant role in the colonial program of the Europeans in the continent. During the decades that followed the abolition of the trade, British diplomacy began to move into the regions of West African interior where it wove a fabric of treaties with the Kings and the chieftains whose cooperation was sought in suppressing the traffic of the trade. British interests carried with it occasional armed intervention to force those chieftains and the Kings to sign those treaties which may sometime go against their will. We should not forget that almost all of the chieftains and the Kings of the West coast interior of this time were people of no letters at all. The only function they had to perform in those documents was to thump print their fingers at the appropriate dotted line on the paper as a seal of authority and acceptance to the terms written from England or France and made binding on the whole community who could not challenge the validity and authenticity of such document in any court of Law. Gradually the British armed intervention began to increase with the cooperation of the Royal Niger Company constabulary, a self-made police force organization introduced by Sir George Goldie the chairman of the corporation to staunch the flow of slaves to the coast, to protect the British traders against other European competitors particularly the French and the Germans and to promote peace and tranquility among the natives.

The missionaries from their own side were busy pressing on the British government to provide for them adequate security for the expansion of their business in Africa especially in the areas of stamping out slavery in any form and to put an end to some other barbarous practices associated with the indigenous religions. The call from this powerful organization of the time prompted the government to post consular officials to service the increasing levels of trade in the ports of the Bight of Benin and Biafra, which actually helped to project the image and the influence of the British in the interior. In 1861 as mentioned earlier Lagos was annexed and became the British colony, yet the British government still considered African project as being an expensive liabilities and its withdrawal from West Africa was expressed in a parliamentary report in 1865. Suddenly its attitude changed just because of its European counterpart's program in the play field, especially France and Germany, who scurried to develop overseas markets and grabbing of territories, which they could conveniently control its potentials from their home base.

This eventually called for the clash of European imperialist's intentions and ambitions in Africa of the 20th century. In 1885 at the Berlin Conference where the European powers gathered to discuss about the welfare of the people of Africa and to which none of the natives of Africa was invited to subscribe, the Conferees enunciated the principle called the "dual mandate", which was interpreted as a program that would best serve the interests of both Europe and Africa. Under this program there was to be free access to the continent by European nations for trade that could benefit both and the successful transfer of European civilization into Africa. The Conference officially acknowledged the British sphere of influence in the Niger Basin, but stipulated that only effective occupation of the region would secure full international recognition. Because of this the pressure of France and Germany in the region spurred British into hastened action to establish an effective occupation of the territory from Lagos to Calabar as the first phase of the annexation program.

The instability created by the Yoruba wars coupled with the activities of other European powers struggling to have their own shares out of the cake made the British authority to move cautiously but inexorably toward colonial domination of the lower Niger Basin. Its expansion moved very rapidly in the last decade of the 19th century. Because of the threats hanging on Yoruba nation from its neighbor in the west – Dahomey and from its north – the Sokoto Caliphate as the evidence of Ilorin Emirate showed, the British governor with the help of the C.M.S officials succeeded in establishing peace settlement in the interior of Yoruba nation. Lagos had now become a cosmopolitan city in nature with modern port facilities of European taste and varied backgrounds of black communities composed of English speaking people from Sierra Leone and of emancipated slaves brought back home from Brazil and Cuba. The government of the colony provided job opportunities it could afford in the civil service for those who were qualified while others thrived in various private sectors of the economy from importation of wares from Europe to local distribution of imported wares to the consumers in both Lagos and in the interior.

Movement of people from the interior to the cosmopolitan Lagos in search of employment and taste of the new civilization was increasing on daily basis. When the construction of roads and rail lines from Lagos to connect the interior began, more and more people began to move en-mass to Lagos thereby calling for government's involvement in the urban planning of Lagos metropolis. The "protection" slogan of 1861 when Lagos became British Colony eventually resulted in the "colonization of Nigeria" through series of steps designed under the trade umbrella and which in 1906 metamorphosed into full control of the British over the territory of what we have today as Nigeria. What transpired during this period is a huge history on itself, which I may not be able to dwell much upon into details on most of the events that occurred during the time. I beg to leave that portion to the historians to give full details and in chronological order because my background differs completely from that area of knowledge. I am more of scientist than historian and this is why I should be taken for who I am in the field of history, which I only branched into out of passion, interest and hobby.

After the Berlin Conference, Britain announced the formation of the Oil Rivers Protectorate, which included the Niger Delta that was already known to be trading partners of the British traders many years back and extended eastward to cover Calabar where the British chose as the new seat of the Consulate-General who was relocated from Fernando Po. The idea behind this move was to oversee and control the market coming down the Niger River from elsewhere in the region and to properly monitor the flow of the market; Vice-Consuls were assigned to ports in those areas that had concluded treaties of cooperation with the Foreign Office. Initially the local rulers were not disturbed from administering their subjects and territories, but Consular authorities took over the jurisdiction of the equity courts formally established by the foreign mercantile communities for the adjudication of trade disputes. In 1894 a re-designated order was approved and the former territory under the Oil Rivers Protectorate became Niger Coast Protectorate with added territories to cover from Calabar to Lagos colony, including the hinterland thereof and also extended northward up the Niger River to Lokoja, which had been the corporate headquarters of the Royal Niger Company. In the Southwest territory military force was used to bring Ijebu, Oyo and Benin into agreeing with the obligations of the prepared treaties while the conquest of Benin City in1897 marked the completion of the British occupation of South Western Nigeria.

In the North of the country treaties were signed with the rulers up the Niger River as far as to Sokoto by 1885, but actual British control over the Northern territory did not take place not until 1900. Reason being that they wanted to firmly establish their hold over the areas closer to the then available means of communication with the home government and also where the means of transportation was easier to them. We should not forget that around this time, the fastest and easiest means of transportation between Europe and Africa was through the Atlantic Ocean. Furthermore, most of the journeys in the interior during those days were either made on foot or by caravans- Horse or Camel driven method.

During the larger part of the last quarter of the century the Royal Niger Company was the only visible British interest that had close interaction with the North through its trading activities along the Rivers of Niger and Benue from Lokoja. The British government's ambition was to occupy Sokoto Caliphate, but they quickly noticed that Royal Niger Company was not sufficient enough for them to achieve this aim and as such the Royal charter granted the company was withdrawn on December 31, 1899 and provided for its owners enough compensation and retention of valuable mineral rights to grease their palms and cool them down.

With the demise of the almighty company the British government now had full control everywhere in the country and by 1900 Fredrick Lugard was appointed the High Commissioner of the Protectorate of Northern Nigeria. Fredrick Lugard was trained as an army officer and had served in India, Egypt and East Africa before being posted to the new Northern Protectorate to apply his experience and wisdom he had acquired from those countries in dealing with the Emirs of the North. In East Africa for example, Lugard was said to have expelled Arab slave traders from Nyasaland and successfully established the British presence in Uganda. It was also on record that in 1894, Lugard joined the Royal Niger Company and he was sent to Borgu to counter the inroads made by the French and in 1897 he raised the Royal West African Frontier (RWAFF) from local levies to serve under the British officers. During his six-year in office as High Commissioner, he tried to consolidate the commercial sphere of influence inherited from the

Royal Niger Company into real territorial concern under an effective British political control.

Some of his primary intentions included the British control of the land and to subdue the local chiefs including the Fulani Emirs of the Sokoto Caliphate. In fact he succeeded in subduing the local resistance, using armed forces where diplomatic measures would not work. He conquered Bornu without a fight but in Kano and Sokoto, his force mounted assaults on those cities. His administrative method of indirect rule, which made him popular and which he used to govern the protectorate through the rulers he had defeated through force gave him triumph and characterized him as the model British Colonial administrator of his time. The cooperating Emirs with the British authority retained their Caliphate titles while those that refused to cooperate with them faced the wrought of the government's firestorm. Things were no longer easy as it used to be in the past because the colonial rule in the North and elsewhere in the country was becoming hardened. The Commissioners were now given more powers as they can on their own depose any Emir or other Rulers who go against their authority either such authority was good or bad and it does not matter to them where such Emir or Ruler came from.

In the case of Lugard in the North, nothing significantly changed in the old system of governance through the Emirs except for the payment of salaries to the caliphate officials who were now transformed into district heads and automatically became agents of the British authorities as they were now responsible for tax collection and peace making. This means that they still had the old wine just in a new bottle.

Although the High Commissioner was given unlimited powers both in his executive and legislative capacities in the Protectorate, but in his wisdom and judgment he did not want to offend the Rulers and their subjects and this was why most of the government's activities were undertaken by the Emirs and their appointed administrators subject to the British approval. Some of the economic developments that occurred during the tenure of Lugard and his successor in the protectorate came when the railroad was

Sir. Frederick Lugard —Gov. of Nigeria from 1912-1919

constructed to transport tin from Jos Plateau, peanut from Kano and cotton from the lowlands below the Plateau to ports on the coast.

All other developments such as education, health and rural infrastructures that the Southern part of the country had been enjoying for years did not fully reached the North for some obvious reasons. Some people attributed this to the inability of Lugard and his successor to open up the road to the North for the missionaries to come there while some had the notion that the Commissioners of the protectorate had special preference for the Islamic religion in order to maintain some certain status quo.

In the Southern part of the country which had been a protectorate since 1894 saw the policy of indirect rule in different forms. In Yorubaland, it was obvious that the people cherish and respect their Rulers and the policy just only needed to be fine-tuned a little bit to suit and accommodate some parts of their customs and traditions. It was therefore not that it was too difficult for the policy to work out fine in Yorubaland; but in the Southeast, where Aro hegemony had been crushed through force, the search for acceptable local administrators to handle the policy met with frustration. As a result, the activities of the government in this area were initially left in the hands of the colonial staffs' resident there, and who were not on the same operating frequency with the Igbo people. This was why the people here vehemently opposed the colonial rule from its start.

Unification of Nigeria into one Entity.

The unification of all the regions, protectorates and the other entities in the country into one unit was as a result of the success of Lugard's indirect rule system he met and expanded upon. It must be clear without any ambiguity that before Lugard came to Africa the system of the government of the old Kingdoms in the land had always been in the form of his new theory. In the Ife, Oyo, or Benin Kingdoms of fourteenth and fifteenth centuries, the European explorers of the time that visited these Kingdoms attested to it in writing the superiority of the government they met and saw in those places and the civilization of the people of the time, which was rated as very high. In the African context, the Kings, Emirs and chieftains had always been recognized as the head of the government of the territory they rule over and all the positions available in the British set-up of government were also available in the old African system of government if not more. If in those days the art of writing was not available to the people of the time that does not mean they were daft. All I believed that Lugard did was that he re-arranged the responsibilities of the officials of the Caliphate and other Protectorates in Nigeria and regrouped the supporting people of various units to match-up with the responsibilities that had been lined up.

For example the District Heads he used to collect taxes in the North under his new arrangement were still the same people that were formerly palace officials doing the same job under the native governments of the Emirs before he arrived. In other Kingdoms such as that of Oyo the similar palace officials to the ones we had in the North were the ambassadors of Alafin in the districts and divisions under the Oyo Kingdom carrying out similar responsibilities to that of their counterparts under the Caliphate system. To me therefore, nothing new that he brought into the system other than the re-arrangement of things to suit the conditions of the time. Understandably Lugard's government in the North laid good foundation for commercial development through the construction of road networks. His restructuring of the labor force to be in line with what was obtainable in the Southern Protectorate of this time was another area of his achievement.

When Lugard was transferred out of the Northern Protectorate, he was sent to Hong Kong as the governor of that country and in 1912 he returned to Nigeria as Governor – General to work on the merger of the Northern and Southern Protectorates, which he achieved in two years later on the eve of the World War I. The new formula of indirect rule had now gained ground throughout the country and the next level of national identification was being expected to come on board. In 1916, Lugard formed the Nigerian Council, a consultative body that brought together some traditional rulers in the country for the first time ever and which included the Sultan of Sokoto, the Emir of Kano and the Alafin of Oyo among others as representatives of different parts of the colony. One of the major programs of the Council was to use the forum as a place for them to express their opinions, which could help the Governor in the execution of his duties. Lugard used this forum only to intimate the traditional rulers of the British policy while given them no role to play except for them to listen and to assent to those policies, which they had no opportunity to study and digest upon.

Lugard's unification program included bringing together the regional administrations of Northern, Western and Eastern regions under one entity with one administration from the center. To achieve this purpose, Lieutenant Governors for the three regions were appointed to provide independent government services. Their duties included the coordinating of autonomous entities that had overlapping economic interests while they had little to say concerning the political and social development of the people. In the Northern Region of the country, the colonial government did not want to offend the Islamic religion and its practitioners. It therefore behooved on them to avoid any confrontation with the Emirs and the Islamic clergies of the territory at the expense of modern development that could have naturally found their ways to the doorsteps of the grass root people of the region. As the Rulers settled down more and more into their new role as reliable and trusted agents of indirect rule, the colonial authorities closed their eyes to the under development of the region and its people pretending to be contented but only trying to maintain the status quo.

The story from the South of the country particularly from Yorubaland was different in that instead of employing the traditional rulers as agents of indirect rule policy, they were only employed as vehicles to move the theory forward. It wouldn't have been two difficult for the imperialists to upturn the minds of the Southern rulers if not because of the Christian doctrine that had gained ground among the people and the Western educational system that had firmly been planted and now bearing bountiful fruits everywhere in the land to which their rulers feared so much. They knew that if they accepted some sort of unpopular program for their people from the colonial dictators, the outcome and the reaction of their people to such action would be too dangerous for them to bear. The indirect rule policy was equivalent to a business venture that employed many agents to represent its interests to the consumers. It therefore became very necessary for the owner of such business to constantly maintain good relationship with his agents so that his business might grow bigger, become prosperous and has a wide range of international popularity. This was the story between the colonial authorities and the local rulers they employed as their agents.

The indirect rule system undoubtedly made some impact on the economic link between the regions but it tended to discouraged political interchange and brought in the serious gap amongst the people of the nation. Lugard's tenure of office as Governor-General did its best in the public works because it was his government that dredged the harbor to accommodate large vessels and began construction works on the roads and railroads that opened Nigeria to economic development. During the World War II, his RWAFF, which now became the Nigerian Regiment recruited Nigerians from both in the North and the South to serve in the War as either laborers or combatant soldiers. These Nigerians played important roles in their actions against German colonial forces in Cameroon and in German East Africa. It was recorded that during this war, the colonial government earmarked a large portion of the Nigerian budget as the country's contribution to imperial defense. Unfortunately no one knew how many Nigerians that were killed in the war and what amount of monetary compensation that was paid to the families of those that died or those that came back home as brave soldiers.

When Lugard was the Governor-General of Nigeria, he tried to bring on board the uniform tax structure, which was the pattern of his traditional system he used while he was the Commissioner of the Northern Protectorate but this time around the policy became a source of discontent in the South and it contributed to the disturbances that the regime saw against the British control. Lugard did all he could to consolidate the British sovereignty in Nigeria but at the same time he was contemptuous of the educated and westernized African elite. Because of the fear he had for them, he at one time recommended the transfer of the capital from Lagos, the cosmopolitan city where the voice and the influence of these people were heard and pronounced to Kaduna in the North. Though the Colonial Office in London refused his spicy request but it was placed on record that Lord Lugard bequeathed to his successor in office a prosperous colony before he left Nigeria.

The immediate successor to Lord Lugard was Hugh Clifford whose regime lasted for six-years – 1919 – 1925. He was an aristocratic professional administrator with liberal behaviors. Before coming to Nigeria, he had served as the Governor of Gold Coast and the experience he had while there made him to conclude that the primary responsibility of any colonial government in Africa was to introduce as quickly as practicable the benefits of Western ideology. In this regard his views were diametrically opposed to those of his predecessor in office because he anticipated the general emancipation of the people irrespective of their religion and ethnicity. He believed that by emancipating the people, a more representative form of government would be put in place. Clifford also emphasized general economic development that would cover the whole territory of Nigeria. He even encouraged business movement by Southerners into the North while he restricted the European participation in business to only capital-intensive business activities. He believed that indirect rule policy encouraged centripetal tendencies, and he therefore argued that to divide the colony into two separate units could be ideal unless a stronger central government was put in place, which would bind Nigeria into more than just an administration that had been fruitful and successful in the South as against that of Lugard's administration views.

There was no doubt about it that Lugard's influence was still weighty in the Colonial Office in London and the respect was there for his immediate past administration in Nigeria. Though Clifford's new ideas were accepted but with reluctance in some areas. The Colonial Office accepted that changes might be appropriate in the South, but it forbade fundamental alterations of procedures in the North. His recommendations as later modified by the officials in London office were embodied in the 1922 Constitution known as Clifford Constitution. Because of the instructions from London, there was nothing done to harm the administration of the North but in the South a new Legislative Council was established in each of the two regions of the Southern part of the country to replace the Lagos Legislative Council and the moribund Nigerian Council. For the first time in Nigeria, direct elections took place outside Lagos to elect the only four elective members of the Council, which comprised of forty-six members. This exercise also marked the emergence of political parties and ultimately brought the growth of nationalism in Nigeria. By 1931, it was reported that strong sentiments emerged in the North against the actions of Governor Clifford and his administration but the South continued to wade through the rough waters, which ultimately gave them the strength and courage to face the realities of life.

PART 3
ECONOMIC DEVELOPMENT

Chapter –10–

Activities of Foreign Merchants in Yorubaland and the Niger Basin.

The relationship between the Yoruba merchants and its foreign partners dated back to late 16th century when the European merchants and the explorers first established forts and trading posts along the West African coast for trade in domestic commodities. When the slave trade was introduced the business relationship grew larger especially between the Portuguese slave traders and Yoruba slave barons who used the advantage of their positions as coastline merchants to boost the trade. The British who joined other European slave trade merchants as newcomers found that they could compete with the Dutch and Portuguese traders in West Africa by forming trading companies rather than doing it on individual trading efforts; they therefore came up with the formation of some companies. The effective enterprise that was introduced first was the company of the Adventurers, which was chartered in 1660 and later renamed African Company in 1672.

In the early 18th century, Britain and France combined destroyed the Dutch business holds in West Africa and by the end of the French Revolution and the Napoleonic Wars of 1799 – 1815, Britain had already established itself fully as the dominant commercial power in West Africa. By the time the slave trade was made illegal for the British subjects, its former slavers began to look for another trade that could prosper them and in this regard they started to explore the interior for palm-oil for the rapidly expanding factories in Britain. The only visible area exposed to them was along the banks of River Niger, which then included the areas of Calabar, Bonny and the Southeastern part of the country that was situated within the palm-oil belt. The palm-oil trade that took over the reign of power from slave trade flourished amid strong competition among the natives of the territory particularly the merchants from Bonny, Brass, Itsekiri and Kalabari.

Unfortunately there was a break in between the period of palm-oil trade in the area, which coincided with the time that the American, Brazilian and Cuban sugar plantations were expanding and thereby called for human labor and a rise in the price of slaves to work in those plantations. Because of the short time business advantage, the palm-oil merchants in the territory found that they could not compete with the slave merchants and this situation prompted most of the city-state palm-oil merchants to shift back to the illegal trade again to catch their profits before the hands of the law caught up with them. This alone was not enough excuse for them to change position as other impediments came their ways.

For example an oil ship normally waited on the coast for a period of between fifteen and eighteen months for it to be loaded up with its cargo for return journey to England, which substantially increased the overhead costs for the foreign merchants and also lowered their profits. The British naval patrol on the sea in search of illegal slave ship with their human cargoes began to prevent the export of slaves by blockading the city-states that were directly situated on the coastline areas. Bonny city-state that was close to open sea and which was easily watched by the British naval patrol squadron could not easily continued with the illegal trade but accepted its faith with fortitude and rapidly moved on with the palm-oil trade. Incidentally Bonny's misfortune brought great prosperity to the Brass slave traders because of their location, which was surrounded by a maze of creeks where slave ships could slip away unnoticed by the British naval squadron. The little illegal slave trading that Bonny traders could do had to be carried out through Brass, which was traditionally an ally of Bonny for centuries back.

Another major set back for palm-oil trade was that the business was being operated on trust – credit system. To stay good in the business, the foreign merchants had to advance the local merchants some money even when the goods were not ready for delivery. The local agents would take the money and disbursed part of it to their buying agents in the field and wait patiently for the season to set in when the goods would be delivered. Trust was not only a source of friction but a strong weapon of commercial competition where everyone connected could accuse each other of cheating, yet no one would give it up because of its effective weapon that could be used against competitors. The verbal agreement between the partners – the European and the African merchants compelled the Africans to sell his oil to the European merchant whose trust he held. The European merchants from their own side never wanted his trust to be totally repaid by a reliable African merchant because once the trust was paid in full the African merchant would be set free to sell his commodity to any European rival of his choice.

To maintain the status quo, European merchants tried every method, honest and dishonest, to keep the African merchants in debt to them, but the African merchants kept their heads cool to master the intrigues of the new business until they became perfect and were able to deal with the foreigners decisively. As the business grew wider and wider, so the problems attached to it became cumbersome. For a new firm to break through or break even, it had to be ready to offer high prices for the product or agreed to ease the terms of the trust, which would tempt the African merchants to break the existing trust between them and their former partners. If African merchants supplied the new firm with commodities that were meant for the old firm, the old firm could forcibly confiscated the goods, which sometime would invite the King or the Chief of the territory where the incident happened to adjudicate on the dispute. The King or the Chief in his judgment may declare a boycott of all trades until the dispute was settled or proclaimed trade boycott to all participants where he was convinced that the European firms had combined to fix prices that would not adequately compensate for the labors of his people.

The regular steamship service between West Africa and Europe, which started in 1852, significantly increased the number of European palm-oil buyers in the Delta region and the small businessmen who were formally not able to afford hiring their own vessels could now ship their commodities to Europe without much hassle. This new development invited traders from Lagos and Itsekiri to join their Delta counterparts in the trade, which in due course encouraged the city-states to extend their trading empires deeper and deeper into the interior of the country. By 1855, the Efik of Calabar had acquired enough trading experience and amassed enough capital to ship their oil direct to Europe by chartered ships, thus now by-passing the English middlemen and raising their profit margin to higher level. The rate with which the Delta native merchants moved business wise baffled and surprised the

British traders and for them to halt their aggressive trading movement, the navy was used as a ploy to threat the bombardment of Calabar in order to weaken their aggressive programs and plans. If not for the use and support of the naval ships on the Delta waters, British firms would not have been equal in any form to the trading capabilities of the native merchants; but unfortunately the moment the natives lost their political control, their economic control and prosperity were lost too.

In Yorubaland where the bulk of British trading interests were concentrated and noticed began immediately after the conquest of Lagos in 1851 and in 1861 when the city became a Crown Colony, a step taken in response to many factors. The British only used the issue of slave trade among other things to order the bombardment of Lagos but their true desire included how their expanding trade interests in the coast line of West Africa could be extended into the hinterland and be protected through the sea. Another reason was to forestall the interests of the other rival colonial powers – France and Germany, which could carelessly slip in through the conflicts of the Yoruba wars that were going on around this time with the help of the coastal chiefs. The palm-oil trade that introduced Trust system of trading technique and which some used as a lever to lift the economic situation of the Africans was seen at other quarters as not the best method to approach African civilization that the hues and cries of the slave trade abolition were all about. The group with the dissenting opinion was the philanthropists who attacked the Trust system of trade from its beginning.

They contended that the expansion of European commerce in Africa did not mean widespread economic development and social reform for the Africans. In their opinion they view the promotion of legitimate commerce as a force to civilize the continent, provided that it was directed to root out the slavery at its source, to alter the subsistence economy on which it was based, to create new wants for the people, to benefit the masses in the interior and to increase the manpower of the nations in Africa. But instead the palm-oil trade, like its immediate predecessor – the slave trade did not do any of these virtues. They argued further that the desired effect of the legitimate commerce that was supposed to benefit all only served the interests of the coastal chiefs who ignorantly exploited the labor of the domestic slaves for the benefit of the unscrupulous European traders.

When the British government fully attained control of Nigeria, its focus included the exploitation of the country's raw materials, its mineral resources and its foodstuffs that were important to western industrial development. To get the full benefits of these products a railroad network was built between the 1890s and the World War II to connect the North and East where tin and coal were discovered and in the case of the upper North where groundnut and cotton were grown in large quantities because of the Savannah terrain of the territory to the ports in the coastal area. Few local motorways were also constructed in the South to connect the cocoa and palm-oil producing areas to the port in Lagos. Major export crops of Yorubaland in the early days of British administration in Nigeria were cocoa, cotton and palm-oil. Cocoa crops was first introduced into Ghanaland from Fernando Po in 1879 by two Ghanaians called the Tetteh Quashie brothers and the crop later found its way to Yorubaland in the 1880s, first at Agege and later spread inland to Ibadan and Ondo regions of Yorubaland. As early as the economic benefits and importance of cocoa crop was discovered by the European industrialists, the export of the produce grew and West African nations such as Ghana, Nigeria and Ivory Coast became the largest exporters of cocoa to European markets. The rise in the value of this produce began to change the life-style of the people from the areas where it was produced. The revenue accrued from the trade around this time almost counterbalanced the amount spent on the importation of consumer goods into the country including food stuffs and other house hold commodities.

In the regions of West Africa, the three imperialist enterprises that were controlling the wholesale and retail trading, the buying of export crops, providing banking facilities and transportation system both on land and on the sea and which dominated the economic life of the period of colonialism for both British and French were as follows:

(1) The Companie Francaise de l'Afriquue Occidentale (C.F.A.O.) that was founded in 1887.

(2) The Societe Commerciale de l'Quest Africain (S.C.O.A.) founded in 1906 and

(3) Unilever, a world-wide organization whose African branch was the United African Company (U.A.C.)

These companies came into existence as a result of series of amalgamations of smaller companies just the way Goldie came up with the Royal Niger Company that in the end installed itself as the dominating trading and functional power along the banks of the Niger River in the areas of its Basin.

155

For example, in 1920 Unilever purchased the Niger Company and in 1929 it joined it with the African and Eastern Trading Corporation to form the U.A.C. These imperialist companies involved themselves in almost all aspects of commerce in the West African territory. In 1927 C.F.A.O. had 33 branches and 154 trading posts, making a profit of about 90% in the years when sales were robust and 25% in poor years. S.C.O.A at the same time had 21 branches and 122 trading centers while U.A.C, which was the dominant British enterprise in West Africa maintained lots of branches and trading posts everywhere along the coast line and in the interior. It maintained many subsidiaries in Senegal, Mali, Guinea and Ivory Coast while C.F.A.O controlled most of the French West African river transportation and was involved in a number of banks and dominated the steamship lines moving produce of the French West Africa to Europe. U.A.C was the only company holding mineral rights to virtually all the mineral deposits of Northern Nigeria and substantially involved in the shipping rights of goods coming in and going out of Nigeria and other British territories in the West African Region.

These companies as powerful as they were could agree among themselves to fix prices when necessary so as to avoid friction of competition and they were not under any moral or legal obligations to give efficient services or cater for the African tastes in the quality or type of goods they brought into the country from anywhere all over the world. The profits they made from the trade were neatly sent back to their home countries and the colonial governments in their areas of operations did nothing to force them to invest in the economy of the countries where the profits were accrued either by taxing those profits going abroad or by direct investment in the technological development of those countries.

In the case of the extraction of tin ore from the plateau deposits and coal from Udi hills in Enugu, Intensive human labor activities were used to bring out those minerals under horrible and deadly conditions, which the workers were subjected to and in most cases with poor compensations given to them after stressful agitations by the then existing labor unions that were only allowed to operate with the guns pointed at the leaders throats. In Ghana and Nigeria, the imperialist companies would repeatedly come together to fix cocoa prices, which had to be paid to the poor farmers who toiled under heavy burdens to get out the finished cocoa crops for exportation to Europe. Whereas the opposite is the case for their finished commodities and goods that were imported into these countries, which their prices would undoubtedly be fixed by them without anyone raising any eyebrow.

When the Africans could no longer accommodate this type of cheating, the farmers union grew up in Ghana and Nigeria to take action to stop the arrogant attitude of these multi national imperialist companies. In 1914, 1916 and 1921, it was on record that some Ghanaian farmers held back their cocoa beans while demanding for higher prices. This sought of action was repeated in 1937 when fourteen firms combined together and led by U.A.C secretly agreed on a fixed price but, when the news was broken, the farmers union in Ghana did not only reject it but refused to sell their produce and as well decided to boycott all the retail shops of those firms involved.

The second merchant group that joined the exploitative category from Europe was the group from Syria and Lebanon, which began to move into West Africa from the Middle East in the 1890s. The business tactic of this group was based on family connection and relationship. The wealthy ones among them would be made to accommodate one or two members from the family set-up; first of all serving him for a number of years as business pupilage until he grows up to master the trade. After sometime the master would now set him up with manageable capital as loan, which he would be asked to repay back to him in part or in full when he might have been fully established himself on the trade. They specialized in small retail trade of domestic wares such as beads, textile and household utensils.

Some of them moved into transportation of goods and people business while some got into kola nut trade. Kola nut business was one of the lucrative trades of nineteenth century because it required less labor than cocoa crops and brought more revenue than it because of its high demand as food and industrial chemical. These reasons prompted many early cocoa farmers in Yorubaland in such places like Agege, Abeokuta and Ijebu areas to change for kola nut planting. One of the greatest set back that affected the African merchant princes of this time was an access to required capital as they had less capital to compete effectively with their European counterparts. Although they were more trusted and had greater influence with more access to the African Kingdoms, but the European merchants had more money to trade with through the help coming to them from the banks and other financial resources, which were under the control of the colonial government.

Interestingly what was going on in the French colonies in West Africa differs significantly from that of the British colonies. In the first place the French considered the land of its colony as state property, which anyone could applied for irrespective of their status and the state would release such right to him. In 1904 the government declared all land vacant and turned them into government property. The reason behind this was to allow French settlers to move to those colonies after the fear of malarial killing of the whites in Africa had been removed through the discovery of quinine drug. Under this program, considerable acreage of land in the colonies was allocated to the settlers, especially in Ivory Coast and Guinea. But unfortunately the low level of agricultural technology as at the time reduced the activities of these settlers on the lands apportioned to them. Most of them found it very difficult to compete with the African farmers who mainly depended on their physical strength to cultivate the land and reap the blessings thereof. After many years of trial, the lands were abandoned for good and they were reverted back to the rightful owners.

In the British West Africa, the allocation of land to settlers was hard because of the stand the educated elite of the regions – Ghana and Nigeria took. This educated group never wanted the type of problems that the settlers in the British colonies in South and Central Africa were given to the African landowners to happen in their countries. In 1894, the British made an attempt to copy the French policy in Ghana when they promulgated the land's bill, which made unoccupied lands, forestlands and mineral deposits the property of the state. The bill was later revoked when it met stiff opposition through protest meetings, petitions, demonstrations and newspaper outcry from the citizens including the chiefs and the educated elite group of the country.

As if this was not enough, three years later another attempt was made to re-introduce the same similar Bill and it again met with tougher opposition. It was as a result of this action that gave birth to the Aborigines Rights Protection Society (A.R.P.S.), which mobilized the people to oppose the Bill. The victory of the A.R.P.S. on this government action was a significant landmark in the history of West Africa. The victory also marked the use of clear lens to watch the activities and intentions of the colonial government throughout the areas of its sphere of influence. In 1912 a land law of similar character to that of Ghana was introduced in Nigeria and it called for the formation of an African Society to oppose the Bill. In 1924, Lord Leverhulme, the chairman of the U.A.C. began to agitate for plantation in Nigeria but his request was turned down because of the tension it would create within the colonial administration. The officials of the administration knew that the educated elite from Creole, Fante and Yoruba had been skeptical of what was happening in Kenya, Congo or even Ivory Coast where the settler-dominated issues were causing trouble. Amid all the series of faults emanated from the colonial rule in Nigeria, the country was able to forge ahead with the few things that the imperialists could give to the people as their own share out of the pie.

Chapter –11–

The Colonial Economic Development in Nigeria:

History remarked that had the British adhered strictly to the letters of the treaties it signed with the Obas and the chiefs of Yorubaland and elsewhere along the banks of River Niger and up the North, their position would have been little more than that of an influence, and not the one of colonial subjugation. It was after the people were disarmed that the Obas and the chiefs realized that they had implicated not only themselves and their generations alone but also that of the generations yet unborn because they were now powerless to do anything to prevent the British from ignoring the terms of those treaties. The British now saw themselves as an outright conquerors and victors. The British and the French economic theory that was propounded for their colonies was that the colonies must be self-supporting, provide export crops for the imperial country and be mandated to buy its manufactured goods in return, but no imperial country was obligated to buy products from its colonies as it was the case with France and its colonies in West Africa during the colonial era. But Britain was more liberal because it usually allowed its colonies to buy and sell in the best markets they could find. But after the World War I, they digressed a little bit when special taxes were levied on palm oil products going to Germany and in 1930 when they excluded Japanese cotton cloth to enter the colonies because of its cheaper prices to English cotton cloth.

The colonies were neglected as far as industrial development was concerned mainly because the imperial countries that maintained colonies in Africa did not want any developing program that would compete with the industries in their home bases. All they were interested in was to get the needed raw materials from the colonies to feed the industries

161

in their countries and after the products were been manufactured, they would bring the finished products back to the colonies to be sold at over 500% profit to the people. The colonial impact would have been less harsh on the people if for instance the imperialists had been willing to established industries that could cater for at least the domestic goods that were necessary for the average living of the people. Everything from cutleries to underwear and footwear were being manufactured abroad and imported into the colonies under the direct arrangement of the colonial officials.

The imperialists were the manufacturers, the importers and exporters, the distributors and the all-in-all of everything concerning the economy of the colonies under their rule. An example of this fact was when groundnut oil mill established in Senegal began to export its product to France in 1927 the French oil millers went against it and killed the ambition and potentials of the project in preference to the home-made oil, which was produced from the groundnuts imported from the same source – Senegal. The colonial administration in Senegal did nothing to make the French oil millers see the project as a development and also an avenue for healthy competition between the two manufacturing companies but instead they watched the project died a natural death, which probably made it not to resurrect before they left that country.

The idea of constructing the railroads, harbors and local roads in any of the colonies was not out of philanthropic gesture but to consolidate the position of colonial ambitions particularly in those areas where the imperialists would gain from such projects. First and foremost the promotion of their trade into the interior of Africa remained paramount to them. Along the coast line of West Africa, it was only Freetown that had natural harbor, all other places had to be artificially constructed and such project around this time gulfed large sums of money from the covers of the colonies. In Nigeria, large amount of money was spent to create deepwater ports at Lagos, which was opened in 1913 and the one at Apapa in 1926. Because of the meager resources of some of the nations in West Africa around this time, some of them could not afford to undertake intensive capital projects on their own. For example the Senegalese people paid through their sweats before the port in Dakar, which was then classified as the best in West Africa could be completed. The Ivory Coast did not get an ocean port not until in the 1930s when the port at Abidjan was developed.

Other nations such as Guinea, Gambia and Liberia got their ports developed after the World War II; Togo and Dahomey did not get one not until the French left the countries in 1960. This cruel attitude of the imperialists, which was extended to other areas of industrial development throughout their stay in the continent and by the time they were leaving much were left to be desired on which way to go for the nations they colonized and benefited immensely from the labors of their citizens and the natural resources of their lands. The intention of the imperialists when they first came and which was made known to the whole world at the Berlin Conference of 1885 was that the best interests of both players on the chess board would be served by allowing European trade to flow freely into the continent while the Africans would be provided with the benefits of European civilization.

The effective take over of the various territories in Africa by the imperialists confirmed that the whites believed that their personal achievements and material gains in the course of coming into this world must be acquired right here on the earth but in order to achieve this they had to effectively blindfold the eyes of people of other races and redirect their course. The strategy they used to achieve this fit was that they told the people to work hard on this earth and expect their rewards for the hardship they may face in the course of their struggle in heaven. The people were so misled and rapaciously put into the cage like a bird to the point that no one from the race could ask such question as to how many of the whites have been to heaven and come back to give an account of the wealth of the oppressed race – the blacks and the poverty level of the oppressors that gave them such impression?

When the imperialists sensed the high number of advantages that could come their ways from the lands in the interior with regards to mineral and food crops potentialities for industrial development in Europe, the colonies were made to finance railway projects from the coast into the interior of Africa to haul goods going abroad through the sea. The railway projects started in those colonies with expected buoyant economy like Nigeria and Ghana in 1896 and it was only Nigeria, which had enough money through the discovery of coal and tin

Locomotive Train - Nigeria in 1896

ore from Enugu in the East and Jos in the North that gave Nigeria the advantage of having two track rail lines while Ghana had only one track and did not reach the Northern part of the country.

Apart from the fact that these railroads were inadequate and of sub-standard to the ones in Europe of this time where the technology came from, no colonial territories were connected to the other like what was done in Europe. The planners of our economy of this time foresaw that if there should be any rail link between Nigeria and Ghana for instance, and with the number of educated elite from those two countries, their time in Africa would be running closer than expected. Most of the planning of the time was done on purpose and with time ticket tagged on them. The motorways constructed by the colonial administration in Nigeria were only feeder roads to feed the haulage trains hauling products from the interior to the ports at the coastal cities and bringing European goods to various important places in the interior.

According to world record, in 1990 the rail system in Nigeria covered only 3500 kilometers of narrow gauge (1.067m) track. The rail system ran on two main lines from the coast in the West from Lagos to Kano, which was commissioned in 1912, and the other track in the East from Port Harcourt to a junction with the Western line at Kaduna, which was completed and opened in 1926. A branch line from Zaria to Kaura Namoda to serve the important agricultural area of the Northwest was completed in 1929. The second line was a branch from Kano to Nguru to haul cattle and other animal products to the South because of the animal breeding advantages of the region. The line was completed in 1930. The third, which comprised of 645 km was from the Eastern line to Maiduguri, which branched at Jos to carry tin ore products to the ports in the coastal area. Until the oil boom era, agricultural commodity had been the chief export products of Nigeria, which mainly consist of cocoa, groundnut, palm oil and palm kernels and timber logs. The demand for imported goods remained high as ever because of the country's lack of much industrialization skills that dated back to the inherited time and program of the colonial days. This would continue to persist until the people of the country is able to free itself from the bondage of colonial mentalities that had fatally destroyed their senses of reasoning, and which generally gives them the impression that the goods manufactured in the country are of inferior quality to those that are manufactured abroad. The people should be correctly informed that three quarters of the products coming into the country from either the developing or less-developed countries of the world are mostly of sub-standard in quality because they are mass-produced for the third world countries where people are less concerned and not bordered to verify the qualities of those products or where the equipments to test or examine them are not available.

The other major reason why we still remain in darkness and being manipulated around by the agents of the same imperialists of the colonial days is the fact that almost all of the African leaders are always susceptible to corruptive and fraudulent ways of life. They can easily be bribed until they run themselves into the nets of the imperialists and be made to believe to their own understanding that to develop African economy to be at the same par with that of the developed continents of the world is a waste of time and energy. Regrettably as beautiful as the geographical position of Africa is with its high taste of landmarks and topography which ranked as one of the best in the whole world for holiday resorts and residential sites and with good weather, I have not heard of any of the American Presidents or British Prime Ministers either in the past or present age that owned a residential house or holiday resort in any of the African nations. But go to Britain, France or America, African leaders do not only own houses but some of them own large estates that are being maintained with the money of the poor nations where they come from leaving the citizens of those countries in penury and as beggars.

Hence all of the West African nations lacked industrial capabilities, most of the nations continued to specialize in primary products, which included food crops, raw materials, minerals, organic oils and timber logs. The secondary products such as industrial machinery, chemicals, transportation and manufacturing equipments that were necessary to make those nations become fully independent are yet to be ordered for from abroad and in the case of where they had been ordered for, obsolete ones with dead engines coupled together from scrap yards and painted as new might be on their ways to Africa. Nigeria for example in 1955 exported 98% of its primary commodities to Europe through Britain while its import level was just 21%; in 1975 its export level was 92% and import was just 19%; in 1985 its export was 98% with 24% of import. From the mineral sector where petroleum products accounted for an increase in its exports through the 1970s, it went up from 13% in 1955 to 35% in 1965, to 93% in 1975 and 96% in 1985. To get the industrial projects off the ground and to move them to production level so that the colonies might be self-sufficient so to say, large sums were required for labor and importation of necessary machineries. In the areas of harbor building and road construction, the technologies that are abound today were just not available at the time under reference and as such costs had to be reduced by the use of forced and unpaid labor. Between the three imperialist powers that dominated West Africa during the colonial days – the British, the Germans and the French, French was the worst among them in the way it administered its colonial territories. It was under the French colonial laws that every male between 18 and 60 years of age were obligated and compelled to contribute a certain number of days as labor responsibility to the state not minding the health situations of such person.

Between 1927 and 1936, close to 15000 men were forced to contribute labor on the Niger project and on the construction of the railway and other state projects. The effectiveness of this forced labor law made many able-bodied men of the country to flee out of their country to look for more quiet and peaceful life-style in some other nations of the West Africa. It was even suggested that the first revolt of the people against the French colonial administration in Niger must have been connected with the forced labor laws. The irony of this was that it was the African chiefs that were appointed as the recruiting agents for the forced labor program. But when the country was up in flames because of the second coming of slavery under the disguised labor laws, the chiefs involved lost their prestige and dignity among their people.

During the time when the law was in use before its abolition in 1946, many young men that numbered up to a quarter of a million traveled to Ghana to work at cocoa plantations to earn good wages. Another 80,000 was said to have traveled to Mali, Guinea and to the groundnut farms in Senegal for the same reason. Conditions under which the laborers in the forced labor program were made to work were horrible and degrading. It was reported that the foods given to them were inadequate, the houses where they lodged them were poor, diseases resulting in death were very frequent and without any medical facilities and attentions.

Under the German colonial administration in the Cameroon, the men recruited from the plateau a region, which was known to be free from malarial mosquito breeding were sent to the plantations on the lowlands where mosquito breeding was rampant. On getting there they would only managed to spend some few days before they die after being bitten by mosquitoes because they had no natural immunity to wade off the poisonous attack of the malarial disease.

Africans who worked under the British rule did not suffer that much as their counterparts under the French and the Germans. The pay was not attractive but still it was better than not earning anything in return for their labor. The British too recruited their labor through the local chiefs, which was then a uniform system in all the colonies. When the coal in Enugu was discovered and production in the mines began, the required labor to work in the mines were recruited through the local chiefs. Those chiefs were paid according to the number of laborers they were able to supply and because of this incentive the chiefs began to force their people to work in the mines because of the increase in the amount of money they would be paid as agents. As the time went by, the people revolted against the outrageous actions of their local chiefs and for this reason the chiefs were that much hated by their people, which obviously resulted into some of them being driven out of their towns. When the colonial administration was informed of the people's action against their local chiefs, they sent army out to arrest those who were responsible for the action. The arrested natives were taken to the colonial court where their towns were fined instead of them individually. The judgment was that their towns should collectively supply 2000 laborers for the construction of the railway that connected Eastern line to the port. The same method was used in Ghana to recruit labor through the local chiefs to work at the Gold mines in the Northern territory of the nation.

At the beginning of the 20th century, the people were being subjected to all kinds of degradations and inhuman torture both mentally and physically. Those natives who worked for the colonial administration had no right to form workers union that may as a body seek redress on their behalf for their grievances. When dispute occurred between the establishment and its workers, it was not only the organizers of the dispute that would be punished but in most cases such punishment would also be extended to everything that surrounded them. In 1925 when the Enugu coal miners went on strike for better pay and improved condition of service, the men were sacked outright and for the next twenty-five years no one from the clans of the organizers was hired by the establishment that was supposedly owned by the government of the people. The end result of such cruel action bordered on the premises that it was not only those workers that were hurt but it also extended the hardship resulting from this wicked act to their immediate families, relatives and the unborn generations of their clans.

The hurtful attitude of the colonial governments in West Africa reached the ears of the black Americans, West Indian and the African youths studying abroad especially those in London. This prompted them to come together to organize the first student organization in London in 1917 and in 1921 it had managed to have 25 strong members; in 1924 its members had risen to 120. In 1925, one Ladipo Solanke a Nigerian and of Yoruba extraction organized the first West African Students Union (W.A.S.U.) which in nature superceded the previous one organized some years back by all nations blacks living in London and which became the center of social and political activities where the West African modern militant nationalism was born. In 1928, one of its leading founding patrons Marcus Garvey gave the organization its first hostel and published a journal that opened up an opportunity for the nationalist writings.

The organization became strong, vocal and served as the mouthpiece of the people of West Africa at abroad. It was noted that some of the later leading statesmen in Africa at one time or the other held executive positions in W.A.S.U. Between 1929 and 1932, the founder – Solanke visited the major cities of the British West Africa to raise fund for his organization's hostel, to organize home base branches and to solicit for the support of the African chiefs on their course. His trip was a successful one that gained a lot of support from the people of West Africa including their Kings, Emirs, Chiefs and noblemen and women. Nana Afori Attah of Ghana, the Alake of Abeokuta and the Emir of Kano became patrons of the union.

In those days, Europe was the only famous continent with which the Africans had close affinity with but as soon as Dr. Nnamdi Azikwe of Nigeria and Dr. Kwame Nkrumah of Ghana returned from America, many Africans began to follow their footsteps and in 1941 a student's union with similar purpose and direction like those of W.A.S.U was established in the United States with its own magazine and had close link with W.A.S.U. headquarters in London. Gradually the organization was becoming more and more expanding with ideas of how to remove prejudices and discriminations that were directed against their race and their continent. Contacts were being sort with the white liberals in Europe, the socialist and communist organizations, all who were anti imperialist for help and support concerning African issue. In 1935 the only remaining pride of Africans and the Negroes all over the world - "Ethiopia" was attacked by the Italians. The rest of the story regarding this attack will be referenced in the continuing chapter.

Chapter –12–

The Young Shall Grow: The Birth of Political Organizations by the African Nationalists:

In the larger context of the picture of this chapter, the whole of West African people and their territories will be treated as one and the same member of family in the sense that all of them began to struggle together from the same camp to release themselves from the same kind of burden and the same sort of treatment they were receiving from their oppressors from Europe countries - the British, French and the Germans. The Italian attack on Ethiopia in 1935 was regarded as an attack on the whole continent and the black race irrespective of where they might be located and under which condition they were being ruled. Ethiopia was in fact the pride of every black race all over the world since Menelik defeated the Italian army at the battle of Adowa in 1896 and ever since it had been looked upon as a symbol of African independence, black great achievements, a noble and ancient history and international race equality. When the whole world was pondering over the Italian's action on Ethiopia's invasion, Mussolini cared less about his country's act of invasion of Ethiopia and stubbornly kicked back with the usual language of racism and white supremacy that had been the European languages on Africa since the time of partitioning. Their excuse had always been that they came to rescue the continent of its primitive and barbaric civilization and to replace their type of civilization with that of European's Christian civilization.

Whereas Italy had forgotten the popular role that the Kingdom of Ethiopia played in the development of Christianity and its doctrine in the Old Testament in the Bible which now became a new philosophical

169

point of a right for it to invade such a civilized Kingdom in the 20th century by those who barely existed during the time when the glory of Ethiopia had been known for its strength, power and popularity with reigns of their internationally recognized Queens and Kings of the great Kingdom. I am positive that during the time of the invasion, the achievements that the Ethiopia Kingdom had had to its credit in the world almanac could in no way be compared to that of Italy.

The Italian action steered the black world into series of protests that were more prolonged, widespread and more meaningful than what the race had ever witnessed in history. Reaction of the black people over this issue was phenomenal and fiercely spread like bush fire that engulfed typical dry woodland during the dry season. Protests were organized in nearly all the principal cities of the then world in support of the Ethiopian people. In New York, London, West Indies, South and West Africa and some other places, people trooped out in thousands to protest against the uncivilized action of Italian government while the young black men of this era offered to be enlisted into the fighting army that would send out Mussolini and his army from the soil of Ethiopia. The West African Students Union of Ladipo Solanke organized an Ethiopian Defense Committee while other groups of African people organized an African Friends of Abyssinia Committee in London, which was referred to as the most Pan-African Committee ever to be organized.

The people behind this committee included J.B. Danquah of Ghana, Jomo Kenyata of Kenya and others from Somali and West Indies. It was the committee members of the Pan-African organization that organized a well befitting reception to welcome Emperor Haile Selassie when he arrived London to begin his exile term after his Kingdom had been taken over by the Italian army. In Nigeria series of meetings were organized by the educated elites to demand for the forceful removal of Italians from Ethiopia. In nearly all the existing principal cities of Yorubaland of this time had a committee organized to intimate their people concerning the situation of things in Ethiopia and to ask them to support the course of the black people in Ethiopia both morally and financially. Some Nigerian young men were desperate to go to war in Ethiopia voluntarily for the release of the territory and its people from the hands of the wicked imperialist agents. One of the important legacies that the Ethiopian invasion left behind for the Africans was that it marked the beginning of a vital step in the growth of unity and determination of the African people to change the world's negative thoughts and realities about the continent by themselves and as its fore-runners only.

Another point was that it aroused the political intellect of the educated Africans of the time, which must be seen as a wider spectacle for them to look at the future of the continent particularly the kind of the needed awareness to be created to monitor the activities of the imperialist agents in Africa. The invasion of Ethiopia would always be referred to as the water fountain from where the political movements in the black African territories drank their first glass of water.

In 1919 the National Congress of British West Africa was established and it held its first Conference in Accra in 1920. The primary aim of the congress was to foster unity among the nations of West Africa by bringing all the elites together for deliberations on the numerous issues confronting the region. The moving spirit behind the congress was Casely Hayford of Ghana, who after consulting with Nana Ofori Atta a recognized chief also from Ghana and R.A. Savage of Nigeria was able to put the organization in place with the support of those who were who in the group of the African elites of West Africa of the time. The Ghana Conference, which was attended by 6 Nigerians, 3 Sierra Leonean, 1 Gambian and 40 Ghanaians, demanded among other things in their resolutions the followings:

(1) Introduction of Franchise
(2) Equal job opportunity between the whites and the blacks in the civil service
(3) Establishment of Higher Institution – University College
(4) Separation of the judiciary from the colonial administration

The Congress thought that by hitting the nail directly on the head would drive the nail through to the required depth in the wood. It therefore decided to take its case straight to London where it was the seat of the mother government in charge of the British colonial administrations in British West Africa. A deputation that included the following people was sent to London to press hard on their requests:

(1) Dr. H.C. Bankole – Bright - Sierra Leone
(2) H. Van Hein - Ghana
(3) T. Hutton - President of the Congress
(4) Chief Oluwa – Nigeria
(5) J. Casely Hayford – Ghana
(6) Egerton Shyngle – Nigeria (Later Adeniyi Jones)

171

(7) H.M. Jones – Gambia
(8) Herbert Macaulay – Nigeria and Chief Oluwa's Secretary
(9) T.M. Oluwa – Nigeria (Son of Chief Oluwa)
(10) F.W. Dove – Sierra Leone
(11) E.F. Small – Gambia

Africa the Ewe people had been divided between
German Togoland. During World War I British and
Togo and, since the British occupied Lome and
reunited. In 1919, without reference to the people,
en Britain and France in such a way that the Ewe
apart than ever before. The Ewe under the leader-
atedly appealed to the British and Americans on the
self-determination. So illogical was the division that
order had their cocoa farms on the other, and this
eation for some and none for others. The Gold Coast
iblicity to Ewe grievances until it was banned by the
the first points raised by the National Congress of
the bartering around of African peoples by the

ss of British West Africa, established in 1919 and
nce in Accra the following year, was in its West
tral expression of the unity of the elite of English-
he moving spirit behind the Congress was Casely
consulted with Nana Oferi Atta and R. A. Savage of
ad the almost unanimous support of the English-
ss. At the Accra Conference attended by 6 Nigerians,
ambian and 40 Ghanaians resolutions were passed
ion of the franchise, equal opportunities for white
rice, opportunities for higher education, and a clearer
ty from the colonial administration. The conference
tation to press its claims in London, since no one
position to act in West Africa as a whole.
ernors were annoyed that the Congress went over
d the Colonial Office that the deputation represented
overnor Clifford of Nigeria was particularly scornful
l ever consider themselves one nationality, and even
Nigeria could ever be a nation. All the governors
iefs could speak for the people. Due to the attitude
leputation achieved nothing in London; but the
xist, holding a Conference in Freetown (1923), in
agos (1930).
t West Africa in the direction the Congress desired
anxious to discourage political agitation) claimed that
ented to the West Africans by the British and not
agress pressure. By 1925 a limited franchise had been

London deputation of the National Congress, 1920. From left to right seated: Dr. H. C. Bankole-Bright (Sierra Leone), T. Hutton Mills (President of the Congress), Chief Oluwa (Nigeria), J. E. Casely Hayford (Ghana), H. Van Hein (Ghana). Standing: J. Egerton Shyngle (Nigeria), H. M. Jones (Gambia), Herbert Macaulay (Chief Oluwa's Secretary), T. M. Oluwa (son of the chief), F. W. Dove (Sierra Leone), E. F. Small (Gambia)

extended to Calabar, Lagos, Accra, Cape Coast and Freetown. Achimota
College was set up in Ghana in 1927 for higher education and the West
African Court of Appeal made the judiciary less subject to the control of the
governors. However, the elected Africans had no power in the Legislative
Council and past pupils of Achimota were discriminated against in the civil
service so that the gains were minor.

Meanwhile the Congress, like political organizations in West Africa before
it, became conservative and in 1930, when Hayford died, the Congress passed
away with him. The common people were never stirred and little effort was
made to bring them into the Congress, so that the governors' contention that
the elite of the Congress represented no one was at least partly true. People
from the interior were dismissed as 'bush'. A party of Ibadan leaders
approached the Congress to take up certain local grievances. They were
treated to such educated snobbery that the Ibadan branch of the Congress
died and could never be revived. The apathy and even fear of elite leadership
was indicated by the few who turned out to vote; seldom more than forty

307

Deputation of West African delegates to London in 1920

Because the British governors of the colonies in the region of West
Africa were not informed before the deputation set at its journey to
London, the governors were annoyed and saw it as a spite on their
positions and because of this they held that grudge against the members
of the Congress until the motives of their journey to London was killed
through their administrative connections with the colonial office in
London.

Though the resolutions of the Congress were well taken in London
and they were promised that everything will be looked into as soon
as possible but as soon as they left the government began to work
on those resolutions through other administrative means. At about

five years later, the government began the implementations of those resolutions as if they were the makings of the British government in the colonies. Of particular interest was the role and comments of Governor Clifford of Nigeria on the visit of the Congress members to London who was said to be very scornful and commented openly that, could West African people ever considered themselves as one nationality? He even laughed at the idea that Nigeria could ever be a nation. Due to the power that was remotely wielded by these governors within the government functionaries in England, the members of the delegation returned to their respective bases without any meaningful answer to their requests.

But the Congress continued to exist, holding its Conferences at different locations of the region. Years later, the British government came out with plans to implement the resolutions of the Congress in the following piece meal fashions:

(1) By 1925 a limited franchise was extended to Calabar, Lagos, Accra, Cape Coast and Freetown.

(2) In 1927 Achimota College was set up in Ghana for Higher Education. West African Court of Appeal (WACA) was also set up to make judiciary less subject to the control of the governors.

(3) Africans were elected into the Legislative Council but with no powers.

(4) Those graduated from Achimota College and employed in the civil service were still being discriminated against as a routine and hidden policy of the imperialist agents.

The divide and rule game that the British governors employed to rule their colonies was now at hand in the general set up of the Congress. The governors had already made their ways into the ranks of the Congress and smashed it into pieces. In 1930 the Congress became conservative and was turned into a play field where the best players could demonstrate their talents and skills in the art of the game. In Ghana the members of the Congress there began to dine at the governor's banquets and parties. In Nigeria big wealthy people who were inwardly satisfied with all that the colonial government had to offer as long as their positions were secured were using the Congress only as a forum to gather large followers for ego purposes.

This type of people outwardly detested the harsh handedness of the colonial administrators in certain areas but at heart they feared major reforms that would affect their business advantages. Unfortunately the common man who were directly affected and who were interested in the real reformation plans had no money to turn things around to their side. For an organization of this type to survive, it has linger heavily on the shoulders of the wealthy patrons; but the danger here is that such an organization would always see itself under the mercy of its financial patrons. Along the line, anything can happen either for good or bad. One of the fatal mistakes that the Congress made was that the foundation of its structures was constructed on the soils of the elites only while they excluded the local chiefs who deal directly with the natives and whose support and input it needed to survive.

As soon as the colonial administrators detected this fault, they swung into action and broke into their ranks and tore down its walls. The divided line created between the two groups – the chiefs and the elites gave the British Administrators every political opportunity to kill the Congress, which they successfully did with less effort. Before Hayford died in 1930, he expressed his disillusionment with anger about the leadership of the elites when he said:

> *The African God is weary of your wrangling, weary of your vain disputations, weary of your everlasting quarrels, which are a drag upon progress and which keep from you, as a people, the good that is intended for you.*

Soonest it became a heart breaking news that this first progressive organization that represented all the political units of West African coast died a premature death as it passed away with the death of its founder J.E. Casely Hayford in 1930.

In 1920 Dr. Mojola Agbebi thus commented about some characteristics bordering on the two sides of African leadership:

> *To pull to pieces, to reduce to atoms, to break, to tear, to disorganize is often the inclination of thoughtless childhood. Such a trait of character is to be met with among some Africans….. Do not tolerate disorder. It is one of the besetting sins of native organizations that every man desires to be the leader. It is the spirit of slavery, and is more manifest among Europeanized Africans than among Africans purely natives. Recognize leadership.*

Dr. Mojola Agbebi who formally bore the foreign names of David Brown Vincent was the leader of the Native Baptist Church who as from 1891 refused to work for any foreign Christian mission inspite of high positions with great remunerations offered to him by the foreign missionaries including the Church Missionary Society (C.M.S.) Dr Agbebi was one of the educated Africans of his time that so much cherished the culture of his people and never deviated from the norms of the African cultural path from his wearing of Yoruba traditional clothing styles to the traditional way of Yoruba marriage ceremony. It was recorded for him that in 1900 when he betrothed his daughter, Ibironke, he did it in the Yoruba traditional way and wherever he went to, he would always be found wearing his voluminous Agbada dress even in the cold weather of Britain and America. From 1904 when he toured Britain and America lecturing on African customs, he left a remarkable cultural legacy for the Negroes in New York, which encouraged them to set aside a date – 11th of October as Agbebi Day in remembrance of African customs and institutions and in support of his evangelistic exertions in Southern Nigeria.

During his address at the Universal Races Congress meeting held at the Senate House, University of London in 1911, where he defended some of the African institutions such as the secret societies and others and which was reproduced throughout West Africa and London, he urged all Africans to make distinctions between the "essentials" and the "non-essentials" of Christianity. He further elaborated on his declaration thus:

> *Prayer-books and Hymn-books, harmonium dedications, pew construction, surpliced choir, the white man's style, the white man's name, the white man's dress, are so many non-essentials, so many props and crutches affecting the religious manhood of the Christian African. Among the great essentials of religion are that the lame walk, the lepers are cleansed, the deaf hear, the dead are raised up and the poor have the Gospel preached unto him.*

If Dr. Agbebi could visualized in the early 20th century that so many things were going wrong in the way his people had accepted and reacted to the new religion and observed that in no distant future if care is not taken, the people would abandon the history of their country for those of England, Greece and Rome and speak no other vernacular language other than English language in their homes, that they would have greater respect for the Kings and the Queens of England than for their Royal Kings, and even eat imported foreign foods in place of their rich and vitaminous foods, fresh from the lands in the villages, then this legendary being of Yoruba extraction to the core must universally accepted as a great philosopher of his time. Most of his predictions that had come to past especially in Yorubaland of today may be summed up in his philosophical ideas of "Europeanized African tenet" that the rush for economic freedom may sometime contribute to the undermining of his people's culture and the upsetting of the society at large.

The other notable personalities to be referenced here regarding the Europeanized African behaviors of the earlier time in West Africa were E.W. Blyden and James Johnson. Both of them were advocates of cultural nationalism and both echoed their views against the denationalization methods of Christian missions in West Africa; the idea which they both termed "a terrible homicide" in 1872 when they both were asking for the establishment of a University in West Africa. As for Blyden, he believed that no greater calamity could befall a race than the loss of its culture. He expantiated further on this that: "the soul of the race finds expression in its institutions and to kill those institutions is to kill the soul – a terrible homicide". Blyden and his works on African nationalism were recognized throughout the length and breadth of West Africa particularly by some of the immediate past African statesmen who accepted Blyden as their inspirer. He was exponent of the view that the different races of the world had special talents distributed among themselves on racial lines. To buttress Blyden's views, we can see today that in the areas of sport and music particularly in America where these two professions are well developed beyond other countries of the world, the blacks are exceedingly rated as champions and leaders of the two areas.

In the case of James Johnson, he was known throughout his lifetime as a hard line advocator of cultural nationalism and in 1908 he carried his philosophy to the Pan-Anglican Conference held in that year. In 1873 when he had an interview with the Secretary of state for the colonies, the Earl of Kimberly regarding the establishment of a University in West Africa, he bluntly told him that by the time their request would be granted, an end shall be put to the presence of white missionaries in West Africa and that the staffing of the proposed University must largely come from the American Negroes who will in turn produce African graduates who would ultimately displace the Europeans.

In his famous correspondence with Hennessy, James Johnson criticized the missionary activities in West Africa in a very strong language that its excerpt deserved reproducing here:

> In the work of elevating Africans, foreign teachers have always proceeded with their work on the assumption that the Negro or the African is in every one of his normal susceptibilities an inferior race, and that it is needful in everything to give him a foreign model to copy; no account has been made of our peculiarities; our languages enriched with traditions of centuries; our parables, many of them the quintessence of family and national histories; our modes of thought influenced more or less by local circumstances; our poetry and manufactures, which though are rude, had their own tales to tell...... God does not intend to have the races confounded, but that the Negro or Africa should be raised upon his own idiosyncrasies...... The result has been that we as a people..... have lost our self-respect and our love for our own race are become a sort of nondescript people.

Both of these great leaders called for the emancipation of the Europeanized Africans from their mental and cultural slavery in which they were growing and stop embracing foreign cultures. Through their spiritual eyes, they saw that this group of people were living in a borrowed continent and existing on the thought and ideas of the people from whom they copied their style of life. If not for the strong opposition of our past and dedicated heroes who refused to sit hopelessly to watch the murder, death and burial of our culture including our languages that represented an important national and racial mark that God has given to us, what could we have been saying today? These cultural nationalists surely realized that the way to elevate people was not to teach them how to entertain the lowest ideas of themselves and make them servile imitators of others. It is very logical that if a society is to be destroyed, the first place to attack is that society's culture and customs. The moment these areas are bombed to ashes, such society is completely destroyed, which was the case with the Africans taken to foreign lands in the slavery days. This is why the offshoots of their first or second generations are now neither here nor there because the original culture had been taken away from them.

Congratulatory messages must annually be going to heaven to meet the past Nigerian nationalists of the 19th – 20th centuries that fought the noble fight against the imperialists when series of attempts were made to strip us off of our culture and languages. The early struggle for our national identity, which began in Lagos in the 19th century, would always recognize the efforts of the African Christians and the native converts of the Yoruba nation of this period. The church was then the cradle of Nigeria nationalism, which was the only place where nationalist expressions could be discussed and where the main focus of nationalist energies resided until 1914 when things began to move to other areas. The foundation of the government we have today in Nigeria came into existence through the efforts and sweats of our past leaders who by one way or the other passed through the training institutions that the missionaries were able to provide for the growth of the natives and the nation.

Almost all of the beneficiaries that enjoyed this privilege owed their gratitude to the kind gesture of the missionaries that established schools in different localities of the land from where the next generations of educated elites developed their talents and skills. The unrestricted access to the Bible, with its notions of equality, justice and non-racialism provided them with a strong weapon, which they used in setting up the bases for the freedom we enjoy today. Many would agree with Professor E.A. Ayandele that the interpretation of "Ethiopianism" in Nigeria context differs significantly from that of other areas in the continent especially from the South and Central Africa's perspective. Interestingly, he was able to equate the situation of the Nigerian nationalists and the natives of this time to the suffering of the Jews and their leaders in the Bible where King David in Psalm 68 aroused the anger and intellectual Supremacy of God over their enemies – the Philistines. The same situation, which the black race found themselves under the rule of the whites in Africa, was not quite different from the type that the Jews found themselves during the Jewish Holocaust period of the World War II under the regime of Hitler in Germany.

In verse 1 of the Scripture mentioned, King David appealed to God that:

Let God arise, let his enemies be scattered: let them also that hate Him flee before Him and in Verse 31 he concluded his supplications by saying that: *Princes shall come out of Egypt: Ethiopia shall soon stretch out her hands unto God in praises.* As King David believed that God would hear his supplications and He did heard him so also the African nationalists of this period believed that their cries unto their Lord and the God of Africa shall be heard and He actually wiped out the tears from their eyes. The nationalists strongly believed that the term "Ethiopia" had come to whip them up, and also to assist them to establish the bacon of the hope of their people as well as to fulfill the promise, which the education they had received from the hands of their oppressors gave to them. They had now become self-conscious and began to nurse the ambition for self-expression and the introduction of self-government, which was a corollary to the theory of equality that they had learnt from the Bible.

The education they had received now began to bring out of them the fruits of its labor and familiarized them with the machinery of the British Parliamentary democracy system, which all the protestant missions were compelled to establish in their territories along the West African coast. It also became natural that before the introduction of Legislative Council in Lagos, the church was the center of social, spiritual and political aspirations of the educated elites and their illiterate converts. It was therefore not a mistake or an accident for educated Africans like Herbert Macaulay, the grandson of Bishop Samuel Ajayi Crowther and the son of Babington Macaulay the founder of the first secondary school in Nigeria – Lagos Grammar School, Dr. Nnamdi Azikiwe of Ibo extraction but of Yoruba breed, both that founded the first political organization with national outlook in 1944 – the National Council of Nigeria and Cameroons (N.C.N.C.), chief Obafemi Awolowo the founder of the Action Group party (A.G.) whose its government ruled the Western Region of Nigeria with creditable achievements recorded for it, Dr. Dikko, a Northern Christian trained as medical doctor in Birmingham by Dr. Walter Miller and his friends, who conceived the strongest political party in Northern Nigeria – Northern Peoples Congress.

It was also not a mistake to assume that the first generation of educated Nigerians were pre-eminently prepared and equipped for nationalistic task through their training and the circumstances of the environment they found themselves. Undoubtedly through the church they all became whatever they were in their respective trades, professions and national callings, be they traders, teachers, clerks, lawyers, writers, politicians, clergies and others. The church made it possible for everyone of them to fulfill their whole being in that through the involuntary monopoly of its educational system, they were able to hold the destiny of their children in its hands.

The departure of the National Congress of British West Africa from the political play field of the people was temporary and short-lived. The ideas it stood for began to trouble the minds of the educated Africans and its philosophical slogan of "Africa for Africans" was generating uncomfortable heat throughout the land. In French West Africa politics was a dangerous occupation because of the French colonial administrator's high handedness towards any native who dared to organized or planned for one. In spite of the French negative attitude towards this move, Louis Hunkanrin of a Senegalese lawyer, and a wealthy Dahomean merchant aided by the support of Blaise Diagne with the contacts they had in Paris, worked together for the recall and investigation of the wicked governor Nonfflard who was particularly burdensome and humiliating the natives with his arrogant officials.

When Hunkanrin returned to Dahomey from Paris, he organized a branch of the League "For The Right of Man", which was used to channel the political course of the people and which, gave publicity in France to poor administration in Dahomey and to demand for reforms. In 1923 when Governor Gaston Fourn who replaced Nonfflard raised taxes by 500% around the time that the main export of the country – palm-oil fell in price, the League stood as opposition leader to the move. People refused to pay taxes, they boycotted the markets and general strike that extended to the port workers in Cotonou was effectively organized. Fourn then ordered for troops from Togo and Ivory Coast and declared a three months state of emergency.

The troops forced the people to pay the taxes, seized firearms, burnt villages and disorganized the whole system of the people. There was not any enquiry to the unilateral actions of Fourn from France. He was able to gather all the leaders of the protest, which included the leaders of the rival Royal lineage of the Yoruba Muslim faction in Dahomey – Sognigbe and Hunkanrin. He exiled and imprisoned them in Mauritania for ten years where it was only Hunkanrin that did not die in his detention. Similar to that of Fourns action would have been attempted in the British West African territories if not for the fact that the educated Africans in those areas had access to lawyers and control of newspapers in their countries, which they could have used to at least legally asked for a commission of inquiry or for redress in the courts against such barbaric actions that would have trampled on the humanity of their people.

The death of the National Congress of West Africa was partly connected with the arrogance of some of the educated Africans who saw themselves as being too superior to come to the level of the natives from the interior when deciding the political and social issues of the entire community with the colonial administrators in the cities of Lagos, Cape Coast and Freetown at the Legislative Council meetings. In all the colonies the educated Africans that became members of the Congress won seats in the elections into the Legislative Council in their respective colonies; while the other members that were not elected through elections were nominated by the British governors because of the intimacy and nexus between the authority and those educated members. The close interaction between the government officials and the legislators now developed into different social levels that in Ghana for example, the native Congress members there were soon entertaining the governor into private parties, which was a sign that their political enthusiasm was ebbing. In Nigeria too some wealthy men in the society began to infiltrate into the hierarchy of the Congress for popularity purposes, which eventually lowered the high respect that people like Herbert Macaulay initially had for them.

When Herbert Macaulay noticed the neglect of the educated Africans on the issues affecting the ordinary natives of Lagos, he decided to form his own political group called the Nigerian National Democratic Party (NNDP) – the first political party in Nigeria. In 1922, the Nigerian Constitution was amended to permit three elected African representatives to sit on the Legislative Council (two from Lagos and one from Calabar) and at the same time a municipal government was set up in Lagos. At the Lagos polls, Macaulay's new party NNDP swept all the seats confirming it to be officially recognized as the first political party in the land with the record victory in the elections of 1923, 1928 and 1933.

Unfortunately the same kind of attitude that the predecessor of NNDP in office was accused of became the order of the day for its members too. After the restoration of Oba of Lagos in 1931 through the case that Albert Macaulay won in the Privy Council on behalf of the Royal King for his being wrongly deposed by the Colonial government for land matters in Lagos, relations between Macaulay and the British

181

governor changed and began to improve. His political party suddenly turned into conservatism and began to support the colonial government, which was its greatest enemy at one time in the past.

The turn around situation became noticed that the members of the party now began to enjoy the British government patronage in the areas of commerce and industry, in positions in the government and at invitations to government house parties. The rebels of the 1920s had now become the princes of the 1930s with affectionate romances from England. The desire for reform was absolutely killed and disappeared into the thin air of the Atlantic, that in 1935 when the Italians invaded Ethiopia, it was only the party that did not support the "Hands off Abyssinia" campaign that all the black race organizations of this time all over the world participated in. The system of divide and rule employed by the governors in the colonies began to work its magical wands as the Democratic Party had now fallen into the self-satisfied conservatism which had crept over the A.R.P.S by 1918 and the National Congress of the British West Africa by the late twenties. This was the way used by the British governors to buy over their critics and maintained their colonial positions throughout the territories under their rule in the West Coast of Africa until a new group from the new generation sprang up to continue the fight for the independence of their people and their lands.

Inevitably the young kids of yesterday were now growing in strength and wisdom and no one could stop their own ideas of how they would want to be ruled and who to rule them. These young lads began to react against the older politicians through their own organization called the Nigerian Youth League. The politics of Nigeria was now taking a new shape and dimension and seriously departing from the old system of the old brigades who saw politics as a club business where people could troop into by the weekends to drink, play pools, relax with girl friends and go back home either half-drunk or fully refreshed. They opposed the conservatism of the old party programs and tried to move away completely from the old idea that political protests was the right of the elites and should be confined only to the cities of Lagos, Cape Coast and Freetown.

They put the larger map of the country on the table for discussions and developments. Based on their philosophy of "National Interest", Eyo Ita in 1932 established in Calabar an industrial school called the West African Peoples Institute where the youths were been prepared to be self-supporting in their localities rather than moving to the cities to look for collar-jobs that may not come their ways till the end of the world. In 1934, the Nigerian Youth Movement (N.Y.M.) was formed in Lagos whose part of its agenda was to encourage national feelings and to make demands for self-determination and Africanization of all the positions in the colonial administration. To show that they were serious, they established branches throughout the country to prove its national outlook and identity. When Dr. Nnamdi Azikiwe returned to Nigeria in 1937 and established his West African Pilot paper, he immediately threw his weight behind the N.Y.M., which eventually derailed the Nigerian National Democratic Party in the elections to the Legislative Council of 1938.

When Dr. Azikiwe had thoroughly understudied those he met on the ground and after he had found out that it will take many more centuries to change the structure of the nation if he had to travel with these people on the same boat, he broke off from them and formed the National Council of Nigeria and Cameroons (N.C.N.C) in 1944 just the same way that Dr. Nkruma of Ghana did in 1949 when he branched out of the United Gold Coast Convention (U.G.C.C) of J. B. Danquah to form his Convention Peoples Party (C.P.P). N.C.N.C through its strong support for the masses of the grass root and for the rights of the ordinary citizens and the workers, it was able to pull together all the ethnic and progressive unions including other voluntary associations in the country to become affiliates of the party. In 1945, the Party stood firmly behind the general strike, which was organized against the hardship of wartime and in 1946 when governor Richards introduced a new Constitution similar to the one introduced in Ghana by governor Burns in the same year, the party kicked against it seriously.

Herbert Macaulay was made the chairman of the party while Dr. Azikiwe was its General Secretary. A tour of the country was organized by the party to raise funds for a delegation to be sent to London to discuss among other things the Nigeria's demand for self-government, but it was so unfortunate to note that it was during this tour that Herbert Macaulay who was then an old person died and the mantle of leadership of the party passed onto Dr. Azikiwe who led the party into Nigeria Independence. The delegation to London talk was still made possible as it represented the cross section of the country that was drawn from the list of the strong nationalists of the nation of the time. Its outcry against the Constitution was that the Nigerians were not consulted in its entire design and that it was only dumped on them without asking for the people's input and opinions. In response to the people's outcry, the British government organized series of meetings at national, provincial, divisional and village levels for their input. The national debate on the matter was held at Ibadan in 1950 with very tense and hot arguments from the delegates and from whence ethnic political unit in Nigeria began to rear its head out of its deep waters.

Problems were now surfacing in the ranks of the N.C.N.C. especially between the Yoruba and Ibo leaders. The Hausa from the North were not at ease with the union between the trio because they were already entertaining the fear of Southern political domination and the Yoruba elements in the party were not happy with the recent rise of the Ibos in the nationalist movement. As a result of all the wrangling here and there, the Ibadan Conference demanded for a federal form of government at the center with strong regional governments for the three distinctive areas of the country – East, North and West.

In 1951, the Action Group was born and stood for the interest of the Yoruba and Edo people, the Northern Peoples Congress was for Hausa/Fulani of the North, and the N.C.N.C was left for the Ibos of the East. Hence some of the former members of the party who were of Yoruba and Hausa extractions now dumped the party and went their ways peacefully. Certainly, ethnic feelings in the leadership of the parties blew open as it now triumphed over that of the national. Gradually the center was becoming weaker and weaker while the Regions were adding more and more feathers onto their bodies. Amid all the troubles that each Region underwent, the Western and Easter Regions were granted internal self-government in 1957. In the same year Alhaji Abubakar was appointed by the British as the Prime Minister at the center to form a unity government of the three political parties participating.

Within the Regions, there was trouble of ethnic clans demanding and agitating for their separate regions and accusing the larger regions of marginalization. In the West for example the Bini people were complaining of Yoruba domination in the political set-up while the Efiks and other clans in the East were complaining of the same thing against the Ibo domination; equally the people of J.S. Tarkar in the Middle Belt hated the Hausa-Fulani domination too. The fear of everyone was that if every clan should be allowed to ask for their rights of statehood, the walls of the country would be torn down in no time and the best thing to do was to give greater powers to the center while mores states could be born but with lesser powers and be made subordinate to the center.

Chapter –13–

The Struggle for and Attainment of Nigeria Independence in 1960:

The attainment of Nigeria independence did not come on a platter of gold as people would have thought of it but it came through protests, dialog, diplomatic arrangements, resolutions of conferences, and with series of enacted Constitutions for the country by the dominating nation of England. The history of modern legislature in Nigeria began in 1862 when the British established the Legislative Council for the Colony of Lagos with the governor at its head, six appointed officials and other four nominated members that included two Europeans and two Nigerians who were designated unofficial members. These people only had the functions of advisory role to the governor as other Legislative powers resided in the foreign governor. Following the amalgamation of Lagos Colony with the Southern and Northern protectorates in 1914 by Sir Fredrick Lugard, Nigerian Council was established to take care of the country's business. This Council was comprised of 36 members out of whom 23 of them were European officials, 7 European businessmen and six traditional rulers of the land from various locations of the country. The new Council was larger than the previous one but yet had only advisory powers with no authority on how the finances of the country were being managed and they had no executive powers no matter how small they might be. By 1912 the Clifford Constitution came on board and it abolished the Legislative Council and the Nigerian Council to usher in the new Legislative Council of 46 members. Out of these numbers, 27 were government official members including the governor himself. The remaining 19 members were shared according to the order of preference. 10 were Nigerians, 15 were the nominees of the governor and only 4 were elected. The major duties of this council were to legislate for the peace, order and good government of the colony of Lagos and the Southern Provinces. As for the North of the country, it was within the powers of the governor to legislate by proclamation for the entire North.

The administration of the country was rapidly changing through the advent of political agitations from the Nigerian educated elites both from home and abroad. Their agitations prompted the birth of another new Constitution named after Richard (the then governor) in 1946and it derailed the Legislative Council and brought in its place the more central Legislative Council with more members to participate in it. Its members were composed of the governor at the head of the country's administration, 13 ex-officio, 3 nominated members, 28 unofficial members who either came in through election or selection. The cotton wool placed on the Nigerian's eyes by their British partners were gradually being removed as the new Council was now empowered to enact laws for the peace, order and good government of Nigeria but the overall approval of such laws still hung on the office and the person of the Governor-General.

By 1951, another meaningful and enlarged Constitution of John Stuart Macpherson came on board and wiped off the central Legislative Council and planted in its place with yet another unit of government called the House of Representatives, which now transformed the governor into the position of the President of the House. Others included 6 European officials, out of which the three Lieutenant Governors of the three regions - East, West and the North were members and 136 elected Representatives from the three Regions according to their sizes in population and landmass. 68 members came from the North being the largest while 34 members each came from both East and West and the remaining 6 members were special members appointed by the governor to represent the interests of those areas with minimum interests and smaller communities that had less louder voices in the order of things in the country. This House of Representative like its predecessors had no power over the bills relating to the public revenue and the public service structures, which were the prerogatives of the mother government in England through its agency the Home Office and to be implemented by its representative in Nigeria, the Governor-General. For the effectiveness of the government to be felt and made manifest to all, the House of Representative was given pseudo-supremacy to veto legislations made by the Regional Houses of Assembly.

From the hues, cries and glamour of the people for independent Nigeria, the Lyttelton Constitution of 1954 came into birth. In it the House of Representatives was retained with allocation of more powers to Nigerians instead of the previous ones that vested all powers in the hands of the foreign governors. The House now had a speaker, 3 Ex-officio members, and 184 native members elected from various constituencies throughout the land. This House unlike its predecessors was now empowered to make laws for its people and as well to discuss all financial matters of the country. In addition to this political achievement, three Legislative Lists specifying about 68 items on which the House of Representatives had powers to make laws; Concurrent List on which the House of Representatives and the Regional Houses of Assembly had concurrent Legislative powers and Residual List made up of some items on which the Regional Legislature had the final say.

The aims of all the Constitutions prepared for the country by the British experts were in preparation for the time when the country would be ripe enough to adopt the Westminster Parliamentary system of government in place in the United Kingdom. The independence Constitution of 1960 completed this arrangement as the Constitution finally established for Nigeria a Parliament made up of a House of Representatives with 320 elected members and a Senate of 44 nominated members representing the structure of the House of Commons and House of Lords in the United Kingdom. This Constitution also ushered in the independence of Nigeria after sixty years of servitude under the British economic and administrative dominance.

In preparation for Nigeria's independence, the major political parties that were to usher in the independence had begun to emerge since in the 1940s and early 1950s as regional parties whose main aims and preoccupations were to control their regions of origin. The two political parties that fell into this category were the Northern Peoples Congress (NPC) from the North and the Action Group (AG) from the West. The third political party, the National Council of Nigeria and the Cameroons (NCNC) was initially the only political party that drew its source from the national fountain until it hit the rock through the politics of regionalism that made it to become the dominant party of the East at independence and the Midwest after independence. Though the party still maintained some pockets of support from the West where it began its political race but the departure of who is who in the politics of Lagos and the West, which made these political heavy weights to align with the Action Group substantially damaged the ranks of the party and made it impossible for it to raise its head above the political waters of these two areas.

The three Regional political parties, which now controlled their Regional Houses of Assembly derived and enjoyed their main support from the major groups in their regions who as well controlled the voting pattern of their people at every election. The NPC had the support of the Hausa/Fulani group, the AG-Yoruba and the NCNC the Igbo group. Apart from these giant political parties, there were many other parties that never achieved national recognition as such. One of them was the radical Aminu Kano's Northern Elements Progressive Union (NEPU) based in Kano and which was opposed to the NPC and its counterpart, the United Middle Belt Congress (UMBC) of the Tivs headed by J. S.Tarka. Both of them became serious political thorns in the flesh of the ruling party at the Northern House of Assembly and senior partner at the Federal government level – NPC.

For political umbrella as a shield, NEPU aligned itself with the NCNC in the East while the UMBC aligned itself with the AG in the West because these two senior political parties supported their demands for separate states to be carved out of the then North. An election was held in 1959 to determine which of the political parties would rule the country immediately after the exit of the colonial administrators but unfortunately none of the major parties was able to single handedly form the government at the center. Although each of them tried and gained majority of the seats allocated to their respective regions but it was difficult for any of them to win overall majority seats to the House of Representatives and as such two of them had to fuss together to produce the required number of representatives needed to form the government. The three parties went into negotiations among themselves and at the end of the day a coalition government of the NPC and the NCNC was formed.

It is worth mentioning here that since the days of Lugard at the head of the colonial government in the North in Kaduna and as Governor-General in Lagos, the British had had soft ground for the Northerners in the politics of Nigeria. When the Northern Peoples Congress came on board in the political play field of the country, the party too was greatly favored by the departing colonial authority. The reason why the

188

negotiations of fussing together to form the federal government of this time between the NCNC and the AG failed after the 1959 elections was because of the seed of hatred that had been planted in the minds of the leaders of both parties during the days of the trouble that divided the National Youth Movement (NYM) along regional lines. It was also as the result of this same problem that prompted Dr. Nnamdi Azikiwe to branch out of the NYM to form the NCNC in 1944.

To top it all the popular carpet crossing episode on the floor of the Western House of Assembly in 1957, which allowed Action Group to form the first government of Western Region played major roles in determining which way was more comfortable for the NCNC to thread. Action Group as a political party to me was not much hated by its opponents as its chieftains for the role they played in the instances mentioned above. The coalition between the NCNC and the NPC on the face of it actually provided a reasonable measure of political stability, which could be interpreted as a North and South consensus that would not have been the case if the NCNC and the AG had formed such a coalition; but with this common sense judgment, the escalation of the country's problems were at their dangerous heights.

The coalition of both parties now produced Dr. Nnamdi Azikiwe of NCNC as the Governor-General of the Federation and Sir Abubakar Tafawa Balewa of the NPC as the Prime Minister. The Leader of Opposition in the Federal House of Representatives obviously went to Chief Obafemi Awolowo. The three political parties in the regions maintained the hold of their respective regions with Ahmadu Bello the Sadauna of Sokoto and leader of the NPC as the premier of the North, Chief Samuel Ladoke Akintola of AG in the West and Michael Okpara of NCNC in the East. Chief Denis Osadebey of the NCNC emerged as the Premier of the newly created Midwest after independence. Some important developments that have continued to affect the governments of Nigeria and the politics of the people in the postcolonial era started during the period of colonial rule that substantially divided the country into two political warring camps, which remained the classic cleavage we see up till today. The first of their miscalculations was the pact that Lord Lugard had with the Northern Emirs to protect Islamic civilization, which short the doors of modern civilization and Western education to their people and to which the people of the South were exposed to thereby given the Southern people a head start in the educational field.

The consequence of such action revealed itself during the struggle for independence, whereby some Northern leaders were afflicted by a constant fear of Southern domination of Nigeria politics and government. When the British administrators realized the effect of this huge mistake, they resulted to the partitioning of the country into two - North and South political play field given the North the territory larger than both the East and West combined. This action again turned the table of domination towards the Southern people accusing the North of political domination not knowing the game being played by their detractors. The colonial administrators knew pretty well that the North had only an image of homogeneity as against the cultural diversity of the people of that region, yet they had to please the Emirs and used the division to compensate them for the mistakes they made earlier but at the expense of the entire people of Nigeria.

The administration of imperialist government in Nigeria left many unresolved problems by the time they left in 1960. When they were creating the artificial regions, they knew that each region contained the nucleus of a majority group that may perhaps dominate the minority group in such regions. The Hausa/Fulani in the North, the Yoruba in the West and the Igbo in the East depicted the ways and manner that the three states were being ruled and controlled particularly with the regional autonomy granted the states. The major groups became the dominating group in each region as well as the major shareholders of the federation. The minority groups, who felt oppressed, cheated and dominated, began to agitate for their own states within the regions especially in the North.

Their agitations led them to an attachment to the political parties that were being known and in control of other states of the federation for alliances. For example, the Aminu Kano's NEPU aligned with the NCNC from the East while J. S. Tarka's UMBC from Tiv aligned with the AG from the West. The effectiveness of these alliances was clearly seen during the campaigns for elections of 1959 whereby the presence of party stewards from Tiv land of the Middle Belt area openly accompanied their leader J.S.Tarka to AG campaign grounds in the West as his protective guardsmen. Same was recorded to Malam Aminu Kano's NEPU's assistance to NCNC campaign meetings either in the East or West where the party stewards of Hausa/Fulani origin gave their support to the campaign meetings of their big political brother's party of the NCNC. Sometime during the electioneering campaign of 1959, this arrangement was used to intimidate the members of the opposing party in the regions and again sometime used to demonstrate or show the greatness in the ancient powers from various places of the regions when people were still recognized as warlords in their respective areas in the country before our coming together as one family member.

To address the issue of minority within the federation, the colonial government in 1956 set up a commission of enquiry into the complaints and fears of the minorities and to explore into details ways of allaying them but the report of this panel never saw the light of the day not until after the independence because the colonial administrators never wanted to border their heads anymore with this kind of complicated problems. In the Independence Constitution of 1960 and that of the Republican Constitution of 1963, the requirements for creating states were clearly spelt out therein. These requirements were stringent enough not to cause panic in the country as against what we began to see later after the creation of many states during the military rule of the country. If those conditions for creating states were strictly followed according to the letters of 1960 Constitution, the process for creating the new states would not have been trivialized, as economic viability of the states created by the military would have been thoroughly considered before their creations at all.

Some of the states that abound all over the country today becomes economic problems to the Federal government that created them. Most of the developments in these states have now become the burden of the Federal government as the people from grass root levels of such states lack financial capability to come to the aid of the state government in creating wealth for their people. All that the state government could provide is the servicing of the employment section of government by paying emoluments at the end of the month from the state allocations from Abuja. The money that was supposed to be used for infra-structural developments at the grass root levels are being mismanaged by either individuals or by group of powerful people in the society. All that we are seeing happening to us today was as a result of the inherited culture through the military intervention that set aside the Constitution of 1960, which were carefully worked out by the people and their representatives after series of Conferences that involved long time negotiations and compromises.

On October 1, 1960, Nigeria became an independent nation from the clutches of its imperial rulers. It was a day of celebration for all irrespective of their age, creed, social status and tribal sentiments. It was indeed a day that the prayers of those who fought for the independence of the nation were heard. The spirits of the dead among them came to rejoice with the living souls as the whole nation was in festive mood. Tafawa Balewa square in Lagos was jam packed by the government dignitaries and invited guests from all over the world. The capital cities of the three regional governments – Enugu, Ibadan and Kaduna went agog for this important national occasion as the people of Nigeria breathe the air of freedom just the way an incarcerated man would breathe the air of freedom after being released either from Kirikiri or Agodi prison houses. It was a day to remember in the life history of a nation that had been incapacitated for 60 uninterrupted years under the bondage of a fellow human being. At the head of the new Federal government and as the new native Governor-General of the new nation was Dr. Nnamdi Azikiwe of the NCNC, Sir Abubakar Tafawa Balewa of the NPC as the Prime Minister and Chief Obafemi Awolowo as the Leader of the Opposition in the Federal House of Representatives. All were dressed gaily in their native outfits except Dr. Nnamdi Azikiwe who took his oath of office in the British Governor-General's official uniform. The decision to put on this outfit may perhaps be out of mark of respect to the out going imperialist administration by the organizers of this occasion or out of the long time interest of the new Governor-General for such an outfit but the occasion had a trait of colonial mentality.

The term of office for some of the government ministers that were working with the Prime Minister under the unity government of Balewa between 1957 and 1960 became terminated or ceased as at this day while only those who belonged to either of the two political parties in the new coalition government retained their positions in office or have another government positions elsewhere. For record purpose, the followings were the first native ministers of Nigeria government that prepared the country for independence:

(1) Sir Abubakar Tafawa Balewa – Prime Minister
(2) Raymond Njoku – Minister for Transport
(3) Jaja Nwachukwu – Minister for Education
(4) Kingsley. O. Mbadiwe – Minister for Commerce
(5) Samuel Ladoke Akintola – Minister for Communication
(6) J. Modupe Johnson – Minister for Internal Affairs
(7) Chief Kola Balogun – Minister for Information
(8) Chief Ayo Rosiji – Minister for Health
(9) Chief Festus Okotie-Eboh – Minister for Labor
(10) Muhammadu Ribadu – Minister for mines

Three years after the attainment of independence, Nigeria proclaimed Republican status for the country with the birth of yet another Constitution named after this status – The Republican Constitution of 1963, which was not a complete departure from the one it succeeded – The Independence Constitution of 1960. The significant changes that affected the old Constitution were that the Queen of England ceased to be the Nigeria's Head of Government as well as either she or her representative will any longer sit in the Nigerian Legislative Houses. The business of the government began in earnest and some of the hidden problems now began to present themselves as national problems of greater dimensions. The seat of the Federal government was in Lagos but the areas of our problems extended beyond Lagos and covered all corners of the country from the Sea coast to the hinterland of the Southern hemisphere and from the banks of Rivers Niger and Benue to the far Northern territory.

The people were becoming very worried and impatient to know when the long awaited national developments would at least come through their villages and when the promises of the 1959 election campaigns would become reality. They forgot in the first place that the new government was an inherited government from the imperialists of distant Europe and that the finances of the country when they were with us were completely managed and supervised by them to the best interest of the big bosses in England and secondly, that we had to sit down on our own to map out our strategies and try our hands on so many things that could show us the ways to solid economic platforms. But instead we saw developments of other nations of the world at their periphery without getting to know their in-depth histories.

Because of the Federal government's inability to tackle the numerous problems it faced within this short period of time in office, it started crying of the existence of wolf where there was none. For the sustenance of a healthy democracy especially in a country, which was just being born newly, the primary duty of the opposing group to the government in power of such nation included the day-to-day policing of that government's activities and report back to the citizens. Under this condition, the opposition group has every right to issue its effective opinions on matters of the business of such government. It is equally the responsibility of the ruling party in government to always look for ways of effective dialog between itself and the opposition members and not to find or manufacture faults that would destabilize or permanently silence opposition group, which may in the process try to turn such nation into anarchy.

The newly established Federal government of this time had not enough shock absorbers to withstand the pressures from the opposition group and as such, they were looking for every possible ways to exterminate the opposition group in the Parliament. For the government to succeed in its plans, it had to corroborate lots of manufactured lies against the Leader of opposition in the Parliament and some members of the Action Group. The case against them was very sensational and widely publicized across the West African coast and at abroad. In the end, those charged for the treasonable felony case were found guilty and sentenced to various terms of imprisonment. Chief Obafemi Awolowo being the leader of the Action Group and a party being accused of planning to subvert the Federal government activities got 10 years in jail while his other lieutenants arraigned for the same offence got sentences ranging between two and five years according to the weight of their roles in the plot. Yorubaland was plunged into total darkness because its touch bearer had been incapacitated and kept behind the bars.

Chief Obafemi Awolowo in the speech he made to the Western Leaders of Thought in Ibadan on May 1, 1967, he emphatically dealt into details the qualities of a good leader to his people when he said that: "The aim of a leader should be the welfare of the people whom he leads" and the welfare he referred to here incorporates the physical, mental and spiritual well-being of the people. It was also in this meeting that in his own words he made a statement that was later misconstrued by his detractors as he was labeled an engineer of secession of the West and Lagos from the Federation. All that he said concerning the issue of the East in his address at this meeting is as follows: "The Eastern Region must be encouraged to remain part of the Federation. If the Eastern Region is allowed by acts of omission or commission to secede from or opt out of Nigeria, then the Western Region and Lagos must also stay out of the Federation". He further advised the two Yoruba political areas that: The people of Western Nigeria and Lagos should participate in the ad hoc committee or any similar body only on the basis of absolute equality with other regions of the Federation.

Where is now the statement of secession from his personal views and observations on the events happening in the country by then that warranted the cries and hues, which prompt national attention on the pages of the news papers accusing chief Obafemi Awolowo as someone who was inciting the West and Lagos to opt out of the Federation? I believed that the above quoted statements credited to Chief Awolowo on the situation of national problems around this time actually helped Nigerians to forge ahead on matters that affected the existence of the nation rather than for people to persecute him again for his opinions. If precautionary steps were not taken based on this statement and West and Lagos were allowed to opt out of the Federation what then could have been left of the Federal Republic of Nigeria? His views obviously became a good meal for those at the head of the Federal government of this period to eat and relax for sometime so as to allow the meal to digest and run perfectly through their system. In the course of the official responsibilities of the opposition party in the Parliament, a criminal rope of Treasonable Felony was hove around the neck of the Leader of Opposition and some members of the Action Group party.

The trial was sensational and popular enough to arouse the congenital aptitude of the international communities and at the end of it all, those charged for trying to derail the process of the newborn baby state were clamped into jail terms of various years. The leading figure of the trumped plot, Chief Obafemi Awolowo got 10years for the part he was purported to have taken on the issue. Another of his trusted lieutenant Chief Anthony Enahoro was grabbed by the Federal authority, charged for fugitive offence and jailed for that offence. The Action Group party was shaken to its foundation while its structures were dismantled and the left over rubbles of it were grounded into sand dusts and blew it over to the Atlantic Ocean for a permanent rest at the bottom of the Ocean. The life that the party programmed to be more abundant for the Yoruba people turned soured overnight as the waters of the land began to dry up. Crisis set in and the people began to run from pillar to post in search for a new means of livelihood. But as a people of strong, courageous and resourceful mindset and the self-confidence they have in whatever they do and the type of people that will always remain undaunted to whatever situations that may come their ways plus their strong will of never to get afraid of their rivals and competitors, they managed to wriggle out themselves out of the programmed troubles that emanated from the domains of their detractors.

In a lecture delivered by Chief Obafemi Awolowo in his capacity as the leader of the Action Group and as well as the Leader of Opposition in the Federal Parliament to Nigerian students at Conway Hall, London, on 3rd September 1961 on the *Philosophy For Independent Nigeria*, he analyzed what a true independence means in its strictest terms when he said that: "Politically, the independence of a country can be viewed from two angles: the corporate and the individual angle. He reiterated further that a country is said to be free only when it has unqualified control over its internal affairs. On the other hand, a citizen of an independent country enjoys individual freedom when he is free to say and do what he likes, subject only to laws enacted by the freely elected Parliament or the popular Legislative Assembly of the land".

In this brilliantly delivered lecture, the leader touched on so many areas of our problems that was too difficult to comprehend about just only a year after independence but which surely came our ways some years later especially during the days of our troubles. In this lecture he philosophically mentioned that: "For a subject people, political freedom is not the end of our journey or struggle and that it is nothing more than a most potent means to the acquisition and consolidation of the economic and other facets of the country's freedom". Chief Awolowo went further to say that political freedom is meaningless unless it goes hand-in-hand with economic freedom and that if anyone cared to read his history aright, such a person will readily concur with him that the prime and sole motivation for imperialist predations, conquests, and rule is economic character, which was a testimony to the European's partitioning of Africa in the 20th century. They divided the territories of the weaker peoples to suit their economic sphere of influence. As a matter of fact, it was when it became obvious to them that economic control would become precarious unless they backed it up with political control that the later was considered and imposed. As such political freedom does not end a country's subjection because a country that does not have economic freedom, wears a heavy and depressing shackles, which are only visible to the discerning eyes according to Chief Awolowo.

Soonest, the crisis in the West began to escalate and it was becoming a fiery problem that the capacity of the nation could no longer be able to contain as it was rapidly moving from one dangerous stage to another. On January 15, 1966, the military staged the first coup d'etat and their action ended the regime of the First Republic. In this take over bid, Nigeria lost some of its illustrious sons that fought with all that they had to offer for the independence of the nation. The tragic loss included the followings:

(1) Sir Abubakar Tafawa Balewa – Prime Minister
(2) Alhaji Ahmadu Bello – Premier of the North

(3) Chief Samuel Ladoke Akintola – Premier of West

(4) Chief Festus Okotie-Eboh – Minister for Finance

(5) Oba C.D.Akran- Government Minister in the West

The devastating result of this action plunged the nation into the appearances of series of army governments that lasted us up till February 27, 1999 when Nigerians went into the poll again to elect a civilian president and two days later the former military ruler – General Olusegun Obasanjo was confirmed the winner of that election. The first Nigeria Coup of January 15, 1966 that brought Major-General Johnson Aguiyi Ironse an Igbo extraction, to power witnessed a brief and disastrous attempt for the nation to practice a unified form of government, with the abolition of Federal structure. The immediate reaction of Northern soldiers to Ironse's program confirmed that the North did not like such unified system as they saw it as an attempt for the Southerners to realize their domination agenda, which had been their fear for many years in the past. The young Northern soldiers swiftly went into action in a July, 1966 counter-coup that brought Lt. Col Yakubu Gowon to power and in which a fine Yoruba soldier and the military governor of the West Lt. Col. Adekunle Fajuyi lost his life along with that of his visiting boss the Head of government Major-General Agui Ironse.

Among the difficulties in Nigeria political structure was that of regional sentiment that had been staying with us since our days of national struggle for independence. After the attainment of independence, the same sentiment still continued to persist and even went with us throughout our long journey during the military administrations. In whatever national role that came our ways, this ugly sentiment would always rear its head above the national water level to debase such role no matter how helpful it might be. An example of this could be found in the premises of national head count (census) and revenue allocation. This two-in-one area falls into the category where wholesome illegalities such as inflated figures, falsification of results, manipulation of figures and grounds for electoral violence usually erupted and not until permanent solution is sought to address the issue, we may continue to experience bitter results from our national cohesiveness and every attempt we make to remain an indivisible unit would always be grounded.

Chapter –14–

An Overview of the Achievements
of the Great Western Region

Government of 1954 – 1962

It was at the First party address of Chief Obafemi Awolowo titled FREEDOM FOR ALL during the Action Group Conference held at Owo on 28th April 1951 that he unfolded the aims and objectives of his political party when he said that - It is our belief that the people of Western Nigeria in particular, and Nigeria in general would have life more abundant when they enjoy:

(1) Freedom from British Rule
(2) Freedom from Ignorance
(3) Freedom from Disease and
(4) Freedom from Want.

These four cardinal points of the Action Group Party in power in the West from 1954 – 1962 were genuinely attended to by the government of the Action Group party and to the expectations of the people of the Region. This government scored pass mark in the execution of the projects it lined up for development during its short period of time in office as it was clearly applauded for a job well done not only by the citizens of the Region but as well as people from the other two Regions of the Federation – East and North. The achievements of the government on Ignorance, disease and want were things of physical appearances on the ground and not an achievement on papers in the office files. How then was it possible that tremendous results were recorded for these various projects that were located at different areas of the Region? The answers are as simple as thus:

(1) The citizens of the Region recognized the importance of these projects to the development of their areas and improvement to their welfare.

(2) The people had implicit confidence in the leadership of their government and as such everyone rallied round the leaders to make sure that the success of those projects became possible.

(3) The government was open to the people it was ruling as there could hardly be an area for shoddy games as it is being practiced today where the government will be turning right and at the same time telling the people that it is now walking on the far-left.

(4) Accountability was the order of the day during this period.

(5) The dividend of democracy was being realized through pressures from the opposition party in the House.

Obafemi Awolowo

By the time the Action Group was born in 1951, the British had indirectly or directly ruled the country for close to 100 years and during these long years the people were wallowing in abject poverty, lack of want and afflicted with all sorts of killer diseases. Whereas the people from their home base in England were living in affluence, enjoying good health and developing their environment at the expense of the resources and people from their colonies.

Based on this fact, Chief Awolowo confirmed in the {*Freedom For All*} paper that: "*An ignorant and poverty-stricken people are the easiest preys to political enslavement and economic exploitation. Diseases of all kinds follow in the wake of want and ignorance*". To remove all these man-made problems that easily found their homes in our society of the time, the leaders of Yoruba of this time set some basic principles to follow and gave guidelines on how they could go about those principles in the following order:

(1) The immediate termination of British Rule in every phase of our political life.

(2) The education of all children of school-going age, and the general enlightenment of all illiterate adults and all illiterate children above the school-going age.

(3) The provision of health and general welfare for all people

(4) The total abolition of want in our society by means of any economic polity, which is both expedient and effective.

It therefore became a duty for the members of the political party that attended this Conference and those at different locations of the Region to declare their irrevocable adherence to the principles enunciated above and to fashion out from the future papers that are to be submitted by Yoruba wise men and women on various subjects that would lift high the status of the Region and on how to implement the party's programs.

Initially the people could not believe how possible it would be that primary education would be made free for children of school age because they saw it as one of the cheapest propaganda that any government would ever offer to its people. As such tongues were wagging that Awolowo's free school program will be totally inferior to the British education system that was in operative during the colonial administration. When it started, people were reluctant to register their children for the program, but because that the government made it compulsory for every parent to register any child of school age under their guardianship or else who-so-ever refused to do so would be prosecuted, fined or go to jail contributed to the success of the program. It was through this strategy that the people knew, realized and felt that the government actually meant business and this was how the Universal Free Primary Education came to life in the West.

In the past during the colonial administration attendance of schools for children of school age in any family was by selection and at the discretion of the family head. Where the Head of the family was a polygamist with several wives, what he would do was to pick one child each from the children bore to him by each woman and send him/her to school while the rest will be denied of education, but when this program came on board the doors to schools were wide opened for every child to compete. This is the main reason why people from the West are still the leading educated people in the country up till today because education in the West is highly competitive among the families in Yorubaland. The implementation and execution of this program bit the imagination of everyone hands down as the people including the detractors of Action Group were taken by surprise when the wise men and women in the Region put every bit of the scheme together to make it become a whole.

This spectacular program and the other important ones that were made possible by the then Western Region government did not happened in vacuum but through the independent and free hands that the Oliver Lyttleton's Constitution of 1954 gave to each Region of the Federation regarding development. It was this Constitution that actually established a true Federation with a central government, including a Federal House of Representative, which was then responsible for the country's foreign relationship with other countries of the world, defense of the nation, the police, the trade and finance policy, major transportation systems such as the development of Railways and shipping industry, and communications. A large degree of autonomy was granted the Regions as they could now elect their own members to the Region's House of Assembly in each Region – East, North and West with legislative powers to make their laws and cater for the welfare of their people according to the weight of their economic resources.

The remnant of the imperial administrators left behind in the country including the governors of each Region only retained limited responsibilities to look after. The old Western Region stood at an advantage position among the three Regions that were made up of Nigeria around this time because of its geographical location through its nearness to the Sea and the Atlantic Ocean as well as its opportunity of early access to Western education. These advantages tremendously uplifted the economic position of the Region and placed it on the richest platform in the country. The other remaining Regions were not equal to the West in terms of development and economic advantages and we should not forget that this was the period when cocoa product took the lead from the palm-oil trade of the past. Eastern Region of the country was mainly recognized as the chief exporter of palm-oil products during the colonial days while the North was good at its exportation of groundnut and Tin mineral products. Undoubtedly the then North was larger in size and population than the two other Regions combined, but it was then the poorest and least educated Region in the Federation.

The West did not waste any bit of the advantages that came its ways to develop the Region into a piece of modern showcase and to the envy of every other states in the region of West coast of Africa. The philosophy of Chief Obafemi Awolowo as the leader of government and the party in power in his Region gave an impression that the party carefully mapped out its strategies before embarking on the process of implementations and executions of the agenda. One would imagine the level of argument on the debate about its people's welfare program at meetings of both the government and the party before they came open with the master plan for the general well-being of the citizens of the Region that every man needed a healthy body, which can be reared only on good food, adequate shelter, decent clothing, a reasonable measure of comfort and luxury, and a whole some environment. That he also needs a sound and cultivated mind, which is free to know and mediate upon the things of his choice. Above all he has natural, conventional and legal rights which must be protected and upheld, with impartiality and inflexible justice from the appropriate organs of the government and party by the society in which he lives.

In fulfillment of these obligations, the government of Western Region under the Action Group party strived to find a state of equilibrium to set the stage rolling for the future citizens of the Region that would carry the mantle of the lined up programs into the next level of our citizenry. It was obvious for the Yoruba wise men and women of this time to recognized the long time that we had waited on line for the development of our people and environment plus the indiscriminate exploitation of the foreigners and of every conceivable inducement that was being given to the foreign investors that came to exploit our natural resources by the past colonial administrators in every reckless manner. For this and other purposes, the West had to take the bull by the horn and showed the whole world that a new page had been opened in the West African history book.

The government swiftly went into action with so many development programs at hand of which the followings were noticed.

(1) The closed door of the education system that was only opened for the advantage of the privileged members of the community in the previous time is now flunk opened to all children of school-going age.

(2) The health program that was neglected and not given any meaningful attention in the past was immediately revitalized as modern hospitals, dispensaries, maternity homes and other facilities were being built and availability of drugs to both in and out patients in those facilities posed no problem at all.

(3) Health and sanitary education were provided through the initiatives of the State Health Department in each province, cities and towns throughout the Region.

(4) The roads connecting one city or town to the other in the provinces were constructed to enhance the free flow of people and goods.

(5) Modern market stalls were being built under the Local Government Budgeting system and allocation to improve trade among women and men alike.

(6) The people of the Region were encouraged to develop the culture of planting economic trees like cocoa, kola-nuts, rubber, oranges and palm-trees to boost the Region's foreign earnings while the government itself embarked on the cultivation of large plantations of these economic trees at different locations of the Region. At the same time the Government physically went into commercial real estate business when it built the famous Cocoa House, the modern stadium complex, the Premier and Gangan Hotels all located at Ibadan, the Western House in Lagos, the Industrial Estate, Low-Cost-Housing program and many other projects at Ikeja, Government participation in industrial development such as wood industry in Sapele, Textile mills at Asaba and Ado-Ekiti, Boat yard building and Plywood industry at Epe, Iwopin Paper manufacturing industry plus the cultivation of pulp tree plantation that was to feed the mill- a project that was not allowed to take off the ground because of the political crisis of 1962 in the West, various other agricultural projects to boost both domestic and foreign trade earnings and many more were credited to the Action Group government of the West.

It is interesting to note here that the opponents of the Universal Free Primary Education program of the West who argued that the project was unrealizable even though it was desirable were the first to enjoy the benefits of the scheme. Chief Awolowo's welfare agenda was equally attacked and criticized that the program was a mid-way house, which at its best would serve no one including the people from the opposing camps and at worst offered itself for appropriation, distortion, and integration into an anti-people programme. But Chief Awolowo insisted that Universal Free Primary Education project was neither the invention of capitalist or socialist, that the scheme was a social objective which every country, whatever its governmental ideology or system, must pursue, as a matter of priority, if it must develop into an egalitarian and truly democratic society of contended and enlightened citizens. The Government of the West placed much emphasis on the structuring of the Local Government, which everyone regarded as a set of myths. Some of them correspond to reality quite closely while others do not, but all of these shaped Yoruba attitudes towards local political authority.

The Myth of Community:

The first myth was the community, which Plato envisioned in the fourth century, B.C as an ideal state of only 5000 citizens, but eight hundred years later, the Utopia's conception through St. Augustine described the perfection of the community not in universal or even national terms but as the city of God. The love of community therefore leads to a preference for government at a local level, because people tend to trust the authorities closest to them than the ones far away from them.

The Myth of Democracy:

The second myth is the democracy that the government of the West upheld in a high esteem. It believed that Local Government is more democratic, more easily controlled by the people than the government at Regional and National levels. Although these two arms of Government have their different roles to play in the lives of the citizens but the grass root concerns of the citizens would be taken care of at the Local Government level better off than at the Regional or National levels.

Myth of Efficiency:

The Action Group opposition party at the Federal Parliament advocating for decentralized power believed in the superior efficiency of the Local Government when dealing with the grass root people who during this time were mostly un-educated people. The party realized the bureaucratic tendencies of the central government that had always been the red tape with which it nearly choked itself. At the central level the bogus expenses on duplicated officers doing the job of one person and remuneration of two or more be paid for such services and where needless secretaries who have secretaries themselves turned the government of the West to invest seriously on the Local Government to avert this sort of inefficiency that it thought to be less flagrant in towns, cities or district council governments. Not that the Regional Government was not efficient but it had its areas of efficiency and areas of inefficiency. Certain functions are probably performed most efficiently at the national level, others by regions, while some by formal or informal organizations. The security of the nation, the control of national monetary system, diplomatic dealings with foreign countries, specialized medical treatments, centralized scientific research, consolidated schools are all instances of economies that could be realized through centralization. But efficiency depends largely on what the government of the then West did to divide the responsibilities of government across the spectrum of its areas of influence.

Myth of Honesty:

At the inception of the modern native government business in Nigeria by the Nigerians, one would expect the few politicians that were around this time to be fairly corrupt because the more successful they were, the more they were to be trusted. Corruption is therefore sometimes thought to be more common in the national government than in its home-town counterparts because the category of people running the national government around this time were the selected few from the society and the society we had then expected some sort of returns from them at their local levels in terms of foods and drinks, which was conspicuously prevailing by then. The judgment of history would support the idea that instances of dishonesty, e.g, bribery, the lavish use of national money for the pleasure of public officials, and kickbacks on government contracts would have occurred more often at local or Regional levels than at the national level, but the situation that prevailed around this time turned the table of dishonesty toward the national level.

An instance to support this sort of attitude was when the nation negotiated to secure a loan of some fairly huge amount of money then with a foreign country. When this loan was packaged at the borrower's country and on its way back into the country, the Federal government officials who traveled out for this purpose came back to report to the nation that on their way back home in the ship in which they were returning home, part of this money was dropped in the Atlantic Ocean. This kind of specialized knowledge that was very common among the members of the government of this period was one of the factors that made the army junta to take over and derailed the Federal Government of Sir Abubakar Tafawa Balewa in 1966. The situation of corruption in the country during the First Republic became a child's play to the new system of corruption that originated and perfected upon during the subsequent army led governments and even the civilian governments that we had after the 1966 coup de'tat. At International scene, the country is now classified as one of the leading countries of the world where corruption has eaten deeply into the fabrics of its national existence, but the fact still remain that for every public official who accepts bribes, there is always a private citizen who offered it.

The political language that was used to describe Chief Awolowo, his political ideology and those of his ardent followers usually put him on the wrong side of the scale. Some people saw him and described him as a socialist or communist but fallen to this school of thought actually labeled him very wrongly because of the limitations they had in the political philosophy of the world he lived. Political views are frequently described in the oversimplified terms of liberal vs. conservative, radical vs. reactionary or left Vs right wing. The group in my view that Chief Obafemi Awolowo belonged to is that of liberal vs. conservative. A liberalist is usually classified as someone who wants change, reform, or innovation, inspired through tolerance for a wide diversity of view points, including new and heretical ones. This was simply what fitted into Chief Awolowo's political ideology. From his time up to the present time we now call modern time of today, self-styled liberals like Chief Obafemi Awolowo usually favor not only freedom of expression for differing opinions from different opinion pools, but a strong, active government that often limits the economic freedom of businessmen in the interest of consumers and employees, and supports the government policies that was to improve the lots of the poor and the victims of oppression, which were his own kinsmen and women.

No wonder then that Chief Obafemi Awolowo in one of his international meetings he remarked that: *Before independence our economy was dominated by Britain and her fellow-members of the N.A.T.O and since independence, we have made no effort to relax this imperialist stranglehold on our economy. On the contrary, we now open the doors of our country wide open to indiscriminate foreign exploitation. Every conceivable inducement is being given to foreign investors of the Western Bloc to come to Nigeria to exploit our natural resources in whatever way they choose. The type of venture, its financial structure, and its location, are left entirely in the hands of the intending foreign investors. The assumption appears to be that foreign businessmen are so altruistic and philanthropic that their main concern would be to help the masses of Nigerian people, and not to enrich themselves at our own expense. In seeking foreign aid for our development, our government has allowed itself to be led into a blind alley by its Western masters and mentors.*

At the other end of the political spectrum of this era were the conservatives who wished to conserve and perpetuated the existing values and institutions left by the colonial administration. They were very skeptical of abstract logic or pure rationality, and preferred instead to depend upon experience and tradition on how things were being done in the past as a guide for future actions. Conservatives are generally known to rely upon individual initiative, private enterprise capitalism, state and local responsibility to solve social problems. Within these two opposing groups in Nigeria politics of the First Republic, Chief Obafemi Awolowo who was in the liberal group was bound to be giving all sorts of names by the politicians from the conservative group and their mentors from abroad. The politics of this time was very complex because the political scientists available as at then were few and scanty and the subject of politics itself was at its infancy in the country.

Careful analysis of political institutions and their legal foundations were too difficult to approach because the practitioners of the nation's politics only knew of one system, which was that of parliamentary system of government, and which was an inheritance from England. Any other system contrary to this would be viewed as reactionary system that was to derail the only one known and those advancing such views would be seriously castigated and labeled communist or a group wanting to destabilize the government. There was no attempt to develop a "value free" objective, which was to be morally neutral method of political analysis and assessment. But the trends today seem to depart away from the old and usher in new political developments that would still need to be thoroughly studied and assessed.

The primary intention of our first government in the West was to educate the citizens as it envisaged that "popular government is but a Prologue to a Farce or a Tragedy; or, perhaps both" according to the words of James Madison of America. James Madison referred to popular government as the government by consent, which was not in the views of the America's founding fathers, period; but informed consent, was what the American republic would need. The American political institutions were designed to take into account human depravity and self-interest as it could happen elsewhere in the globe, but as dynamic and as flexible as these institutions were, the founders believed that more was needed and as such their hope was to raise up men – to improve not just the material conditions of men but the men themselves. This was exactly the intention of Chief Obafemi Awolowo and his lieutenants when the idea of Universal Free Primary Education was being hatched in the incubator.

They wanted the people to be enlightened and virtuous enough to govern themselves and the only means by which the people could achieve this fit would only be through education. There were so many reasons for promoting education, which could be seen as general diffusion of knowledge. Number one is that it would create a natural aristocracy of genius and virtue. This may not necessarily be in the form of wealth, caste or privilege, because genius and virtue are not limited to any particular class, but both scattered randomly throughout the polity. Chief Awolowo's reform of education therefore reached out to all Yoruba citizens – the goal which was to separate the "best geniuses" from the rubbish annually. He stood by his words and put down his feet that all children, no matter what their background, were to be given an opportunity to rise to their potential.

By separating the "wheat from the chaff", Chief Obafemi Awolowo's aim was to elevate worthy persons to guard the sacred rights of our liberty, which became open to all of us today. Make no mistake, our founding fathers knew all too well the tendency of our Region to devolve into oligarchies or tyrannies in which premises we found ourselves during the crisis of 1962 and after, but they equally foresaw it that one day the people would have to rely on themselves to fend off tyranny. This government remained committed and undaunted and continued to build schools that would provide the "best security against crafty and dangerous encroachments on the liberty of our people". From much is desired, much attention is needed to study him properly. If we had had enough time to study Chief Obafemi Awolowo and his philosophical views, the better it would have been for us today, but the little he left for us through his writings and speeches are enough to illuminate our darkened path and ways until we shall be able to get to the highway of progress. For the attainment of his country's independence and total freedom of his people, Chief Obafemi Awolowo fully redeemed the pledge he made by becoming martyr to his course. His life was a sacrifice; his fortune was equally near so; and his sacred honor attended him to his grave; and remains behind him an untarnished legacy to his posterity and his country.

Chapter –15–

Nigerian's Years of Captivity in the Military Confinement – 1966 – 1999

The situations of both economic and politics in the country prior to 1966 military take over contributed immensely to the actions of the Barrack Boys, which later plunged the whole nation into total darkness during its day light period of almost three decades. During the first three years after independence, the government of the nation was being managed by the coalition of the two previously opposing political parties NPC and NCNC that maintained two different political ideologies, which in no way related to each other. The marriage between the two represented a marriage between a deaf husband and a dumb wife. One could anticipate or envisage the living conditions of the two under the same roof and the type of home they would try to build together.

The NPC on its part was a regionalist, Muslim and aristocratic while its partner the NCNC was nationalist, Christian and populist. Apart from the fact that both political parties went into an alliance for a purpose at the centre, the junior partner NCNC supported opponent political party of Mallam Aminu Kano – NEPU in the Regional elections in the Northern Nigeria, which was the home base of the NPC. The Action Group ideology which distant itself from the two in the Federal Government sailing boat could have been a perfect darling to NCNC because both of then had in some instances almost identical ideological programs and both of them from historical perspective began their races from the same point and with the same people of the same mind set. The move was actually made by some leaders of the Action Group but for some obvious reasons it held no attraction to the

NCNC because of the position sharing in the Federal structure from which NCNC anticipated something larger from NPC than what the AG would have offered it if they fused together.

The alliance between the NPC and the NCNC, the parties individually dominating each of the political game field of both the North and the East weakened the AG in the West and in no time its government collapsed because of the division created within the party that reflected cleavages within Yoruba house hold. What the adversaries did not know or realized was that as they were planning the collapse of the government of Action Group in the West so the loss of stability they created gradually began to undermine the political structure of the entire nation, which was under their care. Their political game was to turn away the affection of the people of the West from their progressive leaders and to return West back into the old brigade marshalling on the same spot and waiting on the imperialist commanders to tell them where to go.

But in a very quick return, their alienation program turned the battle against them when in 1966 they met with the strong and trained forces of the Barrack Boys that silenced and removed them from office. Although much damage was done to the already laid down programs of the Action Group government which resulted into bringing the West that was leading in terms of infra-structural development in the nation to the level where the two other brothers remained during and after the independence. Some of the progressive programs put in place by the government in the West were purposely put on hold when some were killed outright in the wombs of their mothers and their fetus discarded into trash bin by the foemen.

During the Action Group crisis in the West, its leadership which formed the official opposition in the Federal Parliament, split into divisions in 1962 as a result of the rift between the topmost leaders of the party and because of differences in the party ideology. From one school of thought it was held that Chief Obafemi Awolowo favored the adoption of *democratic socialism* as party policy, following the lead of Kwame Nkrumah's regime in Ghana. His deputy Chief Ladoke Akintola, from his own side and in reaction to his other leaders mind set attempted to retain the support of the conservative party supporters who had been disturbed by chief Awolowo's rhetoric. He therefore sort for ways where there could be more fascinating relationship with the NPC and to participate fully in the all party federal coalition that

212

would remove the Action Group entirely from opposition and deposited its leaders under the whims and caprices of the senior partner in the Federal Parliament.

While the rancor in the Action Group was stepping up its flight, the foemen fueling the engulfed fire did not give in their efforts in sending combustive materials into the furnace. The whole Western Region had now been engulfed and the leaders were hauling bricks at each other. The streets were no longer safe not only during the nights but as well as the day time too. The House of Oduduwa was attacked as fire was burning everywhere. Chief Awolowo's radical supporters demanded for the expulsion of Chief Akintola both from the party and the government. The governor of the Region by the powers conferred upon him demanded for chief Akintola's resignation as the Premier of the Region and when this demand was not forthcoming within the legal stipulated time, chief Akintola was fired and a successor in person of Alhaji Adegbenro from Egba constituency was named the new Premier and the head of the government of Western Region.

As a counter action, chief Akintola horridly organized a new political party, the United Peoples Party (UPP), which immediately pursued a policy of collaboration with the NPC/NCNC government in the Federal Parliament. In May 1962, chief Akintola resigned from his post as the Premier of the Region under the Action Group government, which later sparked bloody rioting in the Region and forced the effective government to an end as rival legislators introduced violence on the floor of the House of Assembly, which was the reminiscent of what was going on in the streets throughout the entire Region.

The Federal Government never waited for a moment before it declared a state of emergency, dissolved the Regional Legislature and named a Federal Administrator in person of Dr. Majekodunmi who was rumored to be the personal physician to the Prime Minister Sir Abubakar Tafawa Balewa to administer the Region. It was during this period that series of investigations ordered by the Federal Administrator into the activities of the Action Group government and its leaders came on board. Accusations of financial misappropriation and conspiracy to overthrow the seating Federal Government were levied against Chief Obafem Awolowo and his close aides. In the end of it all, Chief Awolowo was arrested and put on trial for treasonable felony case. The authorities alleged that more than 200 activists were to receive military training in Ghana and that tons of ammunition had been smuggled into the country in preparation for a coup d'etat. Obviously Chief Awolowo was found guilty, along with seventeen other prominent members of the Action Group, he was sent to ten years in prison while his other lieutenants got lesser years ranging from two to seven years. Chief Anthony Enahoro who was a trusted confidant of Chief Awolowo and who had been abroad at the time that the coup was to take place was extradited from Britain, tried for similar offence and convicted after being found guilty.

In the course of harnessing the program already laid down to destroy the progressive government of the West, the Federal Government lifted the state of emergency and brought back the dismissed Premier under a new political arrangement that succeeded Action Group government. The new party of Chief Akintola, the United People's Party (UPP) immediately went into coalition arrangement with the NCNC to form the government of the West. Under this new government of NCNC and UPP, chief Fani-Kayode from Ile-Ife constituency emerged as the Deputy Premier while Sir Odeleye Fadahunsi of the NCNC from Ilesha was appointed the Governor of the Region to replace His Royal Higness Oba Adesoji Aderemi, the Oni of Ife who was the first native Governor of West under the Action Group government. The Action Group successfully contested the legality of the action in courts, but a retroactive amendment to the Western Region's Constitution that had validated Chief Akintola's appointment was quickly enacted. The statement that the Prime Minister made to the Parliament on the situation in the West was that the legalities of the case "had been overtaken by events".

The issue of state creation had been on the ground even before the attainment of Independence but as mentioned earlier the past imperialist government did not want to border its head on such complicated and dangerous issue particularly when the height of its agitation was close towards the end of its regime in Nigeria. In 1960 and 1964 the riots in Tivland were related to the agitation of state creation out of the old Northern Region, a move sponsored by the United Middle Belt Congress led by late J.S. Tarka. Another plan was put forward by the Edo and Western Igbo to create the Mid-Western Region out of the then Western Region. The Ijaw and Efik-Ibiobio ethnic groups wanted the coast between the Niger Delta and Calabar to become a new Region in order to end Igbo domination of the area. It was only the Mid-Western Region that achieved the Federal Government blessing and approval despite strong opposition to this move from the Action Group. The creation of the Region was confirmed through plebiscite in 1963.

By the time when the Mid-West Region was carved out of the old Western Region both East and the North that was larger in size and population than the whole of East and Western Regions combined was left untouched. But the political game coming out of the newly created Region was becoming paramount to the political structure of the entire country. There was now the fear that the Igbo dominated NCNC would gain control of the Mid-Western legislature and thereby become more powerful and to derail this notion, a new political coalition between the leaders of the Action Group in the Region and the United People's Party nicknamed the Mid-West Democratic Front was formed to contest the Mid-Western Region elections with the NCNC. This alliance did not work according to plan because the United People's Party accepted moral and financial support from the NPC to wage war against its partner at the Federal level. This prompted many Action Group workers to withdraw their support from the MDF in protest to align themselves with the NCNC thereby given the party a landslide victory in the Mid-Western Regional elections of 1964.

Another important political factor that aroused the awareness of the people was the issue of census. Seats in the House of Representative were apportioned on the basis of population and as such it had enormous and important political implications. The Northern Region's political strength was drawn as a result of 1952 – 53 census, which gave 54% of the country's population to the North and in 1962 a nation-wide campaign was put in place to address the significance of the forthcoming census. The issue of census addressed two national problems: Number one was the connection it has to the Parliamentary Representation in the House and the second one was the role it played in the Federal Revenue allocation to Regions.

It was therefore a powerful tool at the national level. Because of its importance, every effort towards its success was marshaled out but yet there were flops here and there as many enumerators were accused of obtaining their figures from heads of families without physically seeing those who bore the names submitted and in instances where persons were counted more than once. The preliminary result of the 1962 census clearly gave majority population to the South but when a supplementary count was taken in the North, it turned up an additional 9 million persons reportedly missed during the first count. The fictitious figures emanated from falsification of collated results that were well pronounced to all sides and it led to the cancellation of the exercise while a new headcount was arranged by the government.

The results of 1963 census came out with the figure of 60.5mil, which census officials considered impossibly high and a scale down figure of 55.6mil for the entire nation, including 29.8mil in the Northern Region was finally submitted and approved by the Federal Government leaving legislative apportionment unchanged. The outcome of this result stirred a huge controversy among the coalition of parties in the Federal Government whereby some of the NCNC leaders publicly charged the Northern Region's Government with fraud, a claim that was later denied by both Alhaji Tafawa Balewa and Ahmadu Bello the Sardauna of Sokoto who was then the Premier of the Northern Region.

The political maneuvering at the centre which led to the convictions of two of the country's most dynamic politicians, Chiefs Obafemi Awolowo and Anthony Enahoro, severely weakened public confidence in both the political and judicial institutions of the country. Abuses from all quarters were widespread, intimidation of political opponents with threats of criminal allegations, manipulation of the Constitution and the courts, diversion of public funds to party and private use, rigging of elections, and corruption of public officials whose political patrons expected them to put party loyalty above their official responsibilities became an official and legal vices within the system. The detractors of the Action Group government in the West were able to dismantle its structures to rubbles as its members had now disappeared from the floor of the Federal Parliament, thereby altering the political alignments at the national level.

By early 1964, there was no longer and official opposition in the Federal Parliament. Chief Akintola's party now re-named after Albert Macaulay's first political party in Nigeria – the Nigerian National Democratic Party (NNDP) in an effort to attract more support from the House of Oduduwa with the strong backing of the Federal Government now forcefully dominated the Western Region. The political realignment of the country was very deceptive because the basic divisions in the country still remained unchanged. Indeed the alliance between the NPC and the NCNC which was now joined by Chief Akintola's NNDP that destroyed the Action Group now began to fall apart.

The 1964 – 65 General Election:

The 1964 – 65 general elections were the first of such since the attainment of independence in 1960 and it carried many logs of both dead and lively woods with it. The elections which were being regarded as the mother of all elections in the history of the Nation were contested by the two giant political alliances that brought together all the major political parties of the time. The first of such alliance was the Nigerian National Alliance (NNA), which was composed of the NPC, NNDP, and opposition parties representing ethnic minorities in the Mid-Western and Eastern Regions. The second one was the United Progressive Grand Alliance (UPGA) which was composed of the NCNC, the remnants of the AG, and the two minority parties in the North – the NEPU and UMBC. The NNA supported the platform that reflected the views of the Northern political elites and with the alliance it formed with the Yoruba NNDP, it thought that the control of the Federal Government would become an easy venture for it.

From the side of the opposing UPGA, the alliance based its success on the firm control of the two Regions which the senior partner in the alliance – NCNC had been controlling (East & Mid-West) and with the little seats it could capture from the West, Tivland and Kano to secure for it a controlling place in the Federal Government. The strategy of UPGA to win the election was the proposal that it would create more states that would go along the ethnicity lines. It intended to undermine the existing Regional political power base after a reasonable number of states would have been created from the existing Regions so that none of the major ethnic groups – the Hausa, Yoruba and Igbo would ever dominate the Regions anymore.

UPGA was convinced of winning the elections on the condition that it was going to be conducted under free and fair atmosphere and without the interference of the ruling NPC party in the North and NNDP in the West. The alliance was all the while hammering on the intentions of the NNA to rig the elections in those two Regional areas. Because of discrepancies between the number of names on the voting lists and on census returns, the election was postponed for several weeks. Yet UPGA never relent its concerns and outcry about the rigging of the elections by the NNA. When the alliance was not satisfied with the Federal Government arrangements on the election programs, it called its supporters to boycott the elections.

The call for boycotting the elections was effective in the

Eastern Region where polling booths were not opened in fifty-one constituencies that had more than one candidate running for office. In other constituencies in the Region, UPGA candidates were returned unopposed. The results of the elections indicated nationwide that it was only 4 million voters that cast their ballots out of the 15 million eligible voters. The NNA got 198 members elected out from which 162 members were for the NPC from the 261 constituencies returning results. After much delay, the President Dr. Nnamdi Azikiwe agreed to ask Sir Tafawa Balewa to form the government with NNA majority.

The boycott never stopped the elections and in March 1965, supplementary elections were held in those areas of the East and Lagos where UPGA supporters honored the boycott. UPGA candidates were elected in all those constituencies, now bringing the NCNC dominated coalition a total of 108 seats in the Parliament and UPGA now became the official opposition group in the House of Representatives. After the defeat, UPGA was preparing for the Western Region elections slated for November 1965 with the hope of wining the elections, which would make the coalition to control the three Southern Regional governments plus Lagos which had been regarded as Federal territory. Though the control of the three Southern Regions may not preclude the NNA from controlling the Federal Government but would have given the predominantly Southern UPGA a majority in the Senate, whose members were chosen by the Regional legislatures. But again the plans of UPGA was defeated through allegations of mass rigging and voting irregularities by NNDP, heavily supported by its NPC ally when it scored an impressive victory in the elections.

The results of the elections stirred extensive protests among the people of the West, including considerable grumbling among the senior army officers, at the apparent perversion of the democratic process. Within six months after the elections, consistent killings and burning of people and properties claimed more than 2000 lives and hundred of houses throughout the Region. In the face of these disorders, the beleaguered Prime Minister instead of finding solutions to the problems of the West, he delegated extra-ordinary powers to the Regional government to decisively deal with the problem all on their own ways. Around this time, the official relationship between the President and the Prime Minister had gone to its lowest ebb as they were now hardly in speaking terms. Suggestions were moving underground that Nigeria armed forces should be invited to restore order so as to stop the killings and destruction of properties in Western Region.

On January 15, 1966, the army responded and took over the Federal Government in a well coordinated military action. The planners most of them who were Igbo officers assassinated the Prime Minister Alhaji Tafawa Balewa in Lagos, Alhaji Ahmadu Bello in Kaduna and Chief Samuel Ladoke Akintola in Ibadan including some of the Northern and Southern military officers, the Federal Minister of Finance – Chief Festus Okotie – Eboh and Oba C. D. Akran of Badagry who was then a Regional minister in Chief Akintola's government of NNDP in the West. The new Military Government pledged among other things the establishment of a strong and efficient government, which would stamp out corruption, to suppress violence and put in place a government that would commit itself to a progressive program that would eventually lead us to a new and clean elections that would choose leaders of strong and committed conscience for us instead of dictators and semi-illiterates that abounds everywhere in our legislative environments of the past.

Major Kaduna Nzegwu who was one of the leading members of the Coup d'etat was in Kaduna handling the affairs of the North while his other plotters were in Lagos and the West to deal with the Southern affairs. The Nigerian army's commander-in-chief, Major-General Johnson Aguiyi Ironsi was probably kept out of the mutiny but after the successful take over, he quickly intervened to restore order and discipline within the army. In the absence of the President – Dr. Nnamdi Azikiwe who was then undergoing medical treatment in London Hospital, Alhaji Balewa's crumbling cabinet resigned and full authority was vested in the hands of the military. General Ironsi took over as the Commander-in-chief and the Head of the military Government. His government suspended the Constitution, dissolved all legislative bodies, banned all political activities and parties and as an interim measure formed a Federal Military Government (FMG) that would prepare the country for a return to civilian rule. He appointed military governors into each of the Regions and assigned military officers to ministerial positions with instructions to them to implement sweeping institutional reforms. General Ironsi's government came up with unitary form of government, which it thought would eliminate the intransigent regional politics that had been the stumbling block to economic development and the political progress of the nation.

The 1966 Coup d'etat was only popular among the young educated

Nigerians and did not within the high echelon of Nigeria leaders as it put stumbling blocks on their political path. In certain quarters, the Coup was perceived as a plot by the Igbo to dominate Nigeria and likewise many Muslims saw the Coup and the Military Decrees that followed as Christian inspired attempts to undermine the emirate government that had been in place in the North for many past years. Based on these assumptions the troops from the North who were of the Northern Region origin and whose numbers constituted the larger percentage of the Nigerian army infantry of this period became increasingly restive as they were not pleased with the killings of their leaders without any action taken to put on record against their killers either by way of prosecution or otherwise. Because of this the national wounds that the military promised to heal were being expanded and exposed to more dangerous dimensions.

In June 1966 through the abatement by the local officials in the North, people over there carried out a program against the Igbo residents, massacring several hundred of people and destroyed their properties. Many Northerners thought General Ironsi was all out to deprive them of power and to bring in an Igbo-dominated centralized state. This assertion was pure and simple to their perception of things around the time. To actualize a counter program, in July that year, the Northern officers from the army units in Lagos and in the West staged a successful counter-coup, during which General Ironsi, Colonel Adekunle Fajuyi the governor of the West and some other military officers were killed. The then Lt. Col. (now General) Yakubu Gowon from Anga tribe in the Middle Belt as a compromise candidate emerged as the Head of the Federal Government. On assuming power as he was then relatively a young officer enjoying the support of his army colleagues and the chieftains from his Region, he repealed General Ironsi's military decrees and reversed back the nation to federalism while his other important steps that followed this action was the release of Chiefs Awolowo and Enahoro from prisons to help him run the military government of his regime.

Nigerian Civil War:

For the period between 1966 and into 1967 the Federal Military Government (FMG) was pre-occupied with the program of convening a constituent assembly which would revise the Constitution that would usher in a new civilian rule in the country. Equally the tempo of violence had increased especially in the North where attacks on Igbo were renewed with unprecedented ferocity, engineered by the Muslim traditionalists with the connivance of the Northern leaders, which was the belief of Igbo people. The situation sharply divided the army along regional lines to the level whereby troops from the North were being accused of participating in the mayhem. More than a million Igbo people returned home from the North while many of them in thousands were killed. In retaliation some Northerners too were massacred in Port Harcourt and other Eastern cities, and a counter exodus of non-Igbo was underway to their different home bases.

The military governor of Eastern Region Col. Odumegwu Ojukwu was now under pressure from Igbo officers in the army and the civilian leaders to assert greater independence from the Federal Military Government and during this time Col. Ojukwu and his Regional government in the East refused to recognized Gowon's legitimacy as he was not the most senior army officer in the chain of command to take over the reigns of power at the Federal level. The public massacre of the Igbo people on the streets of the North plus the destruction of their properties gave Ojukwu's colleagues the conviction that it was no longer possible to remain within the Federal unit anymore. Amicable settlement was sort through leaders of thought in the country when military commanders and the state governors, including Lt. Col. Ojukwu himself met in Lagos to find solutions to the on-going strife, but all to a failure. In January 1967 the Ghanaian Military Government intervened and invited the Nigerian military leaders and senior police officials to a peace meeting at Aburi – Ghana. But by this time every secession program must have been completed underground by the government of Eastern Region leaving others to float in the air. In an attempt to hold Nigeria together, the military reached an accord which provided for a loose confederation of Regions.

Despite all efforts made to bring Lt. Col. Ojukwu and his Igbo cohort to table, his government in the East rejected all plans for reconciliation and he had to retain all Federal revenues collected in the Region to pay for the cost of resettling the Igbo refugees that were forcibly brought back home from the Northern cities. This was the reason he gave as to why he took such illegal decision. The relationship between Lagos and the East had now reached rupture point as all offers made by the Federal Military Government that met many of Col. Ojukwu's demands were brushed under the carpet. On May 26,

1967 the Eastern Region Consultative Assembly voted to secede from Nigeria. To counter this action, Gowon in Lagos proclaimed a state of emergency, unveiled the program for abolition of Regions and the re-division of the country into twelve states. This action was in cognizance to the agitations of the opposition parties when the going was good and that now the provision eventually broke up the Northern Region thereby undermined the possibility of continued Northern domination. The move was also a blessing and strategic program that won over the minorities and deprived the Igbo heartland of its control over the oil fields and access to the sea.

To win the support of the West General Gowon appointed Chief Obafemi Awolowo and other prominent civilians in the Yoruba community as commissioners, thus broadening his influence and political support. On May 30, 1967 Col. Ojukwu fired back at Lagos with the proclamation of the independent Republic of Biafra given such excuses that the action of his government was in line with the fact that the Nigerian government had failed to protect the lives and properties of the Easterners and its culpability in genocide and depicting secession as an action reluctantly taken after all efforts to protect the lives of Igbo citizens had failed. The rhetoric of the war may not be adequately addressed here because this book is not a place for full details of how the war was fought but just only to mention some important facts about the war.

Of interest here was the Biafran propaganda, which stressed the threat of genocide to the Igbo people that was highly effective at abroad in winning sympathy for the secessionist movement. The propaganda method of the Biafran students studying abroad during the war time over shadowed that of their Nigerian counterparts as it won for them food and medical supplies from some of the European countries. Humanitarian aid, as well as arms and munitions were skillfully organized to reach the embattled Region from international relief organizations and from private and religious groups in the United States and Western Europe by way of nighttime airlifts over the war zone. Those of us who were Nigerians studying at abroad during the war time were much hated and labeled genocide accomplices by some European citizens especially those from the Scandinavian countries.

Biafra's independence was recognized by Tanzania, Zambia, Garbon and the Ivory Coast, and was compromised by most of the African states. Britain gave diplomatic support and limited military assistance to the Federal Government while it was only the Soviet Union that became an important source of supply of military equipment for Nigeria. Although the modern Soviet- build war planes purchased by Nigeria were being flown by the Egyptian and British pilots, interdicted supply flights and inflicted heavy casualties during the raids on Biafran urban centers, but Britain as Nigeria's former colonial boss was expected to do more than it did for Nigeria during the civil war.

In October 1969, Col. Ojukwu appealed for United Nations mediation for a cease-fire as an interim agenda for peace negotiation. But the Federal Government immediately countered this action and insisted that the war must be won by the stronger side. Gowon from Lagos observed that rebel leaders through their proclamation had made it crystal clear that the war was a fight-to-finish war and no concession will ever satisfy them. In December 1969, the Federal forces divided Biafra into two and when Oweri fell on January 6 1970, Biafran resistance collapsed and Col. Ojukwu fled to the Ivory Coast leaving Phillip Effiong his chief of staff behind to hold the dilapidated fortress. Effiong called for an immediate and unconditional cease-fire on January 12, and submitted to the Federal Government authority at a ceremony in Lagos. The war that covered a period of thirty months to execute left a devastating memory for the Igbo people as the number of dead from hostilities, disease and starvation were put at between two and three million people. The Region was completely in ruins in terms of economy, food shortage, lack of medicine and medical supplies, clothing and housing. Cities in Igboland were seriously affected while schools, hospitals, utilities and transportation facilities were destroyed or badly inoperative.

It is important to mention that the genocide slogan that had fueled international sympathy for Biafra during the war was no where to be found by a team of international experts that the Federal Government invited after the surrender to look for evidence of such allegation. The observers testified that they found no evidence of genocide or systematic destruction of properties, although there was considerable evidence of famine and death as a result of the civil war. Immediately after the war the Federal Government made sure that no Igbo civilian was treated as defeated enemies and a program was put in place to reintegrate the Biafran rebels into Nigeria's main stream and family set-up. Tony Ukpabi Asika was immediately named the administrator of the new East Central State which comprised of all the Igbo heartland. The members of Asika's cabinet included members who had served under the secessionist regime. Although Asika was not popular among his people as he was seen as a traitor to the course of Igbo ambition, but in the three years that the state was under his direction, the state government achieved the rehabilitation of close to 70% of the industry that were incapacitated during the war. The Federal Government from its part granted funds to cover the states operating expenses while much of the war damage was repaired.

Nigerian's first term of imprisonment in the military jail house ended in August 1979 when the first election after military take-over in 1966 was held and the Federal Military Government headed by General Olusegun Obasanjo handed over power to a new civilian government under President Shehu Shagari on October 1, 1979. The politics of the second Republic was in every ramification the continuation of the First Republic whereby the National Party of Nigeria (NPN) for example inherited all the features of its former grand parent the Northern People's Congress (NPC). The only slight difference here was the significant support it now enjoyed from the Southern part of the country as against its national outlook during the First Republic when it did not cross the borders of its base in the North. The Unity Party of Nigeria (UPN) was equally the baby child of the Action Group, with Chief Obafemi Awolowo at its head. It enjoyed the same influence that was accorded the AG during the First Republic in the entire Yorubaland.

The Nigerian People's Party (NPP) was the successor of the former NCNC, which was predominantly an Igbo dominated party with Dr. Nnamdi Azikiwe as its flag bearer. The other new political organizations that emerged during the Second Republic were the parties formed by the notable Northern elements like Alhaji Ibrahim Waziri of Borno who was the leader of the Great Nigerian People's Party (GNPP) and the People's Redemption Party of Mallam Aminu Kano, which was a successor to his former Northern Elements Progressive Union (NEPU) of yester-years. Just the way NPC dominated the government of the First Republic so also its baby NPN dominated the Second Republic. NPN had 36 members out of the 95 members in the Senate; 165 of 443 in the House of Representatives and won control of seven states viz: Sokoto, Niger, Bauch, Benue, Cross River, Kwara and Rivers. The party lost the governorship race of Kaduna state where Alhaji Balarabe Musa of PRP emerged as the governor but it controlled the Kaduna legislature. In no time, Alhaji Balarabe Musa was not allowed to enjoy the mandate of the people before he was thrown out by way of impeachment.

Interestingly the politics of the Second Republic was not differ from the one played during the First Republic. The NPN lacked majority in either the Senate or the Lower House (House of Representatives). It was therefore became imperative for the party to look for a partner, which it easily found with its old ally (NCNC) now renamed NPP to form the new Federal Government. Though the alliance was shaky but it managed to forge ahead despite many odds and difficulties. The NPP won three states viz. Anambra, Imo, and Plateau; it had sixteen members in the Senate and Seventy-eight members in the House of Representatives making it easier for NPN and NPP to form a more comfortable coalition to run the Federal Government. There was a great conflict of interest between the two parties, which make the senior partner the NPN to do it alone in most situations.

The UPN which scored the second largest number of seats went back to its former status of the official opposition. The record showed that UPN took five states viz. Lagos, Oyo, Ogun, Ondo and Bendel. It had 28 Senate seats and 111 members in the House of Representatives. The GNPP won two states – Borno and Gongola, had eight Senate seats and forty-three members in the House while PRP, the most radical of all the parties won Kano and the governorship of Kaduna state, had seven Senate seats and forty-nine members in the House of Representatives. The joy of the Second Republic was short lived as the Barrack Boys struck again and returned to the government on December 31, 1983 in a surprised end of the year present to the whole nation. One of the major reasons they advanced was the fraudulent activities that pervaded the elections that saw Alhaji shagari back into office.

Although corruption and the state of the national economy were not put under check as both became concerns to an ordinary citizen. Corruption went so high that some of the government ministers were openly boasting to own private jets and high rises in the principal cities of the country while the citizens of the country were picking their breads crunches from either under the tables or from the gutters. The nations revenue and foreign reserves accrued during the oil boom were being wasted on unnecessary and unviable projects while hunger and famine filled everywhere in the land.

The leader of the Coup d'etat was Major General Muhammadu Buhari from Katsina, whose background and political loyalties associated him closely to the Muslim North. Before becoming the Head of the military government, he had been director of supply and services in the early 1970s, Military governor of Northeast state and Federal Commissioner for petroleum and mines (1976 – 78) during which time Nigeria oil was selling high at international market place. At the time of the coup, he was the Commander of the 3rd Armored Division in Jos. Buhari made an attempt to restore public accountability with the aim to reestablished lost dynamic economy without tampering with the basic power structure of the country.

Reappearing back on the political stage of the country, the army had no specific national agenda other than the issue of corruption, which the army itself had been its baron and election malpractices that became obvious during the last victory of NPN power house. The army thought that hence the civilians could not control the situation, it would be better for them to come back and put a check on the national malady. For Buhari's government to forge ahead with a meaningful agenda it had to continue with most of the political and economic programs of its predecessor in office – the NPN. His government set up tribunals to curb corruption and many scandals were made open to the public. Once again in the life of the nation, civil service was cleansed but not on the purge scale of Muritala/Obasanjo's regime of 1975 when civil servants were indiscriminately purged leaving the civil service almost empty. Buhari/Idiagbon's regime in an attempt to mobilize the country, it lunched a program called War Against Indiscipline (WAI) in which General Tunde Idiagbon was the pillar behind the program. This national campaign preached work ethics, emphasized patriotism, decried corruption and promoted environmental sanitation. The program actually created national awareness in the minds of the citizens especially in its area of sanitation and orderliness in the public places.

This military type of program was actually meant to reform the dead ideas in the life style of the nation and like all other previous reforms introduced in the past, it could only achieved a little because unemployment became the number one enemy of the program's work ethic. The issue of recession floated-in to worsen the intended Nigerian Nationalism slogan it carried along with it. The campaign was enforced haphazardly as some people were executed for their role in the nation's disgraceful compartment while some were given long term jail in prison houses. Those that were let loose from the hook of the regime were those that were well connected to the strong stubs of the big trees in the government circle.

The regime was stifle to criticism as journalists became the object of harassment everywhere they go. The National Security Organization (NSO) whose at its head was Rafindadi during this regime became the principal instrument of repression in which the whole country ever experienced the greatest harassment and insecurity of a secret police force for the first time. Buhari's biggest problem was the National debt. His government went into negotiation with the International Monetary Fund (IMF) to reschedule our debt but for some obvious reasons known to those at the negotiation table, the move failed. The escalation of national debt, the scarcity of goods in the market places, which created economic crisis, the government campaign against corruption and civilian criticism of the military actions on the streets undermined Buhari's position, and in August 1985 a group of army officers under General Ibrahim Babangida seized power and derailed Buhari/Idiagbon,s regime.

General Ibrahim Babangida was of Gwari origin from Niger state and served as a member of the Supreme Military Councils of Muritala, Obasanjo and Buhari's regime and was said to have been involved in the 1975 and 1984 coups. When he took over the government he changed the format of the military government when he appointed Lieutenant General Domkat Bali as the chairman of the Joint Chiefs of Staff and constituted the Armed Forces Ruling Council that replaced the Supreme Military Council of previous military regimes before he came in. He appointed some radicals and technocrats as ministers of his government and made Chief Olu Falae, a seasoned top civil servant and respected technocrat as the Secretary to the Military Government and who later become the country's minister of finance around the same time that Prime Minister John Major of Britain was also the minister of finance of his country.

General Babangida himself assumed the title of President of the country, which he justified under the nations Constitution. His first assignment in office was to assuage the unrest in the country by resolving the excesses of Buhari/Idiagbon's regime. In this direction, he abolished the NSO and its duties were reassigned to less threatening bodies. The press became a little bit freer but with pockets of occasional harassments by the government security agencies. Trials of former politicians were ended and many of the convicted officials for corruption practices were released from jail. Past politicians who had been convicted for criminal offences were under a decree banned from political participation. In December 1985, an attempt was made to remove Babangida's government through coup d'etat organized by some army officers with the joint participation of some down-town civilians but this attempt failed through the quick intervention of his supporters from the army units from Ibadan garrison and other army locations around Lagos.

Dodan Barrack which was then the seat of the Federal Military Government located in Lagos Island witnessed fierce fighting between the rebels and government security agents. University and Polytechnic student's unrest dominated part of Babangida's regime through demonstrations coming from those campuses especially from Ahmadu Bello and Kaduna Polytechnic campuses. During the unrest period, the student movement gained considerable support from the Nigerian Labor Congress and the University Teacher's Union, which organized solidarity national day of sympathy that led to the arrest of many union leaders. As the controversy was dying down, the Nigeria's entry into the Organization of the Islamic Conference, an International body of Muslim States, which Buhari's regime had made the application in 1986, surfaced as Babangida and Idiagbon both whom are Muslims attempted to seek for its approval. The resentment of many Christians led by their association – the Christian Association of Nigeria proved to be a great embarrassment to Babangida's regime.

The worsening recession prompted the regime in 1986 to put in place the Structural Adjustment Program which, Chief Olu Falae was its architect and planner and in the same year, 44% of export earnings were being used to service our foreign debts. Public opinion strongly went against loan from the IMF which was one of the avenues then opened to the nation to move on its economic vehicle that its tires had been deflated. The government from its part committed itself to many of the IMF conditions for loan including more austere measures and with all the stringent economic measures introduced, it made sure that it resisted pressures to reduce the petroleum subsidy so as to allow trade liberalization, and to devalue the Naira. On October 1, 1986, the government declared a National Economic Emergency program which lasted through to early 1988.

During this period, the government de-emphasized large-scale agricultural projects, introduced cut in the wages and salaries of the armed forces, public and private-sector employees and restricted importation of goods and services. It placed 30% surcharge on all imports, which clearly encouraged foreign investors into the country and promoted privatization. Finally, the petroleum subsidy was cut back and all efforts to reschedule the foreign debt without IMF loan failed and the whole situation became worsened by drop in the world oil price. The World Bank had to step in to provide U.S. $4.2billion over three years to support the Structural Adjustment Program. The Nigeria's eligible debt was rescheduled in early 1988 and there was heavy devaluation of the Naira in 1986 followed further devaluation in 1989 and 1990. As a result of the recession, the real income for urban dwellers dropped, while unemployment soared to higher height. In the half of 1980s, the per capita income in the country had falling below US $300 in 1988.

Babangida's program to return the nation to civilian rule was organized through a new body called Political Bureau which he inaugurated in January 1986 to make recommendations on the best ways to approach the issue. The Bureau, which was composed of academics and civil servants, recommended the following progressive ideas to the government in its report:

(1) The body was decidedly at odds with the Structural Adjustment Program and recommended its drop.

(2) It advocated for a strong state presence in the economy and wanted the military regime to completely move-off from the political scene of the country.

(3) It favored the creation of a two-party political system like what is being practiced in either Britain or America, which would be broadly social democratic in ideology, as a means of moving away from the ethnic-based political parties of the past.

Babangida's regime did not like many of the recommendations of the Bureau, but his introduction of two-party system for the country was seen as best of his entire eight years in office and in 1987 a Constitutional Review Committee was inaugurated to review the Constitution for a new take-off.

Some of the noticeable characters of Babangida are that he was deft and tactical and because of his tactful attitude he was nicknamed "*MARADONA*" by his subjects – a name of a world class footballer and a dribbler from Argentina in South American continent. As he was releasing some of the politicians incarcerated by Buhari's regime from the right, he was using his left hand to hound opposition interest groups especially those from the labor and student groups through his infamous

Decree No. 2 that remained in force in 1990 to facilitate oppressive acts. In 1986, he dropped his No. 2 man in his administration, Commodore Ebitu Ukiwe in a surprised manner that astonished the whole nation and appointed in his place Rear Admiral Augustus Aikhomu who was formerly his Chief of Naval Staff. In the same manner he reassigned General Domkat Bali his regime's powerful Minister of Defense and Chairman of the Joint Chiefs of Staff and other ministers at his own will and discretion. Because of the early retirement of senior army officers at the prime of their professional ages, the political landscape of the country was altered as most of them particularly the baby generals who had in the past tasted and enjoyed power as state governors, federal ministers and chairmen of government parastatals are now left with nothing other than to play leading roles in the political and economical fields of the country. This is why the presence of many of them could be seen today at every bus stop of our political landscape.

It was placed on record that it was during Babangida's regime in Nigeria that the promotion and retirement of army generals surpassed any other countries of the world. Major reasons for his actions were connected to political imperatives that led to pensioning off potential opponents or officers of questionable loyalty. Over forty senior officers of the armed forces were either retired or dismissed after Babangida's coup, and about thirty-eight army officers were retired in the wake of the foiled coup attempt of December 1985. By 1989 large number of generals, some of them who were in their forties were retired with full benefits including their pay and allowances for life. Regrettably, the military since the mid 1970s had produced more millionaires in the country because of the close ties that the civilians had with the military regimes with the intention to perpetrate fraud through business of shoddy characters that eventually increased the tempo of corruption opportunities in the country.

What climaxed Babangida's regime in terms of national shamefulness was the annulment of the June 12 presidential election of 1993 in which the entire nation gave their legitimate mandate to Chief M.K.O. Abiola to rule them as their executive president. In the history of our country, this election was regarded as the freest and fairest election ever had but when it was annulled the end result produced a clog in the wheels of our progress. The action clearly distinguished the difference between the two professional bodies – politics and military that the past leaders tried to marry together. The whole world was astonished and swept off its feet when the real reason for the annulment was given by Rear Admiral Augustus Aikhomu the then second in command to General Babangida that chief M.K.O. Abiola who was presumed the winner of the election was not acceptable to the military in spite of the massive support that the Nigerian electorate gave him through their ballots.

As a result of the disrespectful action of the military to the whole nation, tension enveloped the land from the coastal cities in the South to the savanna land in the North. Peace was actually murdered and Babangida who was the man at the centre of the crisis thought that it was one of those calamities that would soon cool off after a while and its dusts would be swept into the Atlantic Ocean. But he miscalculated this time around. He tried to slate another presidential election for November 1993 but his plans were resisted from all sides including the military. When there was no escape route for him to bolt away from the crisis, he abdicated office in shame and hurriedly constituted an Interim National Government (ING) that was headed by Chief Earnest Shonekan an Egba man like Chief Abiola who was denied the mandate of the nation. Chief Shonekan was a former Chairman of the U.A.C. business conglomerate and a serious minded person. Under the hopscotch game arrangement between the military rulers of this period, Chief Shonekan was given the mandate to conduct another presidential election within three months. To ensure the physical continuation of the military in the affairs of the nation, General Babangida left General Sani Abacha who was his Chairman Joint Services Chiefs in service and was given the portfolio of Defense Minister in the Interim National Government of Chief Shonekan.

The whole situation became a scenario of when a thief is put in charge of the security of a city. It would only take God to safely protect such city at the end of it all. The period of the Interim Government was when some ambitious military officers led by General Sani Abacha and their civilian compradors saw Babangida's annulment as an opportunity for them to ascend power. In actual fact, they struck and succeeded in derailing the Interim National Government without much resistance and General Sani Abacha installed himself as the new Head of Government. He annulled all organs of the state, banned all political parties and dismantled the democratic structures that were put in place by his predecessors in office.

The regime of General Sani Abacha would go down into the memory lane of Nigerians as the worst anarchical government that their country would ever had. His regime made all efforts to suppress the activities of political opposition including that of the pro-democracy movement – the National Democratic Coalition (NADECO) and it enforced its rule through the arrest, imprisonment and execution of dissenters, censorship and the development of a police state. Amongst the notable people he detained during his regime included Chief M.K.O. Abiola who eventually died in the prison custody in July 1998; his former military boss and Head of state General Olusegun Obasanjo and an environmentalist, journalist and University Don Ken Saro-Wiwa whom he executed with eight other Ogoni activists from the Nigeria's oil rich region, those who objected to his government's oil lifting policies.

Also under the actions of his sharp sword was the former Deputy Head of State in General Obasanjo's administration and an army General Shehu Musa Yar'Adua whom he carted into prison yard on trump-up allegations and who later died in his jail house in 1997. His regime plunged Nigeria into both internal and international insistence on human rights reforms which seriously affected the progress of the nation through the impact of international sanctions, diplomatic isolation, United Nations condemnation and Nigeria's suspension from the Commonwealth organization. He was prone to public seclusion and whenever he decided to appear in the public, he would always surround himself with throng of soldiers of between 2000 and 3000 strong special Bodyguard unit being taken care of by the state to protect him alone. In 1998, the last year of his life and rule, Abacha appeared from his secluded fortress at Aso Rock to greet Pope Paul II when he was in Nigeria on a state visit. In the same year, he met and held talks with the Palestine Leader Yasser Arafat.

Abacha's regime deserved a little space in this book because of the national atrocities it committed against humanities and the entire nation by re-plunging it back into total darkness that was even worst than the era of slave trading in Africa in the twentieth century. His regime held on to the looting of the national treasury which was the order of the past military regimes that preceded his government. He in connivance with the members of his family was reported to have stolen the staggering amount of US \$4.3bn from the public covers during his four and a half years in office. This was the official amount reported by the Federal Government as money illegally transferred out of public account by General Sani Abacha in the following order:

(1) US.\$2.3bn directly siphoned from the national treasury

(2) US.$1bn from contracts awarded to front companies

(3) US.$1bn extorted from third party foreign contractors

He was alledged to have various foreign accounts stacked with millions of Dollars in banks in the United Kingdom, France, Lebanon and the United States. The Swiss authorities freeze US. $645ml in Bank accounts belonging to General Sani Abacha and his associates when investigations were conducted. There were also stories of vans delivering stacks of banknotes from the Central Bank of Nigeria to the homes of Abacha's family and friends especially in Kano. The extent of his venality was seen to have surpassed that of the more notorious African rulers, such as the late Mobutu Sese Seko of Congo. Transparency International in 2004 ranked Abacha as the fourth most corrupt leader in recent history.

Abacha's political intent was regarded by all as the gravest slap on the intelligence of the people of Nigeria when the five Nigeria's political parties formed to suit his purpose and aspirations in a kangaroo meeting at Abuja collectively endorsed him as their presidential candidate for the elections he slated to be held in November 1998. I will beg to repeat Professor Wole Shoyinka's question in the paper he delivered on "Towards a sustainable vision of Nigeria" on 17 April 1996 when he said that: *We are however, today, a subjugated people. And this is where the mystery lies. Who are these forces that hold ninety to a hundred million people under subjugation? Are they perhaps the inheritors of those imperial forces that succeeded in subduing bits and pieces of the space known as Nigeria?* Our respected Professor like all other authorities on Nigeria history agreed in this paper that there was a formal amalgamation of the country called Nigeria in 1914 by Sir Fredrick Lugard the then Governor-General of Nigeria and that this amalgamation itself was based less on any reality of conquest than on the habit of administration. If by an act of negotiated consent, the people agreed to stay together within the borders of the new artificial structure, the question of *conquest* must be ruled out completely and substituted in its place *"the nation entity"*, which made us to be seen and accorded the status of free people. It is through the struggles and agitations of the nation entity that made us immediately after the independence to repudiate the *Defense Pact* which had been imposed on us by the British government as a condition of independence, yet as a free people, we are today still under subjugation.

Further analysis of Professor Wole Shoyinka's paper kept on asking one and the same question of whom exactly that placed our people under subjugation? He tried to probe his brain further for an adequate answer when he suggested whether these people are perhaps surrogates or inheritors of the old colonial order; and if they are, then, we must be ready to re-tighten our belts as the labor we thought had been completed in 1960 has just begun. On another dimension, our professor searched for another answer when he was not pleased with the answer he thought was the correct one and again he pondered whether they are invaders from outer space and if actually they are, then we must evolve a space-age device and strategy that will dislodge them and send them spiraling back into the hole that spewed them. If under every brain racking we found out that none of the suggestions of Professor Wole Shoyinka fit into the correct answer to this naughty question, then he was right in the end by his own judgment that those who placed us under subjugation are none other than the members of our own nation entity that have to be recognized for what they are – the common felons and the thieves in the same shoes of General Sani Abacha and his cohorts in the military and the civilian sector of our society.

What they have done is to steal from the common resources entrusted to them, and convert it into an instrument of subjugation against the collective owners. It was under the act of this subjugation that General Sani Abacha intended to succeed himself in office without the legal process of democratic principles, and funny enough some elements of political comprador in the society saw nothing wrong in his move as he was unflinchingly supported by the leaders of the five political parties that endorsed his presidential candidacy. Unfortunately for him, he was unable to successfully hatch the eggs of his intention of becoming the first Nigeria military leader that will succeed himself in office when the cold hands of death grabbed him unnoticed on the morning of Monday June 8, 1998 amid different stories and speculations of taking over-dose of vigra while satisfying his sexual lust in the company of prostitutes. His remain was taken to his home city of Kano for interment while his regime ended abruptly.

The leaders of the five political parties that endorsed Abacha's presidential ambition for record purposes – the Grassroots Democratic Movement (GDM), National Centre Party of Nigeria (NCPN), Democratic Party of Nigeria (DPN), United Nigeria Congress Party (UNCP) and the Congress of National Consensus (CNC) were described by Archbishop Olubunmi Okogie of the Roman Catholic Church of Lagos as those who were stupid as they killed themselves by the death of

General Abacha in an interview he had with an American Radio station. The Secretary-General of Ohaneze Ndigbo an Eastern forum of elders immediately after the death of Abacha called for all transition agencies including NECON to be dissolved and reconstituted. The Joint Action Committee of Nigeria (JACON) comprising 52 pro-democracy groups, which was being coordinated by Lawyer Gani Fawehinmi (SAN) in a press release re-iterated the continuation of military in Nigerian political game field as nothing but a continuation of economic persecution and political repression and called on the nation not to take the new military leader- General Abubakar's address to the nation as serious promises as they were empty promises only. The organization reminded the nation that a fight for June 12 is a fight against military enslavement of our society.

Abacha's regime was succeeded by the regime of General Abdul-Salam Abubakar who arranged the elections that ushered in the civilian government of General Olusegun Obasanjo who came from Abeokuta in Ogun state of Yorubaland. He successfully ruled the country for two terms of four years each amid stories of none or poorly performance while in office. The surgery of his tenure in office is prone to further investigation by Nigerians who are the eligible examiners to rate and score his total governing period of close to eleven years as their Head of state under the military and as executive President under civilian rule before he finally retired to his farmland at Otta in Ogun state of Nigeria this year 2007. He finally stepped down from the castle of power at Aso Rock villa in Abuja where he had had the opportunity to live and work for an un-interrupted eight long years as the President of the nation. General Obasanjo, to many of his peers in Yorubaland is known to be a man of many characteristic traits. These qualities in him will one day be diagnosed into details by future Yoruba writers and psychologists. His personality qualities would as well call for an interesting topic to write about as they will be correctly dissected on the theater table of Yoruba House.

PART 4.
EPILOGUE:

Chapter –16–

Yoruba People and their Welfare.

The social security of the citizens of any nation or community includes among other things the elevation of his/her status from zero level to a recognizable height, the protection of his/her life and property, the development of his/her intellectual capability that would make him/her to be useful to the development of the immediate environment where he/she lives and to top it all for him/her to be able to recognize and respect the rules and regulations governing such an entity called his home base. Yoruba people are fortunate enough to have been endowed with the rich land that their *Olodumare* (Supreme God) has given to them as inheritance. They are lucky enough to have been given the most advanced wisdom any nation could possess. They are fortunate enough to accumulate the greatest wealth ever known to black Africa, the fullest measure of freedom ever enjoyed by any people anywhere through the command of their *Olodumare* (Supreme God) who never forsake them even when the Sea was so turbulent and rough for them. With all these blessings, we lost focus on the urgent need to transform all the virtues we have into a concrete form that would modernize our institutions that are put in place to elevate our standard of living as a people and improve upon our decaying environment. Today in Yorubaland, we face an urban crisis - a social crisis and at the same time a crisis of confidence in the capability of our governments to do their jobs.

By the rules of the inherited way of governance that was brought to our land by the imperialists and which represented one of the norms of their culture and alien to ours in all the Kingdoms along the coast of West Africa, the centralized power and responsibility given to Lagos by then and now still in practice at Abuja has produced a bureaucratic monstrosity, cumbersome to understand, unresponsive to the needs of the citizens and ineffective to operate even by the operators of the system itself. Most of the inherited legacies of the imperialists that have outlived their time or outgrown their purposes even in their home countries are still as new as they were at the first time they were entrenched into the government Bible called the General Order (GO) during the third quarter of the twentieth century. The legacy of social experiment we inherited that suits the condition of life in the 19th or early 20th centuries has now left us in limbo or total disarray as the programs of that legacy are completely obsolete and have outgrown their intended purposes.

People tend to forget things easily especially the executors of our government programs that the unprecedented growth and change in life status is continually straining our institutions, and often raised serious questions about whether all policies are still adequate to the times of the moment. It is therefore no accident that we often find increasing skepticism not only from our young people, but among all ranks of our citizenry everywhere in the land – about the continuing capacity of the government to be the one to resolve the challenges we face as a people. There is nowhere has the failure of government been more tragically apparent than in its efforts to help the poor and especially in its system of public welfare.

Tragically today in Yorubaland, the fertile land that the nature has blessed and endowed us with all the good things of life has been abandoned for jobs in the cities. Those jobs that are hard to get and which carries nothing but burdens of endless frustrations and the life-style that was full of uncertainty. People talk about how America is known to be the richest country in the world today but they have forgotten that there are some basic principles of life and the laws of nature that the American people and their government hold onto and respect. They so much cherish and adore the richness of the land that the nature has given to them. They believed that the greatest asset that the nature has ever bestowed on human beings is the provision of land.

Even those communities that have little land space still try as much as they could to manage the little they have to the best advantage of their citizens. Japan is one of such nations of the world with little land space but today the country is building one of the largest airports in the world on waters so as to preserve the little land they have to feed their people. The worst injustice a nation or community can do to hurt itself is when the spirit of hunger abides by the people as we see today in our communities everywhere we go. America is known to be great first and foremost because it is able to sufficiently and adequately feed its citizens. It believed that it is only when a person is properly fed that he/she will be able to think straight and right on all other social contributions to his/her community.

In the Yorubaland of middle to the end of 20th century every family in the land was able to adequately feed itself and yet still had enough to sell to take care of some other domestic commitments like paying for the tuition of their children and wards in the schools, building of houses, buying of clothes and bicycles for the mobility and prestigious position of the head of the family. Ninety percent or more of the houses still standing today in our land were the ones built around this time and they still command the prestige of the day and accommodate our modern generation of people. Though some of them lack some modern facilities like bathrooms and kitchens fitted with modern and sophisticated equipment such as gas pipe lines and electrical gargets, yet they still serve the main purpose for which they were constructed. There was a time in the life circle of our nation when the bulk of our foreign earnings came from the agricultural produce to sustain our economy and for the use to develop our immediate environment. It is obvious and challenging that the modern day people of Yoruba extraction may not have the courage and energy to till the land to produce agricultural products as the people of the 19th century and before. But what is it that has been happening to the national steel plant at Aja-okuta?

This industry with the modern technology that is supposed to come out of it and turn physical energy of the people into mechanical one with great dividend is yet to come out of the woods after more than three decades of its establishment. It is only through the expected technology from the industry that would lift up the spirit of our people and re-energize them to go back to the land to produce enough food to feed the people. If I may ask – How many heads of cattle is the nation breeding annually from Obudu cattle ranch? How many birds (chicken and turkey) do we raise annually from Ikorodu and Agege farm settlements? How many tons of fish do we catch annually from our waters and sea from Lagos creeks through to Okitipupa via Ijebu waterside and to Warri in the Niger Delta Region? Are the fishes in our territorial waters have fewer vitamins to those ones we import from the Scandinavian countries? How many metric tons of different fertilizer grades do we produce annually to enhance food production from our agro-allied industries located at strategic areas of the country?

People seeking for political positions during the campaign season would come out with great manifestoes prepared by their political parties to woo the intelligence of the masses. In these manifestoes, the section of "Poverty Alleviation" of the citizens in most of them will be highlighted or written in bold letters to draw the attention of its readers. Reading through this section, one would find sweet and encouraging promises that could even re-awaking the dead if it is possible on how their political parties would alleviate poverty among our people within their first 100 days in office. Unfortunately when they are voted into office, the money budgeted for the programs to re-channel the course of the poor people would be divided by those who promised Heaven and Earth just less than six months ago when they were appealing to the minds of the poor people to cast their vote for them. Our streets will be completely neglected at nights without street lights.

There will be no hygienic water to drink by the people. The hospitals will be left with no drugs and hospital supplies. Roads leading to the rural areas will be neglected un-cared for. Jobs will not be available to school leavers. Farmlands that are supposed to bring food to feed the people would be abandoned and everyone will be gallivanting about in the streets of the cities hoping for jobs that would never come their ways and their presence in the cities would increase the number of armed robbers that the country is breeding. The existing work force in our communities is poorly organized for the citizens to derive the fullest of its benefits. There is no meaningful link between the governments of the local level, state, the Federal and the local people at the grass root levels, those who these governments are supposed to alleviate their poverty problems. The needy itself do not know where to go to for any help to remove itself from the clutches of poverty. All these remarkable problems contributed immensely to the poor development of serious and accredited social welfare programs in our society.

The program of social welfare received its trade mark in America and Europe during the Great Depression of the 1930s when the Depression brought upon the people its hardest and untold hardship. It was during this time that the governments and other voluntary organizations like the churches came to the aid of the poor people among their citizens as the locust of the Depression affected all the fabrics of the human beings from both continents in particular and the world at large. Ever since then the American government has made it a point of duty to develop the program into a standard one that would continually benefiting the poor people of America irrespective of their color, creed and nationality. The development of people's skills became the task of the government and the people whereby the government provides the facilities to train the people for work, gave the incentive and opportunity to work, and make available enough reward and incentive to people who are physically able to work.

It is a fact that the government cannot provide all the needs of its citizens or absolutely alleviate poverty among the people because poverty is not only a state of income. It is also a state of mind, a state of health and a state of how well one lives and fed. A hungry man is always an angry man, and, an angry man would always end up his/her journey in the domain of disaster if care is not taken. No one is born to become an armed robber or 419 boys but it is the structural building of the society that trains them to become what they are. In our society today where gainful employment is hard to come by after leaving either the university or polytechnic where the minds of our younger generations are being trained for a particular profession that would enhance the development of the society, what type of mind that would develop in such young people after graduating from higher institutions and still roaming the unpaved streets of our cities from one state to another for five or more hopeless years? For someone who is trained as a civil engineer in the university or polytechnic and who for the better part of five good years he/she could not have a job that would actually train him/her on the profession that he/she has chosen, what is to become the state of mind of such young person?

We should not forget that the best place to always see a civil engineer is where standard roads are being constructed or in an office where roads are being designed but in our own case, you find most of our young engineers in the kiosks in front of their parents homes helping people to make internal and external calls on the only cellular phones he/she managed to get through the assistance of either one of his/her uncles living abroad. Are the young engineers of this generation not entitled to all the good livings of life that his/her age mates who have god-fathers in the government are enjoying?

Their counterparts in America for example always get employment immediately after graduation and begin to plan for their lives the way it should be. But our young graduates instead of staying back in the country to develop their communities and environments through the training they have received, their next intention is to find their ways to foreign countries to join their peers who are employed in the dirty and odd jobs from house/office cleaning to security guards or cab driving for survival. Where now is the benefit of the training that we have all contributed both morally and financially to provided for such young man or woman?

My sojourn in Europe, America and some other places of the world gave me an inside knowledge of how their system works. The ways the elderly people in London are being attended to by the government there are very similar to the ways you will find in Washington D.C. There could only be slight variations in the administration of the program because of the difference in situations of people and environment but the basics are almost the same. The basic hospital supplies and treatment one would find in Guy's Hospital in London is similar to what one will find at John Hopkins Hospital – the best hospital in the world in Baltimore Maryland in USA. Variation could be in size or research capabilities but the hospital basics are identical.

The job training opportunities provided by the local governments of Hackney of Lewsham councils in London to the inhabitants of those councils is about the same that one would expect from the local councils in Birmingham or Leeds. The standard of the elderly people's homes in the state of Maryland is what one gets in the state of Delaware. Why are the similarities in all the examples enumerated above? It is simple. Because the Federal government of America or the government of Great Britain set standards for every each arm of the governments under its jurisdictions to follow. In any of these countries, if a piece of land is earmarked for recreational facilities in any local area, no one dare interfere with the government's plan on such land. If a government developmental scheme is to come to an area, the opinion of the people from such area will be sort and their input and contributions on such scheme will be considered. At the end of the day the government's decision on such project will be unanimous and this is the true demonstration of democratic principles.

What of in a country where decisions are only made by the few elements in the government and dump them on the bodies of the citizens of such country? The result at the end of the day is either such projects are abandoned, neglected completely or be made to be more expensive than the original amount that was budgeted for it because of lack of the people's cooperation and support from the on-set. Uncompleted projects of such could be seen in the areas of housing, hospital complexes, school buildings and roads. Before I move on let me stop and ask these questions:

(1) Is it possible for every citizen of Yorubaland for example to obtain visa to go and live either in America or Britain?

(2) Are the good roads, un-interrupted flow of electricity, constant supply of clean water, clean hospital environment and adequate services, work ethics of the labor force, high standard of education, the good health programs for everyone, the efficiency of the transportation sector, the development of water ways to supplement road and train services, provision of holiday resorts, food surplus and others not mentioned that the citizens of America and Europe are enjoying, the design of the Angels from Heaven?

(3) Is there any difference in our schools and colleges curriculum and that of the schools/colleges in either Britain of USA? Or is the teaching of science subjects in our schools diver from the way they are being thought at abroad?

(4) Can our surgeon doctors tell us whether there is difference between the brain structure of a black man and a white man?

(5) If there is no difference, then what is wrong with us?

If the answers to the above questions are relatively positive, I implore us to continue asking God to physically send down to us from heaven the doctors, the engineers, the planners, the builders and the teachers to come down and help us to rebuild everything of ours but if the answers are negative, then something more than terrible and serious is happening to us not in the spiritual realm but physically and mentally.

It will be necessary for us to realign ourselves to the norms of the beliefs of others who are making progress on daily basis rather than sitting on the defense side of matters each time. No one will be able to convince me that someone with no means of living at all will live stupendously than his counterpart who works very hard. We should not forget that the white men came to Africa with the Bible in their left hands and guns in their right hands – using the two objects to colonize us. Not that they have departed from their original belief in God but they knew from the on-set that God has said it that He would no longer send MANNA from Heaven any more for people to eat but instead He commanded the soil to give to them what they desire to eat.

He also gave them the wisdom to produce energy to work on the land so that their physical labor will be reduced and they will have more years to enjoy the fruits of their labor in peace. For this purpose and for the production of their needs He mechanically constructed our brains with no prejudice or discrimination and stock in there billions of cells according to the scientists. What else do we have to ask from Him apart from thanking Him for the wonderful material He has given to us irrespective of our color, creed or nationality?

Unfortunately we re-configured the principles of God to suit our own inadequacies making God to look foolish but He cleverly departed Himself from us and leaves us to work with the model we designed for ourselves. If we had been following His principles and methods with the way we relate to Him in Africa through the Churches and Mosques that could be found in every corner of the continent, I do not think we should still be where we are today. It is high time we should wake up from our deep sleep to reincarnate or re-invent ourselves to the new look that the developed world is currently wearing. We do not need to go to half-way to Heaven to find solutions to our problems as the answers to them are here on the Earth living with us.

In 1969 precisely on the evening of 8th of August, President Richard Nixon addressed the American people on Domestic Programs. In the lengthy Presidential address, he reviewed the government past activities on social welfare of American citizens. What attracted me most in this address was the statement he made toward the end of his address when he said and I quote: *In my recent trip around the world, I visited countries in all stages of economic development; countries with different social systems, different economic systems and different political systems. In all of them, however, I found that one event had caught the imagination of the people and lifted their spirits almost beyond measure: the trip of Apollo 11 to the moon and back. The President re-iterated that on that historical day, when the astronauts set their foot on the moon, the spirit of Apollo truly swept through this world. It was a spirit of peace and brotherhood and adventure, a spirit that thrilled to the knowledge that man had dreamed impossible, dared the impossible and done the impossible.*

Before the journey of Apollo 11 to the moon, no one ever thought that there was a road leading to the moon. We all stay down here watching the beauty of the moon at night at a far-away distance into the sky without knowing that the planet moon also has many similarities with the Earth we live-in here. Though it has some geological variations and due to its age there is difference in the density of the rocks there. The atmospheric condition of the moon surface is quite different from the one we have here on the Earth and this is why it almost lost its gravity. As the exploration of the Moon continues into the future other important revelations as to the mineral contents in those rocks will astonish every one of us. The human journey to the moon had opened our eyes to many things that exist in the moon and under intensive scientific probe more are yet to come.

The spirit of Apollo had re-energized the efforts of the scientists who had almost abandoned their beliefs concerning the structures of the Moon planet, which had been established since the days of Aristotle and Galileo Galilei the great philosopher and scientist whose achievements include the first systematic studies of uniformly accelerated motion, improvements to the telescope and consequent astronomical observations. As all of us in the field of science would remember today that Galileo was named the "father of modern observational astronomy", "father of modern physics", and the "father of science" because of his championing the course of scientific revolution during his days. Galileo who was born in 1564 in Italy and grew up to become a world renowned mathematician, astronomer, physicist and philosopher was also a devout Roman Catholic of his time and yet he did not allowed his faith to deter his scientific discoveries as we of today practice in our society. We have allowed our faith to kill the scientific talents deposited in us by God Himself and this is why we only learn to know the theories and lack further investigations of those theories through adequate practice.

In 1610, Galileo published an account of his telescopic observations of the Moons of Jupiter, using this observation to argue in favor of the Sun-centered, Copernican theory of the universe against the dominant Earth- centered Ptolemaic and Aristotelian theories. In 1612, opposition arose to the Sun-centered solar system which Galileo supported. In 1614, from the pulpit of Santa Maria Novella, Father Tommaso Caccini denounced Galileo's opinions on the motion of the Earth, judging them dangerous and close to heresy. Galileo stood by his discoveries and began to defend them everywhere in the land. By 1624, Galileo had perfected a compound microscope, one copy of which he gave to Cardinal Zollern in May of that year to be presented to the Duke of Bavaria. Because of his beliefs in what he discovered about the solar system, in October 1632, he was ordered to appear before the Holy office in Rome.

Galileo was perhaps the first to clearly state that the laws of nature are mathematical. He remarked this in his book *The Assayer* that "Philosophy is written in this grand book that the laws of universe are mathematical. It is written in the languages of mathematics, and its characters are triangles, circles and other geometrical figures. On 25 August 1609, Galileo demonstrated his first telescope to Venetian lawmakers. His work on this device became an important instrument and a profitable sideline with the merchants who found it useful for their shipping businesses and trading ventures. Galileo was the first to report lunar (Moon) mountains and craters, whose existence he thought that came from the patterns of light and shadow on the Moon's surface and which is now confirmed as real by the astronauts of Apollo 11 and subsequent trips to the Moon by today's scientists.

Galileo's theoretical experimental works on motion of bodies, along with the largely independent works of other scientists, became precursor of the classical mechanics developed by Sir. Isaac Newton. In 1638, Galileo described and experimental method to measure the speed of light when he arranged two observers, each having lanterns equipped with shutters and both of them at some distance to each other. The first observer opens the shutter of his lamp, and the second, upon seeing the light, immediately opened the shutter of his own lantern. The time between the first observers's opening his shutter and seeing the light from the second observer's lamp indicates the time it takes light to travel back and forth between the two observers.

This experiment in physics is today called the "lamp of Galileo". While Galileo's application of mathematics to experimental physics was innovative, his mathematical methods were the standard ones of the days after him. In the area of technology, Galileo made a number of contributions. Between 1595 and 1598, he devised and improved a geometric and military compass suitable for use by the gunners and surveyors. In 1593, he constructed a thermometer, using the expansion and contraction of air in a bulb to move water in an attached tube. In 1609, Galileo was among the first to use a refracting telescope as an instrument to observe stars, planets or the moons.

The church controversy on Galileo's discoveries during his time was the judgment of the time. By 1616 the attacks on Galileo had reached a head, and he went to Rome to plead and persuaded the church authorities not to ban his ideas. But instead of reasoning with him, he was ordered not to "hold or defend" the idea that the Earth moves and the Sun stand still at the center but he defied this decree and continued to discuss his heliocentric hypothecy. In 1633, Galileo was ordered to stand trial on suspicion of heresy. The sentence passed on him included the followings:

(1) He was required to recant his heliocentric ideas: the idea that the Sun is stationary was condemned as "formally heretical".

(2) His proposition that the Sun is in the center of the world and immovable from its place is absurd, philosophically false and formally heretical; because it is expressly contrary to Holy Scriptures, and the converse as to the Sun not revolving around the Earth.

(3) He was ordered imprisoned but the sentence later commuted to house arrest.

(4) His defending Dialogue was banned while the publication of his works was forbidden; including any he might write in future.

Finally he was allowed to return to his villa at Arcetri near Florence, where he spent the remainder of his life under house arrest, going blind and dying from natural causes on January 8, 1642.

On 31 October 1992, Pope John Paul II publicly expressed regret for how the Galileo's affairs were handled, as a result of a study by the Pontifical Council for Culture. Galileo firmly believed that his scientific research was not against the doctrine of his faith as his ideas were confirmed in the Book of Scriptures. In Psalm 104: 5 it was written that: Who lay the foundation of the Earth, that it should not be moved for ever? Obviously according to the discovery of Galileo, Sun is one of the foundations of the Earth which can never be removed. If this theory stands, then, it is a fact that it is the Earth's rotation that gives the impression of the Sun in motion across the sky. His theoretical and practical scientific discoveries about the planet made it possible for Apollo 11 astronauts to make a safe trip to the Moon and come back safely unto the Earth thereby solving the mystery of thousands of years which we considered impossible.

The space given to Galileo Galilei in this book is an avenue to encourage and discover the millions of Galileos in our society which we have inadvertently killed or hospitalized the Galileo's spirits deposited in them by the same God we call upon everyday through our lack of understanding of this very God. To circumvent the true intentions of God about the world we live in through our greed, carelessness and other inherited virus diseases we continued to perfect upon from generation to generation, our inner minds and thoughts were displaced away from the right direction. Our self-centered intuition obviously became an inch-worm that deeply affected every fabric of our societal system.

The history of Social Services or Social Welfare in Europe or America started as a result of the government's gesture to come to the aid of the poor among its citizens during the Great Depression of the 1930s as earlier noted. In 1935, President Franklin D. Roosevelt established social security in America and inaugurated the modern day Federal Welfare Program with a modest small program called Aid to Dependent Children (ADC). Ever since then the social welfare program in America has grown to include lots of subsidiary programs under it. The following units have formed large departments in the Federal and State government administrations in the US:

(1) Child Care
(2) Child Support
(3) Disability Issues
(4) Energy Assistance
(5) Food and Nutrition
(6) Health
(7) Homelessness
(8) Housing
(9) Immigration
(10) Job Training
(11) Seniors Issue
(12) Social Security
(13) Insurance Welfare and other Developmentally & Physically challenged people. Same could be pointed to in many of the European countries too.

Since the beginning of the new European system of government in Africa in the 20th century, the countries in the continent be it small or large have not been serious about how to set up a program that would take care of its people the way it is done in other places of the world except for the time when the maiden governments of the black Africa were beginning to be formed. Those governments of the time included the government of Chief Obafemi Awolowo in the Western Region of Nigeria, the government of Kwame Nkrumah of Ghana and the government of Julius Nyerere of Tanzania. Because of the interest of their people at the top of their hearts the imperialists labeled them communist agents and for this alone their governments were destabilized or rooted out completely. Does it mean that the people running our governments are heartless or they intentionally choose to close their eyes onto the derailing conditions of their fellow citizens?

Whereas if one research into the continents of the world to know which one worships God most, I know Africa will top all the continents of the world. Where now is the effect of our 24 hours praying to Heaven without a minute break? Who is fooling who? Is it God that is fooling us or is it us that is fooling God? I strongly believe that a thief can steal from the whole world but the day he begins to steal from his own home is the day that he is totally finished. Equally a person can tell lies against the whole world but the day he begins to tell lies against himself or herself is the day he/she would begin an endless journey to destruction. Undoubtedly we are threading on the premises of this scenario.

The only remedy for us to hold on to is to retrace back our journey from the dungeon of destruction and make use of the brains of the Galileos in our community. We should retrieve them back home from the foreign lands where some of them are only trying to make two ends meet. We should have a concrete program for those at home presently working as telephone operators on the streets of our cities in an attempt to survive. We should restructure our educational institutions to accommodate serious learning with adequate tools for the teachers in terms of modern laboratories and libraries equipped with books rather than for the students to rely on the teacher's handouts to pass their examinations.

In all the three universities I have attended in my life time, there is none of them that students have to purchase handouts prepared by the professors for the subject he/she teaches. The university library is well equipped and stocked with relevant and adequate books of all courses in the curriculum of the university and also fitted with computer laboratories of the modern age. Why then should there be an exception to our own system whereby if a student refuses to buy handout of the course his/her teacher teaches, he/she would fail that subject at the end of the semester? Is the government aware of this practice?

Regarding our health system, I am sure that if there is a magnifying glass to mirror the number of people dying in most of our sub-standard hospitals because of lack of genuine drugs or the availability of fake and expired drugs on daily basis or those dying on our deathtrap roads or those whose legs and arms are hung onto their hospital bed poles as a result of accidents on motor cycles popularly called OKADA, which has now replaced the use of motor vehicles to transport our people from everywhere in the land, the numbers would be alarming and almost jump above the roof of the tallest building in the land. The Federal Government should take the bull by the horn to enumerate those citizens that are developmentally and physically challenged, those that would require job training, the unemployed and those that would be qualified for genuine welfare program. It is only when these numbers are well documented and ascertained that the government could begin to plan on how to alleviate their burdens or raise their poverty levels.

We should not forget that the world has passed the industrial age and whatever machine that any industry would need to make it function efficiently is now available in the world market place. No American, Japanese or a European motor manufacturer for example would be pleased to see any African country or company rearing its head above the waters in the motor manufacturing industry because African continent is one of the largest market place for their products. Honestly, they would not welcome any competitor from their market place because of the profits they realize from their products. To support this observation, a motor cycle manufacturing plant or its assembly plant should have been a priority project to the Japanese in Nigeria because the number of their motor cycle products in Nigeria alone not to mention across the West Africa Region are enormous – running into millions. But yet they prefer bringing them into the country through the usual system that had been in practice since many decades ago. One need to see the size of their motor plants in the US to evaluate the number of motor vehicles being rolled out annually from these plants and the huge amount of dollars that the plants pays into the covers of the US government treasury as taxes.

Chapter –17–
Where Do We Go From Here?

The future of a nation, community or people is highly unpredictable for certainty as it is to be left for the creator of Earth and Heaven to decide and organize. It is equally right to assume that the future of our very selves depends on our today's thorough planning for tomorrow. If our today's planning for tomorrow is halfway faulty by one reason or the other and it is destroyed either by our enemies or detractors through our inability to release ourselves from their hook and we as people carelessly play into their hands by joining them to destroy us more, then who is at fault? My own judgment would put every reproach or fault on us as a people having the highest magnitude of problems. In the preceding chapters, I mentioned somewhere there about certain modern developments that the Action Group government under the able leadership of leaders of excellence and those that actually wanted good things to happen to their people brought to them when that government was in power in the old Western Region. After the killing and the death of the Action Group and its progressive government, we have witnessed many governments that had come and gone. My question is this: which of them can we give a pass mark on our score board that had even tried to score up to 40% regarding the development of Yorubaland and its people? We read on daily basis on the pages of the news papers or on the internet concerning the eulogies that other people from other communities in Nigeria and West Africa writes about at the grave-yard of the progressive government of the old Western Region led by Chief Obafemi Awolowo each time we celebrate its memorial service. Every remark about that government was continually pointing to every "first things" of modern development that ever came to our great country through the gates of the region called the "old West".

Examples are the first Television station in the whole of black Africa, the first stadium with modern sporting facilities of international standard in Nigeria, the first industrially developed region in the nation, the first people to receive the Western education, the first people to organize its people into political units that fought tirelessly for the independence of all of us, the first people that laid down their bloods and surrendered their sweats and labor when the first rail road in the country was under construction and when the roads that opened up the interior of the land to European civilization and modern commerce were being constructed, the first people that volunteered their labor and expertise knowledge when one of the early Sea ports in West Africa was being constructed and the first people to represent the interest of all of us before the throne of judgment at the courts of the imperialists in foreign land.

Is it not true according to Yoruba proverb which says that – the children of the butcher man who killed and slaughtered the animal turned to be the ones eating the bones while the by-standers eats the flesh, is this not the case with us? The other day I read on the internet concerning the opinion of an Ibo writer who I believed by his age would probably have either being told or read about or researched into the structures of the old Western Region. This young writer must have gathered first class information about the progress made by the Action Group government during its days either through the physical presence of his parents during this time or from some elderly people from his community concerning the quality of that government. In his opinion he was relating to how Chief Olusegun Obasanjo whom he himself is of Yoruba extraction destroyed the more all the legacies left behind by his own people whom the entire nation held at high esteem for their wisdom and contributions to the building of our nation.

Today, we are lucky that television screens can be viewed at every home in the country but only on the condition that electricity supply from the national grid is available. For those who can afford generating set, I congratulate them that they may not be put in total darkness of what is happening in the country and the world. We thank God that Ibadan stadium structure is still standing on its original site at Oke-Ado area of the city. Though the waters in its swimming pool might go dry for some years as a result of shortage of water coming from Asejire water dam to fill the pool like similar story that happened to the national stadium in Surulere, Lagos in the 1980s for almost a decade, but we still give glory to Almighty God that our children can still point towards the direction and be proud of the great job that their grand parents did during their own time. The Cocoa House building at Ibadan, the Western House at the heart of Lagos and Ikeja Industrial complex in Lagos state capital, the Irele oil palm plantation, Oda-Akure cocoa plantation, Ore pulp tree plantation all now in Ondo state; the Agege dairy farm and Ikorodu, Osiele and Miroko Lisabi farm settlements in Ogun and Lagos states are still testimonies to the great work done by the government of the Action Group in the old west.

The boatyard manufacturing factory at Epe, the Lafia canning factory and the Nigeria Tobacco company both located at Ibadan and the construction of modern facilities such as solidly built roads of its' time like the one we had in the past between Idi-Ayunre and Ijebu-Ode, Ife/Ondo, Shagamu/Benin. Owo/Ikare and others; the supply of uninterrupted water supply to those cities that were located within the purview and capabilities of the government of the time, also still stands as testimonies to the good governance of the one time government of our community.

We are to remind ourselves that because of the envy and jealous of the then Western government, the Federal government of late Alhaji Tafawa Balewa cut back the Region's Federal allocation while the two other Region's pockets were filled with money. The then Federal government's action was a replica of what we had just witnessed during the last Federal government of Chief Olusegun Obasanjo toward Bola Tinubu's government of Lagos State. Do we call this marginalization of Yoruba people or what political term can we fashion out for this action? With the non-supportive attitude of the central government of that period, the Action Group government of Western Region proved to the whole nation that pen is actually mightier than sword when it proved beyond every reasonable doubt that it is within the brain compartment that wisdom resides. This government solicited for the use of the brains of Yoruba people to forge ahead with the government's programs and make things possible to develop the Region beyond everybody's expectations.

The Region came out in a surprise move to the astonishment of its paternal father – the Federal government and its two other brothers – the North and the East. How this was done bit everyone hands down because the handwriting of the Action Group government was clearly seen on the bill boards everywhere in the land. Its achievements from all sectors of development provoked and angered its detractors the more and in 1962 the power of its opponents subdued it and this government was floored on the carpet in the ring. This ended the life span of the Yoruba's first grandchild who only enjoyed very little from the benefits of the labor of its grand parents that stood firm on its feet against the imperialist's oppression during the colonial administrative days in Nigeria for the resonance of our freedom as human beings.

Economic Issue:
Comprehensive Energy Sources:

In all of the developed nations of the world I have visited including many countries in Europe, North America, some in Asia, South America and Australia, the backbone of their industrial development is the regular supply of energy which powers their economic vehicle. I cannot see how our nation can make its own impact on the world economy under the present state of our energy supply. We are virtually at the zero level of the scale when compared with what energy supply is in other places of the world. A nation that cannot adequately supply energy to the domestic needs of its citizens would always find it difficult to move on with the pace of industrial achievements going on throughout the world. This is why we still remain where we are today. The fact remains that the abundance of the materials required to make our energy industry grow to the level of other industrial nations of the world are right with us at home. We do not need to import them either from Japan, New York, Sydney or Wellington in New Zealand. The same old story of the bad elements in the ranks of our leadership who only found their ways into the government for the purpose of lining their pockets with public funds would continue to jeopardize the progress of our economic sector. Unless we find a way to wage a serious war against this attitude, we may remain like this forever.

It sometime beats me hollow each time I hear people saying that my country Nigeria is the "giant" of Africa. I always ask myself that giant in which form? What makes her giant? Is it the irregular supply of energy or the lack of adequate clean water supply to her citizens that makes it giant? Is it the high level of unemployment of the graduates from our universities or the high level of corruption at the high places or lack of adequate medical supplies and treatment or the promotion of foreign goods against home made domestic goods that qualifies it to be given such a wonderful title? It may be the lack of security to lives and properties or the gendarmerie we have instead of trained and responsible police officers that classified us for such promotion. Who cares about the security of our lives and properties in the night when we all go to bed? Is it not those who are interested in stuffing stolen Naira notes in empty cases of refrigerators or television boxes in the garages of their official quarters and those who would grow jeep vehicles bought with our monies in private farmlands that are put in charge of the nation's security? Every agricultural land in the world is meant for the growing of food produce such as corns, yams or millets but history has recorded it in Nigeria that some lands can grow jeep vehicles magically. Are these the things that made Nigeria giant?

As at of this moment thousands of young graduates from different universities and polytechnics having qualified in different professions that can move up our country to the level of "giant" are aimlessly roaming the streets without jobs, yet we are the giant of Africa. I believe a giant is suppose to be robust, huge, monstrous, and fearful, command respect and have enough to eat and not the type of giant they call us, the one that cannot stand erect on its two legs. If people are fooling us I think we should stop fooling ourselves and begin to deny it that we are no giant.

What is economic development of a nation when the citizens who are supposed to fly high the balloon of such economy have no places to work? Japan is a country of little land mass located at the far North-East of the globe. It never depended on the countries with massive land space for their domestic needs but instead it developed the brains of its people so as to make their own marks on the world economy. Frankly speaking, Japan is today a nation to reckon with as far as technology is concerned. In our country, its products ranges from motor cars to motor cycles, generating sets, computers, television sets, radio, domestic utensils and others. As clever as the Japanese are, they never thought it for a minute to establish their motor cycle assembly plant in Lagos, Aba or Kano but they prefer bringing in those motor cycles from Tokyo. Reason being that the Japanese government wanted to protect the home labor force of the manufacturing plant in Japan, which provided regular employment to their citizens back home.

If for example the Yamaha motor cycle assembly plant is located anywhere in Nigeria, this will seriously affect the home base factory because 99% of the work force of the assembly would be Nigerians or Africans. On the other side of the coin, half the same number of workers in Japan will be asked to go home without jobs. And not to cause commotion at their home base, which could destroy their national economy, the planners at Yamaha corporate office in Japan would prefer to grease the palms of our leaders in the government to discourage the establishment of such assembly plant knowing fully well that they would recoup from such investment with more profits through the hiking of the prices of their products coming to Nigeria the next season. It is as simple as that. Because of the little amount of dollar paid into the accounts of our leaders in Tokyo, Washington or London, our young graduates from the polytechnics and technical colleges who are to form the middle and upper class group of such plant are made to be roaming about the streets or doing those jobs that are not related to the profession they chose and trained for with the support of everyone of us.

The world scientists have so much advanced many energy supply technologies that are available at every market place throughout the world. What I think we need to do is to go to the market places with our money in our hands to shop for any technology that we can conveniently put into effective use in each location of the country. Honestly, we do not need any laborious and intensified laboratory research or experiment to try on which one would be perfect for us or serve our immediate purpose. Those who have experimented on these technologies and found them workable are also ready to sell their consultancy services along with the products we are buying from them. Energy supply area is our first bus stop to look into and where to train our younger generation for its development. It is only when we have stable energy supply that we can gradually be moving into other areas of economic developments.

Today, there are many sources of energy supply that can be tapped to industrialize either a community or a nation. The followings are the ones using the materials that are abundantly available in our land without any recourse to importing them from any foreign land.

(1) Hydraulic Energy
(2) Solar Energy
(3) Atomic Energy
(4) Oil and Coal Energy
(5) Wind Energy
(6) Thermal Energy of the Sea
(7) Tidal Energy of the Ocean

(8) Global Heat

(9) Geothermal Energy

Out of the above mentioned sources, from Yorubaland for example, we can be proud of the abundance of at least six areas that are sufficiently available to us through the gift of nature. We can choose and pick any of them depending on how we would like to address the issue of our energy needs, which would be necessary for us to use in removing the clog on the wheels of our development. In order of availability in quantity and quality as noted by the scientists, I will begin to explain (not in details) the significance of each source in today's economic development.

Hydraulic Energy.

The continent of Africa leads the whole world in hydraulic energy material with its reserves of thousands of billions of kilowatt-hours, which represented almost half of the total world resources. The total world reserves of hydraulic energy are estimated to be over 60 billion kilowatt-hours per year out of which 90% of the figure are located in the underdeveloped regions of the world. The developed areas of the world which included Europe and America have almost exhausted their hydraulic energy potentials. The Zaire River with its second largest volume of flow (30,000 to 60,000) cubic meters per second is by itself holding more than 700 billion kilowatt-hour, the Sanaga River in Cameroon, which has its source at 1400 meters altitude with a very high flow could deliver substantial energy that could take care of its surroundings which includes the Cameroon Region and part of the Eastern Region of Nigeria. Technically hydraulic resources is not comparable to Uranium ore, which when mined, it could be stolen from the source to any foreign country either through the carelessness of the border guards or by the corrupt practice of the people in the position of authority.

It was only during the early stages of the development of hydraulic energy that electricity from it could only be delivered to short distances. But now that the technology has improved tremendously, the engineers have accomplished greater advances in the long-haul delivery of electricity through the use of the direct current which altogether will force the reactance to disappear. All that is needed is to maintain alternating current at the source and then provide generators that would provide several tens of thousands of volts that would reverse the current making it ready for transmission in direct current. This method had been in practice since 1954 to carry current from Sweeden to the Island of Gotland at Baltic Sea at 200,000 direct-current volts through underwater cable. Electricity supply from hydraulic sources is about the cheapest in terms of raw material supply, which nature has been taken care of from time immemorial and would continue to supply it till eternity.

Solar Energy.

Energy from the sun is a natural gift of the nature which humans have been studying its tremendous use for more than a hundred years ago. It has been calculated that on an average, the sun sends to the Earth one quadrillion kilowatt-hours of energy everyday, a quantity that is comparable to the total sum of all the energy resources in oil, coal, uranium, tidal, global heat and natural gas. The scientists have proved that on each kilometer area on which the sun shines each day receives an energy equivalent to that of an ordinary atomic bomb.

If this result is something to go by, then every effort to probe its usage to the advantage of the people living on the Earth may not be a waste as it has now been proved worthy of the trial. The solar energy can be utilized in either direct or indirect form. The indirect form of its usage is what we see being used in today's commercial applications. All that it required is the solar cells made of semi conductors (silicon, germanium and other conductive metals). This solar energy system is a device in the form of a photovoltaic system, with a peak generating capacity of up to, but not more than two hundred kilowatts, used for the individual function of generating electricity.

The power sector of the country is always on the news everyday due to its inability to perform well to the satisfaction of its customers. Statistics shows that the country has about 6,380 MW of installed electric power generating capacity, consisting of three hydro-based stations and six thermal plants. Unfortunately as the giant of Africa, it is not more than 10% of the rural households and about 40% of Nigeria's population that have access to electricity in this 21st century. It was of recent that the Federal government announced its determination to electrify no fewer than 200 villages with solar power energy under its Master Plan Study for the utilization of solar energy source in Nigeria. We should not forget that this Master Plan program is a brain program of Japanese International Cooperation Agency after Japan had profited immensely from the sales of its generating sets, motorcycles and other household utensils sold annually in Nigeria to Nigerians.

If the Japanese can come all the way from the Far-East of the world to set up their economic superiority and capabilities in all the principal places of the world including Nigeria and now preparing Master Plan for us on how to utilize the energy coming from the Sun that is abundantly available in Africa without interruption, then something terrible is wrong with us. We need to check on our physiological settings to mark out where the element breeding stupidity and shameful ideas in our biological structures hid itself so that it may be removed once and for all. During the commissioning ceremony of a solar power project in Garko Alli, a village in Jigawa state, the Federal Minister of State for power and steel remarked that the Japanese effort in this sector of our development will speedily meet the electricity need of the rural dwellers.

The Minister has forgotten that the solar cells to catch energy from the Sun are to be manufactured from the products of the Japanese Iron and Steel industry – a counterpart of the same department he oversees under the Federal structure. The cells will not be coming to Nigeria free of charge or at any reduced price but with a price tag of the Japanese marketing evaluation. Before the end of the installation contract of the solar project, the Japanese company in-charge must have recouped every Yen invested on such project with profits. The maintenance contract for the rural plants will be another huge contract for another five years or so until Nigeria's technicians will be capable enough to handle the maintenance culture of those projects. It was mentioned under the contract between the Federal government and the Japanese donor agency that the equipment (the generators) to generate electricity in those stations will be on lease to Nigeria government for an undisclosed amount of X dollar for X number of years.

Recently, the Japanese government announced a grant of $30 million dollars to construct transformer sub-stations in Nigeria and Nassarawa, Borno, Benue and Gombe are listed as the beneficiaries of this project according to Narumuya the representative of the Japan International Cooperation Agency in his contributing speech at the commissioning ceremony in Garko Alli village. It is interesting to note that the Japanese is shifting part of its economic base from the cities to the rural areas of Nigeria. The shift would now allow them to consolidate more of their marketing efforts on the new models of generating sets that will soon be coming to Nigeria from Japan to fill the gap that the Federal government has failed to provide to the small local industries that are sparsely located in the large cities. The bigger the capacities of these generating sets are, the fatter the money to be paid on each of them. The Master Plan for solar energy generation in Nigeria that was the baby child of the Japanese business Guru needs to be thoroughly evaluated by our energy experts and advice the Federal government on its pros and cons before we run ourselves into another problem that will hold us down perpetually. Nigerians have the legal right to investigate and know the genesis of this project from the drawing board stages to the execution levels because they are the beneficiaries and furthermore the public fund will be committed toward this Father Christmas project.

Atomic Energy.

Early in the twentieth century, the scientists discovered that atoms of certain radioactive elements can split or fission, if bombarded with fast-moving neutrons. The by-product of this fission becomes two lighter atoms, free neutrons, and energy in the form of heat and light. Scientists then discovered that certain isotopes of the radioactive elements (i.e. variations of the same element with different numbers of neutrons in the nucleus), such as plutonium – 239 or uranium – 235 can emit two neutrons when they fission. These secondary neutrons produced will then collide with each other at nearby nuclei, causing them to fission and release two more neutrons. Each fission reaction will double the amount of neutrons and energy released thereby causing a chain reaction and giving off enormous heat. Similar fission process when controlled will generate the required energy in nuclear reactors to produce electricity for industrial development of a nation and for the production of military hardware such as nuclear weapon or "A – bomb" the type that the America dropped on Nagasaki, Japan, in 1945, which had an explosive yield equivalent to about 20 kilotons of TNT. As powerful as energy release from radioactive elements is, 2000 metric tons of uranium – 235 are the energy equivalent of all the world reserve of petroleum.

Today, there are many uranium deposits scattered all over the places in African continent with promising large quantities of the ore when mined. Before the imperialists granted independence to most of the African states before 1960 and yonder, the then Belgian Congo was the only region that supplied 50% of the world's uranium production. It is for certain that promising radioactive mineral deposits have now been found in Ethiopia, Cameroon, Nigeria, Zaire, Ghana, Uganda, Zambia, Mozambique and South Africa. But a sound of serious warning is necessary to be listening to. A good deal of vigilance must be exercised in the exploitation of these deposits. The major materials of nuclear energy in the rock bodies from these deposits are mainly uranium and thorium, which after extracted from the rock body, the important content can be put into any small container in form of a bottle to be taken out of the country where it is mined. The government of African countries where these deposits are located must take very serious precautions on how to protect those deposits against limitless mechanized mining activities of foreign companies working in the continent. A Nuclear Energy Commission for Africa is strongly recommended to take off the ground immediately for the continental protection of these deposits.

Tidal Energy of The Sea and Ocean.

Tidal power or energy is a form of hydropower that exploits the rise and fall in Sea levels due to the tides, or the movement of water caused by the tidal flow. Tidal power has potential for electricity generation as it is more predictable than wind energy and solar power. For over a thousand years, tidal mills have been in use in Europe mainly for grinding grains. It is therefore an energy that has an efficiency of over 80% in converting the potential energy of the water into electricity, which is more efficient compared to other energy resources such as solar power or fossil fuel power plants. It is a long-term source of electricity especially where there may be a decline in the production of fossil fuel materials. The economy of scale for tidal power scheme is that it has a high capital cost and a very low running cost. As a result of this a tidal power scheme may not produce returns for many years and this may scare-off investors to participate in such projects. It is presently left to the government to finance in the countries where they are in operation. The first tidal power station was the Rance Tidal Power Plant built over a period of six years from 1960 to 1966 at La Rance, in France and it has 240 MW installed capacity. Ever since then, countries such as China, United Kingdom, USA and South Africa have built small Tidal Plants to supplement their countries energy supply.

The scientists have indicated that because the tidal forces are caused by the interaction between the gravity of the Earth, Moon and Sun, tidal power is essentially inexhaustible and classified as a renewable energy resource. In fact, the ultimate energy source of tidal is the rotational energy of the Earth, which will not run out in the next 4 billion years while the Earth's Oceans may boil away in 2 billion years according to their predictions. Will it not be a good idea then if the governments in Yorubaland with the great potentials of the Sea and the Ocean at their disposal come together and exploit the ways they can jointly benefit from this technology that is now moving up the ladder in the countries mentioned earlier?

There are always great advantages waiting for the pioneers of this type of scheme because according to Aristotle "A man is not good at all, unless he takes pleasure in all noble ideas". Why then can't we join the world in exploring the universal technique coming out of this scheme especially when we shall be at the receiving end of its benefits? The source of its inspirational movement to mankind will soon become an explosive range in technology. If we should allow this kind of opportunity to elude us, what shall we then be saying when the Black Monday will eventually knock at our doors in Yorubaland at no distant time?

Wind Energy.

Wind energy is the conversion of the wind power into more useful forms of energy to human, such as electricity, using wind turbines. At the end of 2006, worldwide capacity of wind powered generators was 74,223 megawatts. For the moment it is currently producing just over 1% of world-wide electricity use, but accounts for approximately 20% of electricity use in Denmark, 9% in Spain and 7% in Germany. The technology here is simple. Most modern wind power is generated in the form of electricity by converting the rotation of turbine blades into electrical current by means of an electrical generator. Wind power is currently used in large scale wind farms for national electrical grids as well as in small individual turbines for providing electricity to rural areas or grid-isolated locations. The energy in the wind is plentiful, renewable, widely distributed, clean, and also reduces toxic atmospheric and greenhouse gas emissions when used to replace fossil-fuel-derived electricity. There is an estimated 50 – 100 times more wind energy than plant biomass energy available on Earth. Most of this wind energy can be found from any location with high altitudes and where continuous wind speeds over 160 km/h occur. Eventually, the energy from the wind is converted through friction into diffuse heat throughout the Earth's surface and the atmosphere.

Turbine Site Location:

As a general rule, wind generators are practically located where the average wind speed is 10mph (16km/h) or greater and a pre-selected on the basis of a wind atlas and validated with wind measurements. In this regard, meteorological department plays an important role in determining possible locations for wind parks. The general data of an area from meteorological chart is not usually sufficient for accurate sitting of a large wind power project but specific meteorological data of the intended site that would show constant flow of non-turbulent wind throughout the year and that would not suffer too many sudden powerful busts of wind. Collection of accurate and verifiable data information would therefore be an ideal thing to do before the commencement of such project.

To collect the informed data, a Meteorological Tower has to be installed at the potential site with instrumentations such as anemometers installed at various heights along the tower to determine the wind speed and wind vanes to show the direction of the wind. The taller the height of the Tower the better information is expected because the wind blows faster at higher altitudes as a result of the reduced influence of drag of the surface (Sea or land) and the reduced viscosity of the air. Local winds are often monitored for a year or more with anemometers and detailed wind maps constructed before wind generators are installed.

Throughout the land of Yoruba nation, the land height ranges from between 200 and 500metres above the sea level except along the coastal line where the land is less than 200metres. The temperature in this Region is uniquely fine throughout the year without any recourse to adversity. From the ridges of Olumo rock in Ogun state passing through Ibadan to Ilorin and branching over to Oke-Idanre, Akure, Ikere, Ado Ekiti in Ondo and Ekiti states continuing its journey to the North through Igbomina in Kwara state, don't we have enough place on these mountains and hills where wind farms or parks can be established to provide electricity for our own developments? Is it a matter of must that we should wait on the Federal Government to provide light to illuminate our streets at nights or power our home and business equipment for us when the Federal Government itself is still living in the dark ages when energy from the woods and light from palm oil were used to illuminate homes at night?

I am confident that two or three local governments in a state from Yoruba nation can pull their resources together with the brains of our young graduates from the universities and polytechnics to build a working wind farm which would provide the people of their local governments with the required electricity generation. With adequate supply of energy, people would no longer like to migrate from the rural areas where foods are to be provided to everyone including the city dwellers; the cities itself where people now roam its streets aimlessly to further increase its tensions will have peace to itself. Lagos and other principal cities of Yorubaland fall victim to this type of human drift from the rural areas. If one looks at the present horrible situations of Lagos, we should all agree that the city has now been turned into a city without lungs. It has been afflicted with Congestive Heart Failure (CHF) and if care in not taking, its heart will one day bust into pieces. We can all imagine what could happen to a person walking on the street without healthy lungs.

The data for wind turbine installation throughout the world indicated a total capacity of 73,904 MW out from which Europe accounts for 65% of the total sum (2006). The average output of one megawatt of wind power is equivalent to the average electricity consumption for about 250 American households. Presently the need of electricity current in a household in America is by far greater than that of a household in Yorubaland because in America, people so much depended on electricity to do almost everything possible in their households. Today, wind power was the most rapidly growing means of alternative electricity generation at the turn of the century. In 2005, record showed that both Germany and Spain have produced more electricity from wind than from hydropower plants. The US Department of Energy Studies have concluded that wind harvested in just three of the fifty states could provide enough electricity to power the entire nation, and that offshore wind farms could do the same job.

In recent years, the United States has added more wind energy to its grid than any other single country, and in this year (2007) the capacity is expected to grow by 3 Gig watts (3,000 Megawatts). India for example is now ranked 4th in the world with a total wind power capacity of 6,270 MW in 2006 and wind power generates 3% of all electricity produced in India. On August 15, 2005, China announced that it would build a 1000 – Megawatts of wind farm in Hebei to be completed in 2020 and also set a generating target of 20,000 MW by the same year from renewable energy sources. From between year 2000 and 2006, Canada built up rapid growth of wind capacity moving up the scale from a capacity of 137 MW to 1,451MW and showing a growth rate of 38% and still growing.

Small Scale Wind Power.

Small scale wind power is defined as wind generation systems with capacities of 100 kW or less, which are usually used to power homes, farms, and small businesses. This system I am sure if introduced would conveniently supply electricity to the rural areas and the outskirts of our cities where the national grid may be out of reach to the consumers. In urban areas, where it is difficult to obtain predictable or large amounts of wind energy due to buildings and other structures, smaller system may still be used to run low power equipment. Distributed power from rooftop mounted wind turbines can alleviate power distribution problems, as well as provide resilience to power failures. There are available in the market place some units that are designed to be light-weighted, e.g. 16 kilograms (35lbs), which allowed rapid response to wind gusts typical of urban settings and easy mounting much like a television antenna. Wind power consumes no fuel for continuing operations, and has no emissions that were directly related to electricity production but as do other power production facilities; it consumes resources in manufacturing and construction. Wind power is a clean energy source as its operation does not produce carbon dioxide, mercury, particulates, or any other form of air pollution, as do conventional fossil fuel power sources.

Geothermal Energy.

Scientists and engineers have researched and put into practice on how we all walk on top of renewable energy that is located right beneath our feet. This is called *geothermal energy*, which comes from the supper-hot rocks lying under the Earth's crust. The idea behind this technology is simple too as it only entails the tapping of underground heat to generate electricity. The Earth's core emits enormous quantity of heat from the molten rocks below the Earth's crust, which when combined with water either naturally in hydrothermal reservoirs or artificially resulted in the creation of steam needed to turn a turbine and thereby produce electricity.

The idea behind this experiment was first raised in 1904 in Larderello, Italy, in the region of the valley of the Devil where it was known for boiling liquids that rose to the surface. After considerable studies of this idea, the Italian engineers developed an electricity generator on top of their Hades in an angle between a fault plane and the vertical to give birth to the first geothermal plant. Today, Iceland generates 15 to 20% of its electricity through this means. The ecological advantages that the geothermal energy extraction enjoys over other energy alternatives are enormous. It doesn't compete with food crops like biomass does. It can provide base load electricity without the need for coal, nuclear, or natural gas as backups.

The anticipated problem that could come up for large scale development of geothermal energy is the fact that the planets underground heat is not evenly distributed; but in the 1970s, the scientists have suggested that if they could tap heat located far deeper underground, geothermal energy could be harnessed just about anywhere in the world. Presently the United States is the global leader in geothermal, which provides the same amount of power as the combined output of wind and solar energy. On a country-wide exploration for geothermal energy in Nigeria, the Federal Government could impress such project on the oil drilling companies in the Niger Basin for the establishment of a pilot plant because for the present time geothermal is largely the province of government-backed efforts in America and some other places.

There is a good argument that the Federal Government should steer clear of subsidizing any form of energy production. Why NEPA is a non-performing monstrous government organization is the fact that the same bureaucratic system in the government is what is in every branch of the authority. To me and others I believe that NEPA has grown to become a dead organization and there is no way we can bring it back to life except we all arrange a befitting funeral ceremony for it. When a person is confused about his or her own existence as a human being, the best thing to do for such a person is to arrange and take him/her to a home where he/she would permanently stay for the rest of his/her life under the thorough supervision of the specialists. The Federal Government's involvement in energy production in Nigeria has been fitful, messed-up and seriously counter productive. Its role should be curtailed to the issuance of policies, control and supervision and not as a judge in any case between NEPA and its customers.

It should provide every political backing, funds for research and security to the private companies that are capable of developing research centers for our energy development and to those who are to implement the results coming from the research centers. In some communities in the country, bamboo trees or untreated bush woods are still used to carry life current wires into homes while in some places in Lagos metropolis telephone cables are used to carry currents into some homes and business places. All these anomalies could only be possible with the connivance of either the NEPA officials or from the ranks of its contractors. By the time the Federal Government takes the bull by the horn and the state governments provides lashes to fasten the dogs, the local governments will know how to run faster without being told.

The designers of African governments in Europe in the early days knew very well from the on-set that future governments in Africa would always fall back unto them for decision-making process on the development of their people and this was why instead of teaching us how to catch fish, they always prefer to give us fish to eat at their own terms and discretion. All that have been discussed concerning energy production were already in use in most of the European countries and North America for ages past. But in Africa we only go to them to buy products that have been produced and not the technology on how to produce those products and once they go bad, we throw them off and get into the plane the next morning to go back to Europe, America or Japan to look for their newly introduced products to the market to bring back home without knowing anything about the technology of quality behind them. Every technology has scientific research behind it and every nation of the world has scientists.

No one would therefore tell me that we have no scientists of international substance and quality in Nigeria or we do not produce technicians equal to the same level of intelligence to those of their counter parts in either Europe or America. But what do we make out of them? In Nigeria today for example, once the hydropower station at Kainji built several decades ago and ageing away or the Egbin Termal station shut down, the whole country is automatically put into total darkness and all the businesses that could not afford high powered generators to run their businesses would remain stand still expecting when the miracle of NEPA would come back to rescue them. For how long are we to wait at this horrible bus stop to catch up with the development coach traveling around the globe with specific time-table?

The way a serious nation is identified borders on its seriousness on the good performance of its two vital industries that would help it to develop itself. These two are the Iron and Steel and Energy industries. As one of the first set of Nigerian geologists employed by the Federal

Government in 1971 to explore for all the needed mineral deposits in the country that would make Aja-Okuta a viable and competitive industry, and to this national assignment that we completed at a record time of less than one decade with the assistance of the Soviet Scientists, what is the progress report coming out of our steel industries at Aja-Okuta or Aladja today? How many tons of steel that have been rolled out of these plants say up to the end of year 2006? Have we forgotten that without the production of Iron and Steel, our technologists will never be able to fabricate any object including any modern agricultural equipment that would reduce the intensive labor activities of our people and enhance food production in the country? Without the seriousness of this vital industry, there will never be any time that we will be able to develop our own transportation sector or rebuild our old cities into modern and prestigious cities which would have the same status to the cities of the world where our leaders go to shop with the public resources. Without the functionality of this industry, the technological creativity in us will always be going down the drains because we will be unable to provide the working tools to those who are to develop their creativity talents and lastly we shall remain on the same spot peeping through the holes of the cage that our political leaders locked us into. Aja-Okuta steel plant should equally be regarded as a dead venture like its senior brother NEPA. The nation must be getting ready for befitting burial for the two of them in due course.

With the huge oil money we realize everyday from the international market, what have we been able to substantially do with it in terms of modern development? The train tracks from Lagos to Kaura Namoda or from Ibadan to Enugu had been abandoned for trailer businessmen to haul commodities to and fro those areas where train services were formally efficient. If it is the national policy to abandon train services, is it the trailer trucks with the death-trap roads we have in the country that is to be our alternative in terms of safety of the goods, cost effective to haul the goods and the safety of other road users? What has been happening to our water ways after the British people left us in 1960? Have we forgotten that it was the successful result of the exploration of River Niger that gave the European people and merchants the opportunity to annex substantial areas of Africa as their colonies, and also which afforded them to get away with valuable resources from our land to build their countries into what they are today?

In Yorubaland, our people have been known to be good farmers from its day one as a community and to when we grew into a nation. Before the arrival of the Europeans, we were adequately feeding ourselves without any recourse to importation of foods from anywhere. When the Europeans came, we developed further on the production of food and economic produce like cocoa, rubber and palm oil. When the petro-naira economy came after the Europeans left the decline in food production came with it as people began to migrate into the cities from the farmland. The farmland became desolate and people no longer wanted to be identified with such area any longer. The little food produce coming from the farmers left behind on the farms are not enough to feed the multi-mouths in the cities and alternative food supply is conditionally sort for. This is why today processed tin foods and other food commodities from Europe and elsewhere in the world found their ways into our local markets as alternatives to our home grown foods.

Everywhere in Yorubaland, there is plenty of water, which indicates that it is either we are seating on water or swimming in water that was provided by nature and which is free from little or no impurities, yet hardly could the people have enough good and clean water to drink. Health is wealth as Yoruba adage always says. But in today's modern Yoruba environment wealth is heath and this is true to what is exactly happening. If one is unable to find his/her way to either London or an American hospital but rely on the health services coming from either Lagos Teaching Hospital at Idi-Araba or from the University College Hospital (UCH) at Ibadan, the next stop for such a person will either be at Atan or Ikoyi cementary in Lagos or in the mortuary at Ibadan.

Undoubtedly all the states in Yorubaland have each one state owned university, a polytechnic, one teacher's college and one technical college. In some of the states in addition to above, they have Federal universities and technical colleges. There is no gain saying about it that all these institutions we have in our land graduates students of different professions every year in thousands. But how effectively do we utilize the talents they acquire from those institutions? How do they turn around the knowledge they gain from the universities? The polytechnic graduates are supposed to form the nucleus of our industrial development; which industry absorbs them after graduation? What is the current situation of our young engineers, doctors, scientists, teachers and nurses? Not until when we can identify our problems on a very serious note that we can sit to map out our strategies to combat those problems.

271

The Yoruba language that differentiated us from other nations in the family group is now being eroded away from its home base because it is gradually giving way to a foreign language. In most of the homes in Yorubaland, English language has now become the medium of communication between children and their parents. Are these young children going to learn the language of their mother tongue when they get to either Oxford University in England of Yale University in America? How will they identify themselves with their root when they are completely lost through the inadequacies of their parents? With all the observation of facts said above, I beg to ask my people once again that "Where do we go from here?" because I am now a confused person regarding our next move.

About the Author:

Jacob Oluwatayo Adeuyan is the grandson of late Chief Adeuyan Alebiowu, the first Akogun of Akureland and great grandson of Oba Olokunwolu Osupatadolawa – the Deji of Akureland who reigned between 1834 and 1846. He first served as a Geologist at the Geological Survey of Nigeria, Kaduna and later transferred to Nigerian Steel Development Authority (NSDA) where he served between 1971- 1978 and rose to the position of Senior Geologist before he resigned to establish his Engineering Consulting firm in Lagos – Nigeria. NSDA was the Federal Government of Nigeria's establishment charged with the exploration and exploitation of needed mineral resources for the nation's Iron and Steel industry under the Administration of both General Yakubu Gowon and Generals Muritala and Olusegun Obasanjo.

He holds a Bachelor of Science degree in geology (B.Sc. (Hons) from Geological Exploration Institute Kiev (Old USSR) 1971; a law degree (LL.B Hons) – JD from University of Wolverhampton, United Kingdom (UK), and a masters degree in Business Administration (MBA, Inf. Tech) from Morgan State University, Baltimore Maryland-USA. He has worked in many places of the world for some reputable Engineering and Law firms particularly in the United Kingdom, United States and Nigeria his home country.

He held many political and social positions in some major countries of the world. In England he is a member of the Labor Party and actively participated in the John Major/Neil Kilnock campaign of 1992. In America, he was the chairman Obama for Africa during Obama's presidential campaign of 2008; patron Egbe Omo Yoruba Ti Baltimore (Yoruba Descendant Association) and one of the leaders of the Egbe in USA and Canada. He is also a strong leader of his church – Vineyard of Comfort (Agbala Itura) world wide. He was an old member of the Action Group of Nigeria headed by late Chief Obafemi

Awolowo - Nigeria's political Guru since 1956, foundation member of Nigeria Socialist Workers and Farmers Party headed by late Dr. Tunji Otegbeye since 1959, a strong member of the Nigerian Labor Congress representing the then Ondo province, which later transformed into the present Ondo state as the provincial secretary, under the leadership of Mr. Wahab Goodluck of the blessed memory.

He is happily married with children and grand children and enjoys traveling. He has widely traveled to many places of the world in search of knowledge and social interaction where he is able to establish friendship with people of great substance, who by one way or the other contributed immensely to his well-being and status in life. He has written many books on different topics ranging from religion to politics and from business growth to personality of a past icon in Yoruba society of the 19th century.